OXFORD WORLD'S CLASSICS

THE EUDEMIAN ETHICS

ARISTOTLE (384–322 BC), with Plato one of the two greatest philosophers of antiquity, and in the view of many the greatest philosopher of all time, lived and taught in Athens for most of his career. He began as a pupil of Plato, and for some time acted as tutor to Alexander the Great. He left writings on a prodigious variety of subjects, covering the whole field of knowledge from biology and astronomy to rhetoric and literary criticism, from political theory to the most abstract reaches of philosophy. He wrote two treatises on ethics, called *Eudemian* and *Nicomachean* after their first editors, his pupil Eudemus and his son Nicomachus. *The Nicomachean Ethics* is much better known, but the *Eudemian Ethics* too has a claim to be a mature expression of Aristotle's ethical thought.

SIR ANTHONY KENNY is an Emeritus Fellow of St John's College, Oxford. He is a former Master of Balliol College and Pro-Vice-Chancellor of the University of Oxford and was President of the British Academy from 1989 to 1993. His many books include *The Aristotelian Ethics* (1978), *Aristotle's Theory of the Will* (1979), and *Aristotle on the Perfect Life* (1992). His most recent book is *A New History of Western Philosophy* (2010).

T0054959

OXFORD WORLD'S CLASSICS

*For over 100 years Oxford World's Classics have brought
readers closer to the world's great literature. Now with over 700
titles —from the 4,000-year-old myths of Mesopotamia to the
twentieth century's greatest novels —the series makes available
lesser-known as well as celebrated writing.*

*The pocket-sized hardbacks of the early years contained
introductions by Virginia Woolf, T. S. Eliot, Graham Greene,
and other literary figures which enriched the experience of reading.
Today the series is recognized for its fine scholarship and
reliability in texts that span world literature, drama and poetry,
religion, philosophy, and politics. Each edition includes perceptive
commentary and essential background information to meet the
changing needs of readers.*

OXFORD WORLD'S CLASSICS

ARISTOTLE

The Eudemian Ethics

Translated with an Introduction and Notes by
ANTHONY KENNY

OXFORD
UNIVERSITY PRESS

OXFORD
UNIVERSITY PRESS

Great Clarendon Street, Oxford ox2 6DP

Oxford University Press is a department of the University of Oxford.
It furthers the University's objective of excellence in research, scholarship,
and education by publishing worldwide in

Oxford New York

Auckland Cape Town Dar es Salaam Hong Kong Karachi
Kuala Lumpur Madrid Melbourne Mexico City Nairobi
New Delhi Shanghai Taipei Toronto

With offices in

Argentina Austria Brazil Chile Czech Republic France Greece
Guatemala Hungary Italy Japan Poland Portugal Singapore
South Korea Switzerland Thailand Turkey Ukraine Vietnam

Oxford is a registered trade mark of Oxford University Press
in the UK and in certain other countries

Published in the United States
by Oxford University Press Inc., New York

British Library Cataloguing in Publication Data

Data available

Library of Congress Cataloging in Publication Data

Data available

Typeset by Glyph International, Bangalore, India
Printed in Great Britain
on acid-free paper by
Clays Ltd, Elcograf S.p.A.

ISBN 978-0-19-958643-1

11

CONTENTS

Introduction   vii

Note on the Text and Translation   xxix

Select Bibliography   xxxi

A Chronology of Aristotle   xxxiii

Outline of The Eudemian Ethics   xxxv

THE EUDEMIAN ETHICS

BOOK I   Happiness the Chief Good   3

BOOK II   Virtue, Freedom, and Responsibility   14

BOOK III   The Moral Virtues   37

BOOK IV   Justice   53

BOOK V   Intellectual Virtue   75

BOOK VI   Continence and Incontinence: Pleasure   90

BOOK VII   Friendship   112

BOOK VIII   Virtue, Knowledge, Nobility, and Happiness 141

Explanatory Notes   149

Glossary of Key Terms   189

Index   191

INTRODUCTION

ARISTOTLE was born in 384, fifteen years after the death of Socrates, in the small colony of Stagira, on the peninsula of Chalcidice. He was the son of Nicomachus, court physician to the father of King Philip II of Macedon. After the death of his father he migrated to Athens in 367, being then 17, and joined Plato's Academy there. He remained for twenty years as Plato's pupil and colleague, and it can safely be said that on no other occasion in history was such intellectual power concentrated in a single institution.

One of Aristotle's many claims on posterity is that he was the founder of the discipline of logic. His most important works on the subject are the *Categories*, the *De Interpretatione*, and the *Prior Analytics*. These set out his teaching on simple terms, on propositions, and on syllogisms. They were grouped together, with two works of informal logic, and a treatise on scientific method, the *Posterior Analytics*, into a collection known as the *Organon*, or 'tool', of thought.

While Aristotle was at the Academy, King Philip II adopted an expansionist policy and waged war on a number of Greek city-states, and made himself master of Greece. It cannot have been an easy time for a Macedonian in Athens. Within the Academy, however, relations seem to have remained cordial. Aristotle always acknowledged a great debt to Plato, whom on his death he described as the best and happiest of mortals 'whom it is not right for evil men even to praise'.

Already, however, during his period at the Academy, Aristotle began to distance himself from Plato's most famous doctrine, the Theory of Ideas. In his surviving works Aristotle often takes issue with the theory. Sometimes he does so politely, as where, in the *Nicomachean Ethics*, he introduces a series of arguments against the Idea of Good with the remarks that he has an uphill task because the Forms were introduced by his good friends. However, his duty as a philosopher is to honour truth above his friends. In the *Posterior Analytics*, however, he dismisses Ideas contemptuously as 'tarradiddle'.

When Plato died in 347, his nephew Speusippus became head of the Academy, and Aristotle left Athens. He migrated to Assos on the north-western coast of what is now Turkey, a city under the rule of Hermias, a graduate of the Academy, who had already invited a number of Academicians to form a new philosophical institute there. During his period in Assos, and during the next few years when he lived at Mytilene on the island of Lesbos, Aristotle carried out extensive scientific research, particularly in zoology and marine biology.

Hermias met a tragic death in 345 and about three years later Aristotle was summoned to the Macedonian capital by King Philip II as tutor to his 13-year-old son, the future Alexander the Great. We know little of the content of his instruction: the *Rhetoric for Alexander* that appears in the Aristotelian corpus is commonly regarded as a forgery. Within ten years of succeeding his father, Alexander had made himself master of an empire that stretched from the Danube to the Indus and included Libya and Egypt. While Alexander was conquering Asia, Aristotle was back in Athens, where in 335 he established his own school, the Lyceum, a gymnasium just outside the city boundary. Now aged 50, he built up a substantial library, and gathered around him a group of brilliant research students, called 'peripatetics' from the name of the avenue (*peripatos*) in which they walked and held their discussions.

Aristotle's anatomical and zoological studies had given a new and definitive turn to his philosophy. Though he retained a lifelong interest in metaphysics, his mature philosophy constantly interlocks with empirical science, and his thinking takes on a biological cast. Most of the works that have come down to us, with the exception of the zoological treatises, probably belong to this second Athenian sojourn. There is no certainty about their chronological order, and indeed it is probable that the main treatises—on physics, metaphysics, psychology, ethics, and politics—were constantly rewritten and updated. In the form in which they have survived it is possible to detect evidence of different layers of composition, though no consensus has been reached about the identification or dating of these strata.

In his major works Aristotle's style is very different from that of Plato or any of his other philosophical predecessors. The prose he wrote is commonly neither lucid nor polished, though he could write passages of moving eloquence when he chose. It may be that the texts we have are the notes from which he lectured; perhaps even, in some cases, notes taken at lectures by students present. Everything Aristotle wrote is fertile of ideas and full of energy; every sentence is packed with intellectual punch. But effort is needed to decode the message of his jagged clauses: what has been delivered to us from Aristotle across the centuries is a set of telegrams rather than epistles.

Aristotle's works are systematic in a way that Plato's never were. In Plato's dialogues we flit from topic to topic, and even from discipline to discipline, in a disconcerting manner. In fact the very notion of a discipline, in the modern academic sense, was an invention of Aristotle. There are three kinds of sciences, Aristotle tells us in the *Posterior Analytics*: productive, practical, and theoretical sciences. Productive sciences are, naturally enough, sciences that have a product. They include engineering and architecture, with products like bridges and houses, but also disciplines such as strategy and rhetoric, where the product is something less concrete, such as victory on the battlefield or in the courts. Practical sciences are ones that guide behaviour, most notably ethics and politics. Theoretical sciences are those that have no product and no practical goal, but in which information and understanding are sought for their own sake.

There are three theoretical sciences: physics, mathematics, and theology. In this trilogy only mathematics is what it seems to be. 'Physics' means natural philosophy or the study of things' nature (*phusis*). It is a much broader study than physics as understood nowadays, including chemistry and meteorology as well as biology and psychology. 'Theology' is, for Aristotle, the study of entities above and superior to human beings, that is to say, the heavenly bodies as well as whatever divinities may inhabit or control the starry skies. The eight books of *Physics* and the twelve books of *Metaphysics* that have come down to us belong to Aristotle's contribution to theoretical sciences, as do his *De Anima* and a number of minor psychological treatises.

In the realm of productive sciences, Aristotle wrote two works, the *Rhetoric* and the *Poetics*, designed to assist barristers and playwrights in their respective tasks. The latter was meant to resolve the quarrel between philosophy and poetry that Plato had famously begun in his *Republic* by banishing the poets. He presents a theory of tragedy that enables him to respond to Plato's complaint that playwrights, like other artists, were only imitators of everyday life, which was itself only an imitation of the real world of the Ideas.

If we turn from the productive sciences to the practical sciences, we find that Aristotle's contribution was made by his writings on politics and moral philosophy. His contribution to political science was both theoretical and empirical: he wrote a *Politics* in eight books, and made

a copious collection of the constitutions of various states, of which
one, *The Constitution of Athens*, was rediscovered in the nineteenth
century.

The standard modern corpus of Aristotle's works contains three
substantial treatises of moral philosophy: the *Nicomachean Ethics*
(*NE*) in ten books, the *Eudemian Ethics* (*EE*) in eight books, and the
Magna Moralia in two books.[1] The relationship between these three
is complex and controverted, and of all the intellectual treasures
bequeathed to us by Aristotle few have had a more extraordinary history than the *EE*.

In the early centuries after Aristotle's death no great use was made
of his ethical treatises by later writers, and in the earliest surviving
list of his works none of our treatises appear under the names by
which they are now known.[2] In the catalogue made in Rome in the
first century BC by the bibliophile Andronicus, the *EE* and the *Magna
Moralia* are listed, but not the *NE*. The earliest testimony to all three
of the traditional titles of the ethical works is a remark of the Platonist
Atticus, a contemporary of the emperor Marcus Aurelius.

Between Aristotle's death and the second century AD a dozen
authors cite Aristotle's ethical writings; all but one of them take their
quotations from books that form part of the *EE* rather than from
purely Nicomachean books. Indeed, in this early period there are
traces of some doubt whether the *NE* is a genuine work of Aristotle;
both Cicero and Diogenes Laertius entertain the possibility that it
is the work of his son Nicomachus. But this early primacy of the
Eudemian over the Nicomachean treatise comes to an abrupt end
with the work of Aspasius in the second century AD, who wrote a line-
by-line commentary on several books of the *NE*.

Since that time it has been almost universally agreed that the *NE* is
not only a genuine work but the most important of the three treatises.
From the Byzantine period, twenty MSS of the *NE* survive, but only
two of the *EE*. The entire *NE* was translated into Latin in the Middle
Ages, but only fragments of the *EE*. Since the time of Albert the
Great commentaries on the *NE* have appeared about once a decade,

---

[1] There is also a pamphlet entitled 'On Virtues and Vices', which is universally
regarded as spurious.

[2] In the list attached to the Life of Aristotle by Diogenes Laertius there appear an
Ethics in five books, a book on the influence of the passions, and a book on friendship.
It is just possible that these seven books are what are now Books I–VII of the *EE* (see A.
Kenny, *The Aristotelian Ethics* (Oxford 1978), 42).

whereas the *EE* has had only half-a-dozen throughout its history. In the nineteenth century it was treated as spurious, and republished under the name of Aristotle's pupil Eudemus of Rhodes. In the twentieth century scholars commonly followed Werner Jaeger[3] in regarding it as a genuine but immature work, superseded by an *NE* written in the Lyceum period. Throughout the Middle Ages, and since the revival of classical scholarship, it is the *NE* that has been treated as *the* Ethics of Aristotle, and it is indeed the most generally popular of all his surviving works.

There is a special problem about the relationship between the *NE* and the *EE*. In the manuscript tradition three books make a double appearance: once as Books V, VI, and VII of the *NE*, and once as Books IV, V, and VI of the *EE*. It is a mistake to try to settle the relationship between the *NE* and the *EE* without first deciding which was the original home of the common books. It can be shown on both philosophical and stylometric grounds that these books are much closer to the *EE* than to the *NE*. It now seems to be the majority opinion of scholars that the original home of these common books was indeed the *EE*. Once these books are restored to the *EE* the case for regarding the *EE* as an immature and inferior work collapses: nothing remains, for example, of Jaeger's argument that the *EE* is closer to Plato, and therefore earlier, than the *NE*. Moreover, internal historical allusions suggest that the disputed books, and therefore the *EE* also, belong to the Lyceum period.

There are great similarities, in structure and content, between the undisputed parts of the *NE* and the *EE*. Both treatises give the notion of happiness a fundamental role in ethics, and both begin and end with an analysis of the concept. Both assume a similar account of human nature, and of the different psychological and mental faculties. Both discuss the nature of voluntariness and choice, and offer definitions of moral virtue based on the concept of the mean. As well as virtue in general, both discuss individual virtues in detail. Both address the difficult topic of pleasure, and both treat at length of the nature of friendship.

In addition to these similarities, there are significant differences in content. The *NE* presents philosophical contemplation as supreme happiness, and the *EE* identifies happiness with the exercise of all the

---

[3] Werner Jaeger, *Aristotle: Fundamentals of the History of his Development*, trans. R. Robinson (Oxford 1948).

virtues, moral as well as intellectual. The *EE* treatment of voluntariness and choice is more systematic and is more firmly embedded in
a general theory of human agency. In the *EE* individual virtues are
treated more briskly than in the *NE*, and less emphasis is placed on
pride and more on gentleness. The treatment of friendship in the *EE*
may well be thought more altruistic and less self-absorbed than that
in the *NE*.

There are also differences in style between the treatises. The *EE* is
often tauter and more concise than the *NE*, and it makes much more
use of technical terms of Aristotelian logic and metaphysics. It regularly employs signpost phrases and cross-references to link parts of its
discussions together and to bring out their structure. These features,
and many other tiny peculiarities of style, reappear in the common
books that stand in the MSS of both the *NE* and the *EE*.

The stylistic differences that separate the *NE* not only from the
EE but also from almost all Aristotle's other works may be explicable
by the ancient conjecture that the *NE* was edited by Nicomachus,
while the *EE*, along with some of Aristotle's other works, was edited
by Eudemus. As for the *Magna Moralia*, while it follows closely the
line of thought of the *EE*, it contains a number of misunderstandings
of its doctrine. This is easily explained if it consists of notes made
by a student at the Lyceum during Aristotle's delivery of a course of
lectures resembling the *EE*.[4]

Aristotle on Happiness

In all Aristotle's ethical treatises, the notion of happiness (*eudaimo-
nia*) plays a central role. The *EE* begins with the inquiry: what is a
good life and how is it to be acquired? (1214a15). We are offered five
candidate answers to the second question (by nature, by learning, by
discipline, by divine favour, and by luck) and seven candidate answers
to the first (wisdom, virtue, and pleasure, honour, reputation, riches,
and culture) (1214a32, b9). Aristotle immediately eliminates some
answers to the second question: if happiness comes purely by nature
or by luck or by grace, then it will be beyond most people's reach
and they can do nothing about it (1215a15). But a full answer to

---

[4] The account given here of the relationship between the Aristotelian ethical treatises
is controversial. I have expounded and defended it in *The Aristotelian Ethics* and, with
corrections and modifications, in *Aristotle on the Perfect Life* (Oxford 1992).

the second question obviously depends on the answer to the first. Aristotle works on that by asking the question: what makes life worth living?

There are some occurrences in life, e.g. sickness and pain, that make people want to give up life: clearly these do not make life worth living. There are the events of childhood: these cannot be the most choiceworthy things in life since no one in his right mind would choose to go back to childhood. In adult life there are things that we do only as means to an end; clearly these cannot, in themselves, be what makes life worth living (1215b15–31).

If life is to be worth living, it must surely be for something that is an end in itself. One such end is pleasure. The pleasures of food and drink and sex are, on their own, too brutish to be a fitting end for human life: but if we combine them with aesthetic and intellectual pleasures, we find a goal that has been seriously pursued by people of significance. Others prefer a life of virtuous action—the life of a real politician, not like the false politicians, who are only after money or power. Thirdly, there is the life of scientific contemplation, as exemplified by Anaxagoras, who when asked why one should choose to be born rather than not, replied, 'In order to admire the heavens and the order of the universe.'

Aristotle has thus reduced the possible answers to the question 'what is a good life?' to a shortlist of three: wisdom, virtue, and pleasure. All people, he says, connect happiness with one or other of three forms of life: the philosophical, the political, and the voluptuary (1215a27). This triad provides the key to Aristotle's ethical inquiry. The Eudemian treatise contains detailed analyses of the concepts of virtue, wisdom (*phronēsis*), and pleasure. And when Aristotle comes to present his own account of happiness, he can claim that it incorporates the attractions of all three of the traditional forms of life.

A crucial step towards achieving this is to apply, in this ethical area, the metaphysical analysis of potentiality and actuality. Aristotle distinguishes between a state (*hexis*) and its use (*chrēsis*) or exercise (*energeia*).[5] Virtue and wisdom are both states, whereas happiness is an activity, and therefore cannot be simply identified with either of them (II.1, 1219a39). The activity that constitutes happiness is,

---

[5] The *EE* prefers the distinction in the form virtue–use of virtue; the NE prefers it in the form virtue–activity in accord with virtue (*energeia kat'aretēn*).

however, a use or exercise of virtue. Wisdom and moral virtue, though different *hexeis*, are exercised inseparably in a single *energeia*, so that they are not competing but collaborating contributors to happiness (V.13, 1144b30–2). Moreover, pleasure, Aristotle claims, is identical with the unimpeded exercise of an appropriate state: so that happiness, considered as the unimpeded exercise of these two states, is simultaneously the life of virtue, wisdom, and pleasure (VIII.3, 1249a21).

To reach this conclusion takes many pages of analysis and argument. In order to lead up to the analysis of happiness which is the burden of the treatise, Aristotle must make a preliminary analysis of several other concepts. First, there is the concept of human agency itself: Aristotle shows how that differs from the activity of other agents, and this leads him to explore the nature of voluntariness and choice. Next, he must show the relation between action and virtue. Virtue unexercised is not happiness, because that would be compatible with a life passed in sleep, which no one would call happy (1219b19). Thirdly, he must analyse the concept of virtue itself. Human virtues are classified in accordance with Aristotle's anatomy of the human soul and its faculties. Virtues come in two main kinds: moral and intellectual. Aristotle gives a general account of the moral virtues as being concerned with a mean. He goes on to give a detailed account of a number of principal moral virtues, ranging from courage to justice. Then he discusses the intellectual virtues, the excellences of the truth-seeking faculties of the soul. He shows how the best forms of human activity involve the coordination of both moral and intellectual virtue. After a digression on human qualities that fall short of virtue without being actual vices, Aristotle takes up the topics of pleasure and friendship before presenting his final account of happiness.

Aristotle's Psychology

For Aristotle, not only human beings have souls, so do animals and plants and all living beings that have the capacity for self-sustenance, growth, and decay. The soul, we are told in the *De Anima* (II.1, 412a20ff.), is the form of an organic body, a body that has organs, that is to say, parts that have specific functions, such as the mouths of mammals and the roots of trees. The soul is not only the form, or formal cause, of the living body: it is also the origin of change and motion in the body, and above all it is also the final cause that gives the body its teleological orientation.

The souls of living beings can be ordered in a hierarchy. Plants have a vegetative or nutritive soul, which consists of the powers of growth, nutrition, and reproduction (*De An.* 415a23–6). Animals have, in addition, the powers of perception and locomotion: they possess a sensitive soul, and every animal has at least one sense-faculty, touch being the most universal. Whatever can feel at all can feel pleasure: and hence animals, who have senses, also have desires.

The human soul has parts that exercise functions similar to those of these lower forms. When we talk of parts of the soul, we are talking of faculties: and these are distinguished from each other by their operations and their objects. The power of growth is distinct from the power of sensation because growing and feeling are two different activities; and the sense of sight differs from the sense of hearing not because eyes are different from ears, but because colours are different from sounds (*De An.* 415a14–24). Corresponding to the soul of plants, there is in humans a vegetative soul, responsible for nutrition and reproduction. Any virtue of the vegetative part of the soul, such as soundness of digestion, is irrelevant to ethics, which is concerned with specifically human virtue (*EE* II.1, 1219b22, 38).

Like animals, humans have the power of sense-perception, and at the level of the soul where the senses provide the cognitive element, there is an affective part of the soul, the locus of spontaneous felt emotion (1219b22). This is introduced in the *EE* as being a basically irrational part of the soul which, unlike the vegetative soul, is capable of being controlled by reason. When brought under the sway of reason it is the home of the moral virtues such as courage and temperance (1219b28–30, 1220a10).

For Aristotle as for Plato the highest part of the soul, unique to humans, is the mind or reason, the locus of thought and understanding. Aristotle makes a distinction between practical reasoning and theoretical reasoning, and makes a corresponding division of faculties within the mind. There is a deliberative part of the rational soul (*logistikon*), which is concerned with human affairs, and there is a scientific part (*epistemonikon*), which is concerned with eternal truths (*EE* V, 1139a16, 1144a2–3). The rational soul is the seat of the intellectual virtues.

Aristotle on Human Agency and Responsibility

Aristotle places his account of human agency within a very general theory of causation and origination (*EE* II.6, 1222b15–1223a20). Some causes have their causation caused by a previous cause; others are uncaused, or ultimate, causes, and these Aristotle calls 'sources' or 'originators'. Living things beget their kind, and axioms in geometry provide the ground for the theorems derived from them. Both of these, for Aristotle, count as instances of origination. Among such sources some are causes of motion or change, while others (most obviously mathematical axioms) are not. The first causes of change are called by Aristotle 'controlling sources'. Some such agents control necessary movements and others control contingent movements. God is the controller of the necessary motions of the heavens, but the contingent events of human affairs have contingent causes. Some such events are the results of chance, and some are the results of human intervention. It is thus that Aristotle assigns to human beings their place in the universe of causation. Man is the controlling source of human conduct: and the sphere of human conduct is provided by those contingent matters that are 'in our power'. When we want to evaluate human conduct, we must restrict the field still further, to voluntary actions, that is to say, actions that are 'in our power to do or not to do' (1225b8, b36, 1226a28, etc.).

In saying that there are some things that are in our power to do or not to do, Aristotle is subscribing to the thesis that was later called 'the freedom of the will', and in the strong form which came to be named 'liberty of indifference'. Some later philosophers championed a weaker form of freedom which was called 'liberty of spontaneity'. We cannot, they maintained, do otherwise than we actually do, but we do have freedom in the sense that we can do what we want to do. In chapter 7 of Book II Aristotle explores the possibility that voluntariness can be defined in terms of wanting.

Desire, he tells us, comes in three forms: volition, appetite, and temper. Volition is intellectual wanting: the kind of desire that only language-users can have, such as the desire to act justly. The other two are forms of sensory desire, whether positive (as in hunger and lust) or negative (as in the desire to punch someone in anger). After a number of complicated dialectical moves Aristotle rules out the sensory desires on the grounds that we do many things voluntary without appetite or anger. He goes on to rule out volition on the grounds that we often voluntarily act against our better judgement. Hence, he rejects the idea that voluntariness consists in any kind of liberty of spontaneity.

However, in order to define voluntariness we need to refine the notion of liberty of indifference. I may do something that it was in my power not to do and yet not do it voluntarily because I did not know what I was doing. So Aristotle says that the voluntary—as a subclass of the things that are in my power to do and not do—must be defined as action performed in a certain state of awareness (1224a5–8). The agent must know who is affected by his conduct, the nature of any instrument he is using, and the likely effect of his action. Aristotle goes on to give examples of possible errors that would undermine the voluntariness of what is done (1225b1–8).

It seems that not only error may render an action involuntary, but also compulsion of various kinds. In his treatment of this topic in chapter 8 of Book II, Aristotle makes a distinction. Physical compulsion does negate voluntariness—indeed, if someone seizes my hand and uses it to strike a third party, that is not really my action at all. But coercion by threat does not necessarily do so. A bad action I perform unwillingly to avoid a greater evil may still be something that I do voluntarily and am therefore responsible for.

Finally, Aristotle introduces the notion of *prohairesis*, or purposive choice. Any action that is chosen by an agent is voluntary, but not every voluntary action is chosen. Many voluntary actions are performed on the spur of the moment, but for Aristotle an action is chosen only if it is performed as a result of deliberation—and deliberation of rather a special kind, referring the proposed action to an overall plan of life. The notion of choice is important for Aristotle because choice is essential for fully human action, and without choice action is strictly neither virtuous nor vicious. Choice involves both cognition and wanting: volition for an ultimate end, and belief about the way to achieve that end. It is intelligence qualified by desire, or desire qualified by thought (V.2, 1139b5).

Aristotle on Moral and Intellectual Virtue

The moral virtues are dealt with in the second and third books of the *EE*. These virtues are not faculties like intelligence or memory, nor momentary passions like anger and pity, but abiding states of character. What makes a person good or bad, praiseworthy or blameworthy, is neither the simple possession of faculties nor the simple occurrence of passions. It is rather a state of character that is expressed both in choice (*prohairesis*) and in conduct (*praxis*) (II, 1220b1–20, 1227b8). Virtue is expressed in purposive choice, that is to say, a prescription for action in accordance with a good plan of life, and choice in turn will be expressed in conduct (V.2, 1139a31).

The actions that express moral virtue will, Aristotle tells us, avoid excess and defect. A temperate person, for instance, will avoid eating or drinking too much; but he will also avoid eating or drinking too little. Virtue chooses the mean, or middle ground, between excess and defect, eating and drinking the right amount (II.3, 1220b21 ff.). To illustrate his point Aristotle offers a list of virtues, including the traditional ones of courage and temperance, but including others such as liberality, sincerity, and pride. In the third book he treats individual virtues at greater length, sketching out how each of them is concerned with a mean.

The doctrine of the mean is not intended as a recipe for mediocrity or an injunction to stay in the middle of the herd. Aristotle warns us that what constitutes the right amount to drink, the right amount to give away, the right amount of talking to do, may differ from person to person. Virtue is concerned not only with action but with emotion. We may have too many fears or too few fears, and courage will enable us to fear when fear is appropriate and be fearless when it is not. We may be excessively concerned with sex and we may be insufficiently interested in it: the temperate person will take the appropriate degree of interest and be neither lustful nor frigid (1221a18, 22).

The virtues, besides being concerned with means of action and passion, are themselves means in the sense that they occupy a middle ground between two contrary vices. Thus, courage is in the middle, flanked on one side by foolhardiness and on the other by cowardice; generosity treads the narrow path between miserliness and prodigality (1220b36–1221a12).

While all moral virtues are means of action and passion, it is not the case that every kind of action and passion is capable of a virtuous mean. There are some actions of which there is no right amount, because any amount of them is too much: Aristotle gives adultery as an example (1221b20). There is no such thing as committing adultery with the right person at the right time in the right way.

The doctrine of the mean seems to many readers truistic. In fact, it is a distinctive ethical theory which contrasts with other influential systems of various kinds. Traditional Jewish or Christian doctrine gives the concept of a moral law (natural or revealed) a central role. This leads to an emphasis on the prohibitive aspect of morality, the listing of actions to be altogether avoided: most of the commands of the Decalogue, for instance, begin with 'Thou shalt not'. Aristotle does believe that there are some actions that are altogether ruled out, as we have just seen; but he stresses not the minimum necessary for moral decency but rather the conditions of achieving moral excellence.

But it is not only religious systems that contrast with Aristotle's treatment of the mean. For a utilitarian, or any kind of consequentialist, there is no class of actions to be ruled out in advance. Since the morality of an action, on this account, is to be judged by its consequences, there can, in a particular case, be the right amount of adultery or murder. On the other hand, some secular ascetic systems have ruled out whole classes of actions: for a vegetarian, for instance, there can be no right amount of the eating of meat. We might say that from Aristotle's point of view utilitarians go to excess in their application of the mean, whereas vegetarians are guilty of defect in its application. Aristotelianism, naturally, hits the happy mean in application of the doctrine.

In his account of moral virtue Aristotle constantly refers to the role of correct reasoning in determining the mean (1222a34, 1229a1 ff.), and to the judgement of a wise person (1232a36). In order to complete this account, he has to explain what correct reasoning is, and what wisdom is. This he does in Book V, in which he treats of the intellectual virtues.

Wisdom is not the only intellectual virtue, as he explains at the beginning of the book. The virtue of anything depends on its *ergon*, its function or job or work or output. The job of reason is the production of true and false judgements, and when it is doing its job well it produces true judgements (V.2, 1139a29). The intellectual virtues are then excellences that make reason come out with truth. There are five states, Aristotle says, that have this effect: art (*technē*), science (*epistēmē*), wisdom (*phronēsis*), understanding (*sophia*), and intelligence (*nous*) (1139b17). These states contrast with other mental states such as belief or opinion (*doxa*) that may be true or false. There are, then, five candidates for being intellectual virtues.

Technē, however, the skill exhibited by craftsmen and experts such as architects and doctors, is not treated by Aristotle as an intellectual virtue. Skills have products that are distinct from their exercises—whether the product is concrete, like the house built by an architect, or abstract, like the health produced by the doctor (1140a1–23). The exercise of a skill is evaluated by the excellence of its product, not by the motive of the practitioner: if the doctor's cures are successful and the architect's houses are splendid, we do not need to inquire into their motives for practising their arts. Virtues are not like this: virtues are exercised in actions that need not have any further outcome, and an action, however objectively irreproachable, is not virtuous unless it is done for the right motive. Finally, though the possessor of a skill must know how it should be exercised, a particular exercise of a skill may be a deliberate mistake—a teacher, perhaps, showing a pupil how a particular task should *not* be performed. No one, by contrast, could exercise the virtue of temperance by, say, drinking himself comatose.

It turns out that the other four intellectual virtues can be reduced to two. *Sophia*, the overall understanding of eternal truths that is the goal of the philosopher's quest, turns out to be an amalgam of intelligence (*nous*) and science (*epistēmē*) (1141a19–20). Wisdom (*phronēsis*) is not concerned with unchanging and eternal matters, but with human affairs and matters that can be objects of deliberation (1141b9–13). Because of the different objects with which they are concerned, understanding and wisdom are virtues of two different parts of the rational soul. Understanding is the virtue of the theoretical part (the *epistēmonikon*) which is concerned with the eternal truths; wisdom is the virtue of the practical part (the *logistikon*) which deliberates about human affairs. All other intellectual virtues are either parts of, or can be reduced to, these two virtues of the theoretical and the practical reason.

The intellectual virtue of practical reason is inseparably linked with the moral virtues of the affective part of the soul. It is impossible, Aristotle tells us, to be really good without wisdom, or to be really wise without moral virtue (1144b30–2). This follows from the nature of the kind of truth that is the concern of practical reason.

What affirmation and negation are in thinking, pursuit and avoidance are in desire: so that since moral virtue is a state that finds expression in choice, and choice is deliberative desire, it follows that if the choice is to be good both the reasoning must be true and the desire must be right, and the latter must pursue just what the former asserts. This is the kind of thought and the kind of truth that is practical. (1139a21–7)

Virtuous action must be based on virtuous choice. Choice is reasoned desire, so that if choice is to be good both the reasoning and the desire must be good. It is wisdom that makes the reasoning good, and moral virtue that makes the desire good. Aristotle admits the possibility of correct reasoning in the absence of moral virtue: this he calls 'cleverness' (*deinotēs*) (1144a23). He also admits the possibility of right desire in the absence of correct reasoning: such are the naturally virtuous impulses of children (1144b1–6). But it is only when correct reasoning and right desire come together that we get truly virtuous action (1144a16–18). The wedding of the two makes intelligence into wisdom and natural virtue into moral virtue.

Practical reasoning is conceived by Aristotle as a process starting from a general conception of human well-being, going on to consider the circumstances of a particular case, and concluding with a prescription for action.[6] In the deliberations of the wise person, all three of these stages will be correct and exhibit practical truth (1142b34, 1144b28). The first, general, premiss is one for which moral virtue is essential; without it we will have a perverted and deluded grasp of the ultimate grounds of action (1144a9, 35).

Aristotle does not give a systematic account of practical reasoning comparable to the syllogistic he constructed for theoretical reasoning. Indeed, it is difficult to find in his writings a single virtuous practical syllogism fully worked out. The clearest examples he gives all concern reasonings that are in some way morally defective. Practical reasoning may be followed by bad conduct (*a*) because of a faulty general premiss, (*b*) because of a defect concerning the particular premiss or premisses, (*c*) because of a failure to draw, or act upon, the conclusion. Aristotle illustrates this by considering a case of gluttony.

We are to imagine someone presented with a delicious sweet from which temperance (for some reason which is not made clear)

---

[6] See A. Kenny, *Aristotle's Theory of the Will* (London 1979), 111–54.

commands abstention. Failure to abstain will be due to a faulty general premiss if the glutton is someone who, instead of the life-plan of temperance, adopts a regular policy of pursuing every pleasure that offers itself. Such a person Aristotle calls 'intemperate'. But someone may subscribe to a general principle of temperance, thus possessing the appropriate general premiss, and yet fail to abstain on this occasion through the overwhelming force of gluttonous desire. Aristotle calls such a person not 'intemperate' but 'incontinent', and he explains how such incontinence (*akrasia*) takes different forms in accordance with the various ways in which the later stages of the practical reasoning break down (VI.3, 1147a24–b12).

From time to time in his discussion of the relation of wisdom and virtue Aristotle pauses to compare and contrast his teaching with that of Socrates. Socrates was correct, he said, to regard wisdom as essential for moral virtue, but he was wrong simply to identify virtue with wisdom (1144b17–21). Again, Socrates had denied the possibility of doing what one knows to be wrong, on the grounds that knowledge could not be dragged about like a slave. He was correct about the power of knowledge, Aristotle says, but wrong to conclude that incontinence is impossible. Incontinence arises from deficiencies concerning the minor premisses or the conclusion of practical reasoning, and does not prejudice the status of the universal major premiss which alone deserves the name 'knowledge' (1147b13–19).

Pleasure and Happiness

The pleasures that are the domain of temperance, intemperance, and incontinence are pleasures of a particular kind: the familiar bodily pleasures of food, drink, and sex. If Aristotle is to carry out his plan of explicating the relationship between pleasure and happiness, he has to give a more general account of the nature of pleasure. This he does in *EE* VI (1152b1–1154b31).[7]

Aristotle offers a fivefold classification of pleasure. First of all, there are the pleasures of those who are sick (either in body or soul); these are really only pseudo-pleasures (1153b33, 1173b22). Next, there are the pleasures of food and drink and sex as enjoyed by the gourmand and the lecher (1152b35 ff., 1173b8–15). Next up the

---

[7] See Kenny, *The Aristotelian Ethics*, 233–7.

hierarchy are two classes of aesthetic sense-pleasures: the pleasures of the inferior senses of touch and taste, on the one hand, and on the other the pleasures of the superior senses of sight, hearing, and smell (1153b26). Finally, at the top of the scale are the pleasures of the mind (1153a1–20).

Different though these pleasures are, a common account can be given of the nature of each genuine pleasure. Pleasure is defined as the unimpeded activity of a disposition in accordance with nature (1153a14).

To see what Aristotle had in mind, consider the aesthetic pleasures of taste. You are at a tasting of mature wines; you are free from colds, and undistracted by background music; then if you do not enjoy the wine either you have a bad palate ('the organ is not in good condition') or it is a bad wine ('it is not directed to the most excellent of its objects'). There is no third alternative. The organ and the object—in this case the palate and the wine—are the efficient cause of the activity. If they are both good, they will be the efficient cause of a good activity. But pleasure itself causes activity not as efficient cause, but as final cause: like health, not like the doctor.

After this analysis, Aristotle is in a position to consider the relation between pleasure and goodness. The question 'is pleasure good or bad?' is too simple: it can only be answered after pleasures have been distinguished and classified. Pleasure is not to be thought of as a good or bad thing in itself: the pleasure proper to good activities is good and the pleasure proper to bad activities is bad.

If some pleasures are base, that does not prevent the chief good from being a pleasure of a kind, just as it might turn out to be knowledge of a kind, even though certain kinds of knowledge are bad. Given that every disposition has unimpeded exercises, it may be that the unimpeded exercise of all of them, or of one of them, is what happiness is; and, if so, it is perhaps necessary that this is the thing most worth choosing. This activity is a pleasure. (1153b7–11)

In this way, it could turn out that pleasure (of a certain kind) was the best of all human goods. If happiness consists in the exercise of the highest form of virtue, and if the unimpeded exercise of a virtue constitutes a pleasure, then happiness and that pleasure are one and the same thing.

Plato, in the *Philebus*, proposed the question whether pleasure or *phronēsis* constituted the best life. Aristotle's answer is that properly understood the two are not in competition with each other as candidates for happiness. The exercise of the highest form of *phronēsis* is the very same thing as the truest form of pleasure; each is identical with the other and with happiness. In Plato's usage, however, '*phronēsis*' covers the whole range of intellectual virtue that Aristotle distinguishes into wisdom (*phronēsis*) and understanding (*sophia*). Shall we ask whether happiness is to be identified with the pleasure of wisdom, or with the pleasure of understanding?

In the *EE* happiness is identified not with the exercise of a single dominant virtue but with the exercise of all the virtues, including not only understanding but also the moral virtues linked with wisdom (II.1, 1219a35–9). Activity in accordance with these virtues is pleasant, and so the truly happy man will also have the most pleasant life (VIII.3, 1249a18–21). For the virtuous person, the concepts 'good' and 'pleasant' coincide in their application; if the two do not yet coincide, then a person is not virtuous but incontinent (VII.2, 1237a8–9). The bringing about of this coincidence is the task of ethics (1237a3).

Though the *EE* does not identify happiness with philosophical contemplation, it does give it a special place. The exercise of the moral virtues, as well as intellectual ones, is, in the *EE*, included as part of happiness; but the standard for their exercise is set by their relationship to contemplation—which is here defined in theological rather than philosophical terms.

whatever choice or possession of natural goods—bodily goods, wealth, friends, and the like—will most conduce to the contemplation of God is the best: this is the finest criterion. But any choice of living that either through excess or through defect hinders the service and contemplation of God is bad. (VIII.3, 1249b15–20)

The Eudemian ideal of happiness, therefore, given the role it assigns to contemplation, to the moral virtues, and to pleasure, can claim, as Aristotle promised, to combine the features of the traditional three lives: the life of the philosopher, the life of the politician, and the life of the pleasure-seeker. The happy man will value contemplation above all, but part of his happy life will be the exercise of political virtues and the enjoyment in moderation of natural human pleasures of body as well as of soul.

Justice and Friendship

An ethical system like Aristotle's, which makes the agent's happiness the ultimate aim of moral action, appears to modern minds impossibly self-centred. Unless a philosopher seeks to make it true by definition, it is surely wrong to maintain that one's own happiness is the only possible aim in life. A person may map out his life in the service of someone else's happiness, or for the furtherance of some political cause which may perhaps be unlikely to triumph during his lifetime. A wife may be convinced that she will never be happy unless she leaves her husband, and yet stay with him for the sake of the children. Perhaps Aristotle did not maintain, at least in the *EE*, that happiness was the only possible aim, but he certainly thought it was the only proper aim. But surely it is a central feature of morality, as we understand it today, that it concerns our relationships to other people and to the claims they have on us?

I believe that the attempt to make one's own happiness the foundation stone of ethics is a fundamental defect in Aristotle's system. But it must in fairness be pointed out that within this framework he did devote much careful thought to the individual's relationships to others. His reflections on these matters are to be found in the *EE* in Book IV (on justice) and Book VII (on friendship).

Aristotle makes a distinction between universal and particular justice. Universal justice, he tells us, is complete virtue, considered not in the abstract but in relation to one's neighbour. Each of the virtues he has considered in the earlier books is incomplete unless this relation to others is incorporated in it. Many people can exercise virtue in their own affairs, but not in relation to their neighbour. 'The best person is the man who exercises virtue not for himself but for his neighbour—a more difficult task' (IV.1, 1130a28).

Particular justice is a specific virtue in its own right: it concerns the things that would nowadays be the province of the criminal and civil courts. Aristotle offers us several subdivisions: there is distributive justice (governing the allotment of the proceeds of military or commercial ventures) and rectificatory justice (the compensation for losses incurred either through defaults on contracts or as the result of crimes). Distributive justice involves taking into account the merits of the individuals between whom the goods are to be distributed—though it is not clear whether a person's 'merit' depends on his original contribution to the project or on his social status within a particular constitution. The consideration of distributive justice leads Aristotle into a disquisition on the nature of money and the purposes of commercial exchange. He adumbrates theses that later developed into the medieval doctrine of the just price, the economists' concept of the free market, and the Marxist labour theory of value. In treating of rectificatory justice Aristotle does not offer a justification of punishment, but devotes his attention to methods of restoring the status quo between wrongdoer and victim. In treating of political justice, he endeavours to sort out the relation between the natural and conventional elements in the constitution of a just society.

For Aristotle, justice and friendship are closely connected. He begins his book on friendship (the longest single book in the *EE*) by quoting a saying that the promotion of friendship is the special task of political skill. 'True friends do not wrong one another. But people will not act wrongfully if they are just.' Therefore justice and friendship are either identical or very close to each other.

Aristotle's word for friendship (*philia*) also covers love, and Book VII treats of many kinds of loving relationships: those between husband and wife and between parents and children as well as those with comrades and business partners. There are three different kinds of friendship, Aristotle tells us: those based on virtue, those based on utility, and those based on pleasure. At times this tripartite division seems to operate as a straitjacket confining his empirical observations, and it leads to a complex and implausible account of why a virtuous man has any need for friends at all. But the book is full of psychological insights on such matters as the factors that put a strain on relationships of different kinds and lead to their break-up.

The relationship between husband and wife is sometimes presented as a partnership between equals, but more often the husband is the clear master of the household. Children, in Aristotle's view, should be seen and not heard, and not even seen too often. '[M]others love their children more than fathers do', he tells us, 'because they are likely to regard the children as more their own work. For people judge work by its cost, and the mother suffers more, in childbirth' (VII.8, 1241b9).

The Afterlife of Aristotle's Ethics

The first great Christian moral philosopher, St Augustine, shared Aristotle's eudaimonism, though the ultimate satisfaction that he held out as the aim of morality was to be obtained not in this world but in the next. Augustine taught, of course, that we must love our neighbour, as we are commanded to do by the God whose vision we seek. But the concern for the welfare of others is presented as a means to an ultimate goal of self-fulfilment.

The eudaimonism of Aristotle and Augustine continues in the work of St Thomas Aquinas, who thrust Aristotle's ethical thinking into a central position in Christian morality. Not only did Aquinas write insightful commentaries on the Aristotelian corpus, but one of the four volumes of his immensely influential *Summa Theologiae* is virtually a commentary on the *NE*. He Christianized Aristotle by adding the 'theological' virtues of faith, hope, and charity to the Greek 'cardinal' virtues of wisdom, temperance, courage, and justice.

While Augustine and Aquinas had followed Aristotle in placing happiness at the apex of their ethical systems, they accepted, as Aristotle did not, the idea that human beings must obey a natural law laid down by a creator God. Aquinas concurred that such things as murder, abortion, and usury were all violations of the natural law of God. But he structured his ethical system not around the concept of law, but around the idea that virtue was the route to self-fulfilment in happiness. It was the fourteenth-century Franciscan Duns Scotus who gave the theory of divine law the central place that it was to occupy in the thought of Christian moralists henceforth.

Simultaneously, Scotus removed happiness from its position of solitary dominance in ethical theory. He agreed with Aquinas that human beings have a natural tendency to pursue happiness; but, in addition, he postulated a natural tendency to pursue justice. This natural appetite for justice is a tendency to obey the moral law no matter what the consequences may be for our own welfare. Human freedom, for Scotus, consists in the power to weigh in the balance the conflicting demands of morality and happiness.

Throughout the Middle Ages, and even after the Renaissance, the *NE* continued to exercise great influence in moral philosophy; the *EE*, on the other hand, was almost totally neglected. Only fragments of it were translated, though one of these fragments, the second chapter of Book VIII, enjoyed wide popularity under the title *De Bona Fortuna*.

In the Renaissance period Latin translations of the *EE* (minus the disputed books) began to appear, and emendations to the Greek text were made by a number of scholars including Isaac Casaubon (1559–1614). The first, brief, commentary was composed by the Jesuit Silvester Maurus and published in 1668. But it was only in the nineteenth century that serious scholarly editions began to appear. However, so long as it was believed that the work was by Eudemus, and that the disputed books belonged to the *NE*, there was no incentive to publish or translate the *EE* in its entirety, and almost all nineteenth- and twentieth-century editions and translations deprived it of three of its most important books. Here, at last, the *EE* appears for the first time in a modern language in complete and untruncated form.

NOTE ON THE TEXT AND TRANSLATION

THE text of the *EE* I have translated is that presented in the Oxford Classical Texts series, edited by R. R. Walzer and J. M. Mingay (Oxford: Clarendon Press, 1991). I have taken the text of the common books from the edition of the *NE* by Ingram Bywater (1894, reprinted many times).

The MSS of the *EE* are in many places corrupt, and all editors and translators have had frequent recourse to emendation. The OCT helpfully presents a copious critical apparatus, listing the emendations of many scholars. Critics have thought, however, that the OCT editors were a little too ready to amend the MSS (see J. Barnes, 'An OCT of the *EE*', *Classical Review*, NS 42 (1992), 27–31). In places where I thought it was possible, with a little patience, to make good sense of the MSS reading, I have preferred it to the text printed in OCT. In other places, I have accepted the amended text of the OCT except where it seemed that some other emendation was clearly preferable. In very rare cases I have proposed amendments of my own. Whenever I have departed significantly from the OCT text of the *EE*, this is made clear in the Explanatory Notes. There were very few similar problems with the Bywater OCT because the MSS of the *NE* are in much better shape than those of the *EE*.

In translation I have not attempted to reproduce the order of words or clauses in the Greek MSS, or the punctuation of the OCT editors. I have aimed to produce clear and readable English that preserves Aristotle's sense, rather than to achieve word-for-word correspondence with the original. The decisions I made about the translation of key words in the vocabulary are recorded in the Glossary. Here, too, where a Greek word has many meanings, I have preferred to produce versions appropriate to the context, rather than to achieve absolute consistency across the whole treatise.

The numbering system, with references such as 1214a1, is that nowadays universally adopted: it derives from Immanuel Bekker's 1831 Berlin edition of Aristotle's works. The marginal numbers correspond to those of the Greek text, so that occasionally in the translation the correspondence is not exact. I have also noted the division into books and chapters (e.g. Book III, chapter 2), and added headings within the books.

I am greatly indebted to previous translators into modern language of the undisputed *EE* books, and in particular to the works of Solomon, Rackham, Woods, Dirlmeier, and Décarie listed in the Select Bibliography. I am also indebted to the editors and commentators whose conjectures appear in the critical apparatus of the OCT. For the common books I owe gratitude to the long series of translators and commentators up to the present day, and in particular to the translations of Broadie and Rowe, of Terence Irwin, and the Ross translation in the Oxford World's Classics series, revised and annotated by Lesley Brown. My greatest debt is to Jonathan Barnes, who read through the penultimate draft of the translation with enormous care, and saved me from some serious errors and countless minor ones.

SELECT BIBLIOGRAPHY

MOST of Aristotle's works appear in the original Greek in volumes of the Oxford Classical Texts series, and many of them appear with a translation in volumes of the Loeb Classical Library. All of the surviving works are to be found in English in the two-volume Oxford Translation, edited by J. Barnes (Princeton 1984). The Clarendon Aristotle series (Oxford 1963–) contains translations of selected texts, with detailed philosophical notes. Many of Aristotle's works are available in translation in Penguin Classics or in Oxford World's Classics.

On Aristotle in general

Barnes, J., *Aristotle* (Oxford, 1982).
—— *The Cambridge Companion to Aristotle* (Cambridge, 1995).
—— *Aristotle: A Very Short Introduction* (Oxford, 2000).
Shields, C., *Aristotle* (London, 2007).

On Aristotle's ethics

Bostock, D., *Aristotle's Ethics* (Oxford, 2000).
Broadie, S., *Ethics with Aristotle* (Oxford, 1991).
—— and Rowe, C., *Aristotle, Nicomachean Ethics*, trans., introd., and comm. (Oxford, 2002).
Hardie, W., *Aristotle's Ethical Theory*, 2nd edn. (Oxford, 1980).
Irwin, T. H., *Aristotle, Nicomachean Ethics*, trans., with introd., notes, and full glossary (Indianapolis, 1999).
—— *The Development of Ethics*, i (Oxford, 2007).
Kenny, A., *The Aristotelian Ethics* (Oxford, 1978).
—— *Aristotle's Theory of the Will* (London, 1979).
—— *Aristotle on the Perfect Life* (Oxford, 1992).
Kraut, R., *The Blackwell Guide to Aristotle's Nicomachean Ethics* (Oxford, 2006).

Translations of and commentaries on The Eudemian Ethics

Décarie, V., *Aristote, Éthique à Eudème* (Paris, 1978, 2007).
Dirlmeier, F., *Aristoteles. Werke*, vii: *Eudemische Ethik* (Berlin, 1969).
Fritzsche, A. T. H., *Aristotelis Ethica Eudemia* (Regensburg, 1851).
Harlfinger, D., and Moraux, P. (eds.), *Untersuchungen zur Eudemischen Ethik* (Berlin, 1971).
Rackham, H., *Aristotle, The Athenian Constitution, The Eudemian Ethics*, Loeb edn. (London, 1935).

Solomon, J., *The Eudemian Ethics*, in *The Works of Aristotle*, ed. David Ross, ix (Oxford 1915); rev. J. Barnes (Princeton, 1984).

Susemihl, F., *Eudemi Rhodii Ethica* (Leipzig, 1884).

Woods, M., *Aristotle's* Eudemian Ethics: *Books I, II and VIII* (Oxford, 1982).

Because three of the books of the *Eudemian Ethics* appear also in MSS of the *Nicomachean Ethics*, they are commented on by all the commentators on that treatise. There is a full bibliography to be found in the Oxford World's Classics edition, with a translation by David Ross and notes and an introduction by Lesley Brown (Oxford 2009).

A CHRONOLOGY OF ARISTOTLE

(All dates are BC)

399 Trial and death of Socrates in Athens; Plato was around 30 at the time.

384 Aristotle born in Stagira, northern Greece. His father is a doctor at the court of Macedon.

367 Aristotle goes to study in Athens; joins Plato's Academy.

347 Death of Plato, whose nephew Speusippus succeeds him as head of the Academy. Aristotle leaves Athens. He travels to Asia Minor and marries Pythias, the daughter of Hermias, who hosts him in Assos, Asia Minor.

342 Aristotle becomes tutor to Alexander, son of Philip II of Macedon.

338 Battle of Chaironeia, at which Philip II defeats Thebes and Athens, and becomes master of the Greek world.

336 Death of Philip; he is succeeded by his son Alexander.

335 Aristotle returns to Athens and founds his own 'school', the Lyceum. After the death of his wife, he lives with a slave-mistress, Herpyllis, by whom he has a son, Nicomachus.

323 Death of Alexander; anti-Macedonian feeling prompts Aristotle to leave Athens.

322 Death of Aristotle at Chalcis in Euboia.

OUTLINE OF *THE EUDEMIAN ETHICS*

BOOK I. HAPPINESS THE CHIEF GOOD

1. Happiness is the noblest, the best, and the most pleasant of human goods.
2. The nature of happiness and its preconditions.
3. Opinions about happiness.
4. The three lives of philosophy, virtue, and pleasure.
5. Opinions about what is worthwhile in life.
6. The method of inquiry.
7. The greatest of human goods.
8. What is the chief good?

BOOK II. VIRTUE, FREEDOM, AND RESPONSIBILITY

1. Happiness and the virtues, moral and intellectual.
2. Character, powers, and passions.
3. Virtue as a mean.
4. Virtue, pleasures, and pains.
5. Further remarks on the mean.
6. Human power and responsibility.
7. Voluntariness and its opposite.
8. Voluntariness, choice, and compulsion.
9. Concluding definition of voluntariness and involuntariness.
10. Deliberate choice.
11. Virtue, ends, and means.

BOOK III. THE MORAL VIRTUES

1. Courage.
2. Temperance and intemperance.
3. Gentleness and cruelty.
4. Liberality.
5. Pride.
6. Magnificence.
7. Other good and bad qualities of character.

BOOK IV. JUSTICE

Justice: its sphere and nature: in what sense it is a mean

1. The just as the lawful (universal justice).
2. The just as the fair and equal (particular justice).
3. Distributive justice, in accordance with geometrical proportion.
4. Rectificatory justice, in accordance with arithmetical proportion.
5. Justice in exchange, reciprocity.
6. Political justice and analogous kinds of justice.
7. Natural and legal justice.

Justice and choice

8. The scale of degrees of wrongdoing.
9. Can a man be voluntarily treated unjustly, and other questions.
10. Equity, a corrective of legal justice.
11. Can a man treat himself unjustly?

BOOK V. INTELLECTUAL VIRTUE

1. Intellectual virtue and the divisions of the intellect.
2. Truth and right desire.
3. Scientific knowledge of the necessary and eternal.
4. Art—knowing how to make things.
5. Wisdom—knowledge concerned with the ends of human life.
6. Intelligence—awareness of the first principles of science.
7. Understanding, intelligence, and science.
8. Wisdom and political science.

Minor intellectual virtues concerned with conduct

9. Skill in deliberation.
10. Judgement, a critical skill.
11. Common sense in ethics.

Relation of wisdom to understanding

12. What is the use of wisdom and philosophy?
13. Relation of wisdom to various kinds of virtue.

BOOK VI. CONTINENCE AND INCONTINENCE: PLEASURE

Continence and incontinence

1. Six varieties of character.
2. Discussion of current opinions about continence and incontinence.
3. Solution to the problem about the incontinent man's knowledge.
4. Solution to the problem about the sphere of incontinence.
5. Brutish and morbid forms of incontinence.
6. Incontinence in respect of anger is less disgraceful than plain incontinence.
7. Softness and toughness, weakness and impetuosity.
8. Intemperance worse than incontinence.
9. Relation of continence to other states of character.
10. An incontinent man cannot be wise, but he may be clever.

Pleasure

11. Three views hostile to pleasure and the arguments for them.
12. Discussion of the view that pleasure is not a good.
13. Discussion of the view that pleasure is not the chief good.
14. Discussion of bodily pleasures and the exaggeration of their importance.

BOOK VII. FRIENDSHIP

1. The nature of friendship.
2. The basis of friendship: virtue, utility, or pleasure?
3. Friendship and equality.
4. Friendships between unequals.
5. Friendship and likeness.
6. Self-love.
7. Friendship, concord, and goodwill.
8. Benefactors and beneficiaries.
9. Friendship, justice, and partnerships.
10. Civic friendship.
11. Special problems about friendship.
12. Friendship and self-sufficiency.

BOOK VIII. VIRTUE, KNOWLEDGE, NOBILITY, AND HAPPINESS

1. Virtue and knowledge.
2. Luck, good fortune, and happiness.
3. Complete virtue and nobility.

THE EUDEMIAN ETHICS

BOOK I · HAPPINESS THE CHIEF GOOD

*Happiness is the noblest, the best, and the most pleasant of human
goods**

1. THERE is an inscription on the porch of the temple of Leto in 1214a
the shrine at Delos* that runs as follows:

> Noblest of all* is perfect justice, best of all is a life of health; 5
> Most pleasant of all is to win one's heart's desire.

The man who composed those verses was expressing his view that
goodness, nobility, and pleasure belong to different things. But we
cannot agree with him. For happiness, being the noblest and best of
things, is the most pleasant of all as well.

There are many matters and features of nature that present problems
and need to be investigated. Some of the disciplines that treat of these 10
contribute simply to the acquisition of knowledge; others are concerned
also with getting things and doing things. From time to time we shall
have occasion to treat of matters of purely theoretical philosophy, in so
far as they are relevant to our inquiry; but our first concern is to investigate what constitutes a good life, and how it is to be attained.*

When people chance to be called 'happy', is this something they
owe to nature, like tall people, or short people, or people of colour? Or 15
has it been acquired by learning, so that happiness is a form of knowledge? Or by a kind of training? After all, human beings acquire many
characteristics neither from nature nor by learning, but by habituation—bad characteristics by bad habituation, and good characteris- 20
tics by good habituation. Perhaps people are made happy in none of
the above ways, but in one or other different manner. Are they like
people possessed by a nymph or a divinity, getting carried away by the
inspiration of some kind of spirit?* Or is happiness a matter of for- 25
tune? After all, many people are willing to identify happiness with
good luck. What is clear is that it is in all or some or one of these ways
that happiness comes to people. For almost every change originates
from one or other of these sources (provided we use 'knowledge' in a
broad sense * to include all activity arising from thinking). 30

Happiness, and a blissful and noble life, would seem to consist above all in three things that appear to be of all things the most worth choosing. Some say that the greatest good is wisdom;* others 1214b say it is virtue,* and others again say pleasure. People disagree about the size of the contribution that each of these makes to happiness, and claim that one element offers more than another. Some rate wisdom as a greater good than virtue, while others rate virtue above wisdom, and others again rate pleasure above the other two. Some 5 say that a happy life is an amalgam of all three elements, or of some pair of them, while others think it consists in just one of them.

The nature of happiness and its preconditions

2. All this considered, everyone who has the power to live according to his own choice should set up for himself* some object for a noble life—whether honour, or reputation, or wealth, or culture—with a 10 view to which he will govern all his conduct, since not to have one's life organized with reference to some end is a mark of great folly. Above all, he must first determine in his own mind, with care and without haste, where in our human condition the good life resides, and what are the necessary conditions for people to possess it. For a healthy life is not the same thing as the necessary conditions for 15 healthy living, and there are many other cases where a like distinction holds. So a noble life is not the same as those things whose lack would make nobility of life impossible. (Some of these necessary conditions are not specific to health or to life, but are more or less common to any and every state or activity; for instance, unless we 20 are breathing and awake and capable of moving there is hardly anything, whether good or bad, that we can take any part in. Other conditions—and they are important to notice—are specific to individual natures. In the case of physical well-being, eating meat and taking exercise after meals are conditions of a kind quite different from the above.) Here is the root of the controversies about the 25 nature and causes of happiness: some people treat as parts of happiness items that are no more than its necessary conditions.*

Opinions about happiness

3. It would be a waste of time to examine all the opinions about happiness held by different people. Children, invalids, and lunatics have 30 many views, but no sane person would trouble himself about them.

What such people need is not argument but something else: either time for their opinions to mature, or else medical or penal correction—for medical treatment is no less correctional than flogging. Likewise, we do not need to consider the opinions of the multitude, who speak at a venture on almost every topic and especially on this one. On this topic, at least, only the opinions of philosophers need to be taken into account, for it is absurd to offer reasoning to those who need not reasoning but chastisement. Every inquiry, however, and not least the quest for the highest and best life, throws up its own problems, and so it is well to place these latter opinions under scrutiny. For one way of proving a thesis that is contested is to refute the arguments of its opponents. 1215a

Moreover, such considerations should especially be borne in mind with respect to the matters to which our entire investigation must be directed. We are looking for the things that enable us to live a noble and happy life ('blissful life' is perhaps presumptuous*) and what prospects decent people will have of acquiring any of them. For if a noble life is something that results from chance or the course of nature, it would be a hopeless dream for many people; its acquisition would be beyond their powers no matter how strenuous their endeavours. But if it is something that depends on a person's character and conduct, then it will be a good both more widespread and more divine: more widespread because it will be accessible to more people, and more divine because happiness will reside in the personal development of character and conduct. 5 10 15

The three lives of philosophy, virtue, and pleasure

4. Most of the controversies and difficulties will become clear if we offer an appropriate definition of how to think of happiness. Does it consist only in a particular character of one's soul, as some senior philosophers have thought?* Or is it necessary for one not only to have a particular character, but more importantly to exhibit that character in one's actions? 20

We can distinguish different kinds of life. Some of them, such as lives spent in the vulgar arts, or commerce, or in servile occupations, make no claim to be a flourishing existence, but are pursued only out of need.* (By vulgar arts I mean arts pursued only for the sake of celebrity, by servile occupations I mean the work of sedentary wage-earners, and by commerce I mean buying and selling by retail.) 25 30

But just as there are three items reckoned as elements of a happy life—the three mentioned earlier as the greatest of human goods,
35 namely, virtue and wisdom and pleasure—so too we see three lives that all who have the opportunity for choice choose to live, namely, the political life, the philosophical life, and the hedonistic life.*
1215b The philosopher aims to devote his life to wisdom and the contemplation of truth, the politician to noble deeds (conduct that manifests virtue), and the hedonist to the pleasures of the body. And
5   so, as we have said before, different people call different people happy. Anaxagoras of Clazomenae* was once asked who was the happiest person. 'Not anyone that you would think,' he replied, 'but someone who would seem very odd to you.' He gave this answer because he could tell that the man who asked the question thought
10 it was impossible for anyone to be called happy unless he was great and beautiful or rich. But he himself, no doubt, believed that any man who leads a painless, blameless, and upright life, or is engaged in some divine contemplation, is as blissful as the human condition allows.

Opinions about what is worthwhile in life

15 5. There are many problems on which it is difficult to make a sound judgement, and none more so than one that everyone thinks is so easy that they need no special qualification to solve it: namely, what in life is worth choosing, and what is there whose attainment would totally satisfy one's desire.* There are many contingencies of life
20 that make people want to throw it away: diseases, torments, tempests, and so on. Clearly, right from the start, if given the choice, people in such straits would have preferred not to be born at all. Then there is the kind of life that people lead as children; no one in his right mind could tolerate returning to such a state. Moreover, there are many events that involve neither pleasure nor pain, or in-
25 volve pleasure only of an ignoble kind; episodes of such a kind make non-existence preferable to life. Altogether, if we were to heap up all the things that people do and undergo involuntarily (in the sense that nothing of them is wanted for its own sake), we would be offering no reason for choosing to be alive rather than not, even if we were to throw in an infinite stretch of time.
30 Further, no one who was not an utter slave would put any value on existence solely for the pleasures of food and sex, in the absence

of all the other pleasures that are provided to humans by knowing
and seeing and using any of their other senses. It is clear that for
a person making such a choice there would be no difference 35
between being born a beast or a human. Certainly the ox in Egypt,
whom they venerate under the name of Apis,* has access to more of 1216a
these pleasures than many a monarch. The same goes for the pleasures of sleep: what difference is there between sleeping an uninter-
rupted sleep from one's first day to one's last, for a thousand years
or more, and living the life of a plant? Certainly plants do seem to 5
share some such kind of life, and so do babies, for babies when they
first come into existence within their mothers have a continuous life
but sleep all the time. From all this it is obvious that inquirers have
little success in finding out what is well-being and what is the good
in life.

Someone who was puzzled about these matters once asked 10
Anaxagoras, was there any reason why one should choose to be born
rather than not? He is said to have replied, 'To survey the heavens
and the order of the whole cosmos.' So for him it was knowledge or
science that made the choice of life worthwhile. On the other hand, 15
people who celebrate Sardanapallus or Smindyrides of Sybara,* or
some other dedicated hedonist, appear to equate happiness with
enjoyment. There are others again who would choose no kind of
wisdom nor any bodily pleasures in preference to deeds of virtue. 20
Not everyone makes this choice for the sake of reputation; some act
well even when they are not going to get any credit. However, most
statesmen do not deserve the name, for they are not truly statesmen.
A statesman is someone who chooses noble deeds for their own sake, 25
whereas most politicians take up their career for personal gain and
advancement.

From what has been said it is clear that everyone relates happiness to one or other of three lives: the political life, the philosophical
life, and the hedonistic life. If we take the last first, there is no prob- 30
lem in identifying the nature and quality and sources of the pleasures associated with the body. The question is not what such
pleasures are, but whether and how far they contribute to happiness.
Suppose that a noble life should indeed have certain pleasures associated with it: what we have to ask is whether it is these bodily pleasures that we should associate with it. No doubt the happy person
must share them in some way or other, but perhaps it is on account 35

of quite different pleasures that he is rightly thought to live a life that is pleasant and not merely painless. But these matters must be investigated further later on.*

First, we must consider virtue and wisdom, and discover the nature of each of them.* Are they parts of the good life, either in 1216b themselves or through the conduct to which they give rise? After all, even if not everyone links them to happiness, they are so linked by all people who are worth taking into account.

The elder Socrates* believed that the goal of life was to know virtue, and he used to ask what justice is, what courage is, and so 5 with every part of virtue. This was an intelligible way to proceed, since he thought that the virtues themselves were pieces of knowledge, so that once you know what justice is, you are a just person.* After all, as soon as we have learnt geometry and architecture, we become geometers and architects. And so he used to 10 ask what virtue is, rather than how or whence it comes into being. This is appropriate in the case of the theoretical sciences, because there is nothing else to astronomy or physics or geometry over and above the knowledge and understanding of the subject matter of these disciplines. Nothing indeed prevents them being useful to us 15 for many of our needs; but that is something coincidental. In the case of productive sciences, however, the aim of the science is different from the science itself and not a mere matter of knowledge: health is different from medicine, and law and order (or the like) is not the same as political science. The knowledge of what is noble is 20 indeed a noble thing; but in the case of virtue the most valuable thing is to know whence it arises rather than to know its nature. For what we want is not simply to know what courage is, but actually to be courageous; and we do not want simply to know what justice is, but rather to be just ourselves. It is parallel to the way in which we want to be healthy rather than simply to know what health is, and to 25 the way we aim at physical well-being rather than at mere knowledge of its nature.

The method of inquiry

6. About all these matters we must seek conviction through argument, using people's perceptions* as evidence and example. The best thing would be if everyone turned out to be in agreement with 30 what we are going to say; if not so, that all should, on reflection,

reach at least partial agreement. After all, everyone has something of their own to contribute to the truth, and we must start our proof from such points. If we begin with things that are said in a manner that is true but unenlightening, we shall make progress towards enlightenment, constantly substituting more perspicuous expressions for ones that are more familiar but confused.

In every discipline there is a difference between philosophical 35 and unphilosophical manners of expression. Even in political thinking it is misguided to treat as irrelevant an inquiry into not only what is the case, but why it is the case.* In every discipline that is the way a philosopher proceeds: but great caution is needed here. Since it seems that a philosopher should never speak at a venture, but always with reason, some people offer reasons that are irrelevant or 1217a unsound, and often get away with it. (Some people do this in error; others are sheer charlatans.) By such arguments even people of experience and practical ability can be caught out by people who lack even the capability for practical or strategic thinking. This 5 comes about through want of culture: for want of culture is precisely the inability to distinguish between arguments that are appropriate, and those that are inappropriate, to a given subject matter.

It is well to make a separate judgement about a conclusion and 10 the explanations on which it is based, because, as we have just said, there are often cases where one should attend not just to the results of arguments, but rather to people's perceptions. (As things are, if people cannot see a flaw in the argument, they cannot help believing what has been said.) Moreover, it often happens that what appears 15 to have been shown by argument is in fact true, but not for the reason offered by the argument. (There can be a proof of a truth from a falsehood, as is clear from the *Analytics*.)

The greatest of human goods

7. So much by way of prologue. Let us begin our discussion by starting, as was said, from the first, unclarified, opinions, and seek 20 then to gain* a clear view of what happiness is. It is generally agreed that it is the greatest and best of all human goods. We say 'human', because there may well be happiness for some higher form of being, say for a god. None of the other animals that are by nature inferior to human beings have any claim to this title: no horse or bird or fish 25 is happy. Nor are any other beings, unless they have by definition

some share of the divine in their nature.* To be sure, they can have
a better or worse life, but it is by sharing in good things in some
30 manner that is different from happiness.*

That this is the case is something to be examined later. For the
present let us say that among good things there are some that fall
within the scope of human action and some that do not. Why do we
make this point? Well, there are some things, including some good
things,* that are not susceptible to change at all, and these things
may well by nature be the best things of all. Then again, there are
35 some things that fall within the scope of action, but only for agents
more powerful than us.

There are two ways in which things fall within the scope of action.
There are the things that are the purposes of our action, and the
things that we do in order to bring them about: thus, we count health
and wealth as being within the scope of action, and also the things
we undertake in order to produce them, such as a healthy lifestyle or
a commercial venture.

40 It is evident that we must lay it down that happiness is the chief
good among the things that fall within the scope of human action.

What is the chief good?

1217b 8. So we must inquire what this chief good is,* and in how many
senses the expression is used. People's perceptions about this can be
summed up in three opinions.

Some say that the chief good is Goodness itself,* and Goodness
itself has the properties of being the first of goods and of causing by
5 its presence the goodness of all other good things. Both these properties—I mean, being the first of goods, and causing by its presence
the goodness of all other goods—belong, it is claimed, to the Idea of
Good.* For, they say, it is of this Idea that good is most truly predicated, while other things are called good because they participate in
10 it or resemble it. If this shared Idea were eliminated, so too would be
all the things that participate in it and thus share its name. That is
the way in which what comes first is related to what comes after. So
Goodness Itself is the Idea of Good; and, moreover, it, like any other
15 Idea, is separable from what participates in it.

A thorough investigation of this belief belongs to a different discussion, which would inevitably bear a closer resemblance to
logic*—for that is the only discipline that deals with destructive

arguments of general application. But if we must make a summary   20
judgement, let us make two remarks. First, the claim that there is
an Idea of Good, or for that matter an Idea of anything else, is too
abstract and vacuous; the thesis has been examined in many
ways, both in our popular and in our philosophical works.* Secondly,
even if there really are such things as Ideas, including the Idea of
Good, they are altogether useless either for a good life or for
actions.

For good is predicated in many ways—in as many ways, indeed,   25
as being.* Being, as has been explained elsewhere, signifies essence,
or quality, or quantity, or time, and in addition active or passive
change. Good occurs in each of these categories. In the category of
substance there is mind and God, in the category of quality there is   30
justice, in the category of quantity there is proportion, in the category of time there is opportunity, and in the matter of change there
is teaching and being taught. Just as being is not a single thing
including all the things mentioned, neither is goodness.

Nor is there a single science* of being or goodness. Even goods
classified in parallel categories (e.g. opportunity and proportion) are   35
not subjects of the same science: different sciences investigate
opportunity and proportion in different cases. Thus, in nutrition it
is medicine and gymnastics that determine opportunity and proportion, but in the conduct of warfare it is strategy. Thus, for each
different kind of activity there is a different science. So there could   1218a
hardly be a single science whose province was Goodness itself.

Again, where things can be ranked as prior and posterior,* there
is not in addition some common thing that is separate from them all.
That would mean that there was something prior to the first of the
series: the common separate thing would have priority since if that
common element were eliminated, the first item would be elimin-   5
ated also. Take the case of multiplication, and let us suppose that the
first case of multiplication is multiplication by two. Then there
cannot be some separate element, multiplication *tout court*, that is
common to all cases of multiplication. For that would then be prior
to multiplication by two.

Alternatively, even if one were to say that the common element is
separable, does it turn out to be the Idea? They say that if justice is   10
a good, and courage too, there is also Goodness itself.* 'Itself' thus
gets added to the definition of what is common. What would that

mean except that it is eternal and separate? But a thing that is white for many days is no whiter than something that is white for only one, so that what is good would not become more good by being eternal. Nor is the common good identical with the Idea because the common good belongs to all goods.

15   Goodness itself should be demonstrated in a manner quite opposite to the way in which they do it nowadays. Nowadays they start from objects whose goodness is a matter of controversy, and go on to demonstrate goods whose goodness is uncontroversial. Thus, they start with numbers,* and go on to demonstrate that justice and health are goods, on the grounds that these latter are orders and
20   numbers, and goodness belongs to numbers and units, because the One is Goodness itself. But they should start with the uncontroversial goods like health and strength and temperance, and go on to show the greater nobility of what is unchanging. For all these things exemplify order and repose; so if they are good, the latter things are even more good, since they exemplify them to a greater degree.

25   There is also something wrong with the proof that the One is Goodness itself, on the grounds that it is something that the numbers tend towards. This is far too bald an assertion without any clear statement of what this tending consists in. How can there be any desire in things that lack life? People should take more trouble, and not maintain without argument things that even if argued for are
30   not easy to believe. And to say that all things tend towards some one good is not true: for each thing has a desire for its own special good, the eye for sight, the body for health, and so on.

The problems just listed urge us to deny that there is any such thing as Goodness itself, and to say that if there were, it would be no use to political science. That, like other disciplines, has its own par-
35   ticular good, in the way that physical well-being is the particular good of gymnastics. Further, there is what is written in the text:* the Form of Good is either useful to no discipline or useful to all in the same way. Further, it is not within the scope of action.

1218b   Likewise, the common good is not identical with Goodness itself (for this common element would be present even in a tiny good), nor is it within the scope of action. For the task of medicine is not to ensure that any old good should be where it belongs, but that health should be. So too with all the other arts. Goodness is manifold, and
5   one part of it is nobility. Some parts of goodness are within the scope

of action and others are not. What is within the scope of action is the kind of good that provides a purpose, and nothing of the kind is to be found in things that are unchanging.

It is obvious, then, that neither the Idea of Good, nor the good that is common, is the chief good that we are looking for: for the one is unchangeable and unattainable by action; the other, while it is changeable, is not attainable by action. What really is the chief good is the purpose or end that is the cause of what leads to it and is 10 the first of all goods. It is this, then, that goodness itself must be: the end of everything attainable by human action. It is that which is the object of the science which is supreme over all others, namely political and economic science and wisdom. This supremacy marks off these disciplines from others: whether they differ from each other is something that will have to be explained later.*   15

An end stands in a causal relation to the means subordinate to it: that is shown by the method of teaching. Teachers prove that the means are severally good by giving a definition of the end, because the purpose is one form of cause. They say, for instance, that since to be healthy is such-and-such, necessarily what conduces to health must be so-and-so. Healthy items, for instance, are an efficient cause 20 of health; but it is only the cause of health's coming into existence; it is not the cause of its being a good. No science proves its own first principles, and no one demonstrates that health is good, unless he is a sophist rather than a doctor—for sophists will prove anything by inappropriate arguments.

The good as the end of man and the best of things attainable by 25 action: that is the object of our study. We must now inquire in how many ways this chief good is realized; that is what is best.

BOOK II · VIRTUE, FREEDOM, AND RESPONSIBILITY

Happiness and the virtues, moral and intellectual

30 1. NEXT we must take a new starting point and discuss what follows.* All goods, according to the distinction made also in our popular writings, are either external or internal to the soul, and among the goods thus distinguished, the goods in the soul are preferable. For wisdom and virtue and pleasure are internal to the soul, and it is
35 universally agreed that some or all of these constitute the end of life. Internal to the soul there are states and powers on the one hand, and activities and processes on the other.

Let us add to this assumption the further statement that virtue is
1219a the best condition or state or power of whatever has a use or has work to do.* This is clear from induction; in all cases this is what we suppose. Because a cloak has a use and has work to do, there is such a thing as the goodness or virtue of a cloak, that is to say, the best state for a cloak to be in. So too with a boat, a house, and other
5 things. The case is the same with the soul, for it too has work to do.

Let us assume that the better the state, the better the work it does, and that as one state is related to another, so too is the working of the one related to the working of the other. Again, each thing's working is its end. From these assumptions it is clear, then, that the working
10 is better than the state, since the end, as an end, is the best thing, for it was assumed that the end was that best and ultimate thing that is the purpose of everything else. It is evident, then, that the working is something better than the state or condition.

But there are two different ways in which we speak of work. In some cases the work is a product distinct from the operation, as the
15 work of the housebuilder's craft is the house and not the building of it, and the work of medical skill is health rather than healing or curing. In other cases, the work is nothing other than the operation, as seeing is the work of sight, and understanding is the work of mathematics. So it follows that when the operation of a state is its work, the operation is something better than the state itself.

Having made these distinctions, let us say that the work of a thing

is the same as the work of its goodness or virtue, but not in the same
fashion. For instance, a shoe is the work of the shoemaker's art and 20
also of his shoemaking; and if there is such a thing as the virtue of
the shoemaker's art, then the work of a good shoemaker is a good
shoe.* So too in other cases.

Let us postulate that the work of the soul is to be alive*—or to
exercise life while awake, since in sleep the soul is idling and at rest. 25
So, since the work of the soul and of its virtue must be one and the
same, the work of its virtue will be a virtuous life. This, then, is the
complete good, which, as we saw, is happiness. This is evident if you
recall that we assumed that happiness is the best thing, and that the
ends, that is to say, the best of goods, are in the soul, and that things
in the soul are either states or activities.* From these assumptions, 30
and from the premises that an activity is better than a disposition,
and that the best activity is the activity of the best state, and that
virtue is the best state, it follows that the activity of the virtue of the
soul is the best thing of all. But happiness, as we saw, is the best of
all things; consequently, happiness is the activity of a good soul. We
also saw that happiness is something complete, and from this and 35
the premises that a life can be complete or incomplete, and that
virtue likewise can be total or partial, and that the activity of what is
incomplete is itself incomplete, it follows that happiness is the activity of a complete life in accordance with complete virtue.

Is this a correct statement of the genus and definition of happiness?
Well, universal opinion testifies to that effect. Doing well and living well 1219b
are regarded as the same thing as being happy, and each of these, both
living and doing, is an employment and an activity. (The life of action is
a life of employment: it is the coppersmith who makes the bridle, but
the horseman who puts it to use.) Another popular view is that one
cannot be happy just for one day, or while a child, or only for the prime 5
of one's life. And so Solon's dictum was well judged: call no man happy
while he lives, but only when his life has reached completion. For nothing incomplete is happy, as it does not make up a whole.

Further, if virtue is praised, it is because of the works that express
it; the works themselves are matter for congratulation. It is those
who actually win who receive the crown, not those who have the 10
ability to win but do not do so. Again, it is from their works that one
judges what sort of a person someone is.

Furthermore, why is happiness itself not an object of praise?

Because it is the reason why other things are praised, either for leading up to it, or by being parts of it. So felicitation and praise and
congratulation are all different from each other. Congratulation is
15 bestowed on an individual action, praise is for being a certain kind
of person, and felicitation pertains to the end.

From all this it is evident how to solve a problem sometimes
raised: how can it be, since all men are alike when asleep, that for
half of their lives the good are no better than the bad? The reason is
that in sleep the soul is not active but idling. For this reason too, if
20 there is some other part of the soul—say, the nutritive—the goodness of this is not a part of total virtue, any more than the goodness
of the body is. For in sleep the nutritive part is more active, while the
sensory and appetitive parts are ineffective. However, to the extent
that they have any kind of involvement in what is going on, the
25 dreams of virtuous men are better, unless they suffer from some
disease or decay.

This leads on to an examination of the soul,* since virtue belongs
to the soul, and not just coincidentally. As it is human virtue that we
are investigating, let us assume that in the human soul there are two
parts, each endowed with reason,* but each in a different fashion:
the natural role of one is to give orders, and the role of the other is
30 to listen and obey. (If there is something that is non-rational in some
other way, let us ignore that part of the soul.) It makes no difference*
whether the soul is divisible or is indivisible; either way it has distinct powers, including the ones just mentioned. Compare the way
in which in a curve the concave and the convex are inseparable, and
35 a straight line may be a white line, though straight is not white—the
identity is coincidental, and not a matter of substance.*

Any other part there may be in the soul, the vegetative part for
instance, should also be disregarded: it is the parts we mentioned
earlier that are peculiar to the human soul.* (Accordingly, the virtues of the nutritive and growth-inducing parts of the soul are not
40 human virtues either.) For if a part belongs to a human being qua
1220a human being, reasoning must be present as a governing element,
and conduct too; and what reasoning governs is not reasoning itself,
but desire and the emotions, so that these parts must be included.
And just as physical well-being is constituted by the virtues of the
several parts, so is the virtue of the soul when it is complete.

5   There are two kinds of virtue: moral and intellectual. For we

praise not only just people, but also intelligent people and men of understanding. For praise, we assumed, was given both to virtue and to its works; these states, though not themselves activities, have activities that belong to them. The intellectual virtues incorporate reason: they do so by belonging to that part of the soul that possesses the reason that, qua rational, gives orders. The moral virtues, on the other hand, belong to the part that is irrational but is by nature obedient to the rational part. When we say that someone is clever or is possessed of understanding, we are not describing his character as we are when we say that he is gentle or foolhardy.

After this, the next thing we must do is to investigate moral virtue, what it is and what are its parts (which comes to the same thing), and what are the means of producing it. As in other matters, all researchers start with something already in hand, so in conducting our search we must make use of statements that are true but unclarified to try to achieve an outcome that is both true and clear. At present we are in the same position as if we knew* that health was the best condition of the body, and that Coriscus was the swarthiest man in the marketplace, without knowing what or who they were. Such a position may be helpful as a step towards the knowledge of each of the two.

Let it be assumed first of all that the best disposition is a product of the best things, and that in each field of activity the best deeds are an exercise of the virtue proper to that field. For instance, it is the best exertions and nourishment that produce physical well-being, and people's best exertions are themselves an exercise of physical well-being. Let it be further assumed that each condition is destroyed by a particular application of the very same things that produce it, as health is by food and exertion and climate. These matters are clear from induction.

Virtue, therefore, is the sort of disposition that is produced by the best motions of the soul, and which is exercised in the best working and feeling of the soul. The same things applied in one way produce it, and applied in a different way destroy it; and it finds its exercise with regard to those things that promote or destroy it, disposing the soul for the best. A clue: virtue and vice are concerned with what is pleasant and what is painful, for punishments take effect through these, and punishments are a kind of therapy that, like others, works through opposites.

Character, powers, and passions

2. It is evident, then, that moral virtue is concerned with what is pleasant and what is painful. Now, character (*ēthos*), as the word 1220b itself indicates, is developed from habit (*ethos*), and an agent acquires a habit when it eventually becomes operative in a particular fashion as the result of the repetition of a certain motion under some non-innate impulse. (This is something we do not see in inanimate agents: a stone, even if you throw it upwards ten thousand times, will never do that except by force.) So let character be defined as a 5 quality governed by the prescriptions of reason, which inheres in that part of the soul which, although non-rational, is capable of obedience to reason.*

We must say, then, what it is in the soul that makes our character traits to be of a particular kind. It is our capacities for emotion (our susceptibilities, as they are called) and our attitudes to these emotions that are what make people call us either sensitive or insensitive 10 in a particular fashion. Here comes the division, made elsewhere, between emotions, potentialities, and states. By emotions I mean things like anger, fear, shame, desire, and in general anything that as such is generally attended by feelings of pleasure or pain. These are 15 passive experiences* and their occurrence does not imply any trait of character. It is the potentialities that do this, those potentialities, I mean, in respect of the emotions that make us call a person irascible, insensible, amorous, bashful, or shameless. What is responsible for whether these emotions occur in accord with reason, or in opposition to it, is states of character: things like courage, temper-20 ance, cowardice, intemperance.

Virtue as a mean

3. In the light of these distinctions we must observe that in every divisible continuum there exists excess, deficiency, and a mean, which may be either relative to each other or relative to us—in gymnastics, for instance, in medicine, in architecture, in navigation, and 25 in any practical pursuit, whether scientific or unscientific, skilled or unskilled. For change is a continuum, and practical activity is change. And in all cases it is the mean relative to us that is best, for that is as knowledge and reason ordains. Everywhere, indeed, this produces the best state, and this is clear from induction and from reasoning.

Contraries eliminate one another, and extremes are contrary both to 30
each other and to the mean. The mean, you see, is either of the contraries in relation to the other, in the way that the equal is larger than
the smaller, but smaller than the larger. Hence, moral virtue is concerned with certain means, and is itself a middle state. We must
ascertain, therefore, what kind of a middle state is virtue, and what 35
sorts of means are within its scope. By way of example, let us take
and examine each item in the following table:*

irascibility	impassivity	gentleness	
foolhardiness	cowardice	courage	
shamelessness	bashfulness	modesty	1221a
intemperance	insensibility	temperance	
envy	[unnamed]	righteous indignation	
gain	loss	justice	
prodigality	illiberality	liberality	5
boastfulness	dissembling	candour	
flattery	surliness	friendliness	
servility	churlishness	dignity	
softness	toughness	hardihood	
vanity	diffidence	pride	10
extravagance	shabbiness	magnificence	
cunning	naivety	wisdom	

These affections, and others like them, occur in the soul, and all take
their names from being either excessive or defective as the case may
be.

Thus, an irascible man is one who gets more angry than he should, 15
and more quickly, and with too many people, while an impassive
man is one who falls short in respect of persons, occasions, and
manner. A foolhardy man is one who does not fear things he should
fear, and is afraid neither when nor as he should be; a cowardly man
is one who fears things that he should not, and when he should not,
and in a manner he should not. Similarly, an intemperate man is one 20
who desires what he should not and goes to excess in every possible
way;* an insensible man is one who lacks desire even for things
that are most natural and would be better for him, and is as void of
feeling as a stone. A greedy man is one who grabs gain from every
possible source; one who rejects it from everywhere or almost everywhere is a loser. A boaster is a man who pretends to have more than 25

he has; a self-deprecating person pretends to have less. A flatterer is one who offers another more praise than is right; a surly person offers less. To be too ready to please is servility; to do so never or rarely is to be churlish. Again, a man who cannot put up with any
30 pain, even when it is beneficial, is soft. Strictly speaking there is no name for a man who can bear any and every pain, but in an extended sense we can call him stiff, hard, and tough. A vain man is one who rates himself too high, and a diffident man is one who rates himself too low. Again, a prodigal man is one who goes to excess in every kind of expenditure, and an illiberal man is one who never spends
35 enough. The case is similar with the shabby man and the ostentatious man: one goes beyond what is decent and the other falls short of it. A cunning person is out to get what he can by any means from any source, while a naive person does not take even what he is entitled to. A man is envious if he is too often distressed by the good fortune of others, for the envious are distressed by the prosperity even of
40 those who deserve to prosper. The opposite character is more diffi-
1221b cult to find a name for, but there is a kind of man who goes too far in not being distressed by the prosperity of the undeserving. (He is tolerant, like a glutton who will swallow anything, while envy makes his opposite disgruntled.)

There is no need to add to the definition that the relation specified in each case should not be merely coincidental. For no science,
5 whether theoretical or productive, adds this clause to its definitions, either in exposition or in practice; it is there to guard against crafty verbal quibbles. Let us give this abstract definition of the virtues, and define it more precisely when we are speaking of the contrasted states.

These affections themselves, however, have different forms with
10 different names depending on whether the excess is in time, or in intensity, or in relationship to the object provoking the passion. I mean, for instance, that a man is called quick-tempered if he gets angry sooner than he should, bad-tempered or choleric for getting angry more than he should, bitter for nursing his anger, violent and truculent for the vindictive acts in which he vents his anger. Men are
15 called gourmets or gourmands or drunkards in accordance with the form of intake in which they are susceptible to unreasonable overindulgence.

We must not overlook the fact that not all of the faults listed can be regarded as a matter of how something is done, if *how* means experiencing to excess. An adulterer is not a man who seduces other men's wives more than he ought (there is no such thing); adultery in 20 itself is a form of depravity, with a name that indicates not only what has occurred but also its moral quality. So too with assault. That is why when men reject accusations they admit they had intercourse but deny it was adultery (they acted in error or were coerced), or they admit they hit someone but deny it was assault. The same holds 25 in other similar cases.

Virtue, pleasures, and pains

4. Having noted all this, we must next say that since there are two parts of the soul, there is a corresponding division of the virtues. Those belonging to the rational part are intellectual virtues, whose work is truth, truth either about the nature of a thing or about how 30 it comes into existence. The other virtues belong to the part of the soul that is non-rational but capable of desire (for not every part of the soul, supposing it to be divisible, has desire). It follows that a character is vicious or virtuous by pursuing or avoiding certain pleasures and pains.

This is evident from the distinctions we made between emotions, susceptibilities, and states. For susceptibilities and states are con- 35 cerned with the emotions, and the emotions are characterized by pain and pleasure. From this and from our earlier assertions it fol- lows that every moral virtue is concerned with pleasures and pains. For whatever naturally makes a soul better or worse provides it with 40 its scope and subject matter. It is on account of pleasures and pains 1222a that we call men vicious, for pursuing and avoiding the wrong ones or in the wrong way. That is why everyone is willing to offer casually a definition of virtue as insensibility or unconcern in the matter of pleasures and pains, and of vice as the opposite. 5

Further remarks on the mean

5. The following assumptions have been made. Virtue is the kind of state that makes people doers of the best actions, and best disposed to what is best. The best and chief good is what is in accord with correct reasoning. This, in turn, is the mean between excess and defect rela- tive to ourselves.* It needs must follow, then, that moral virtue is in 10 each case a middle state concerned with certain means in pleasures

and pains and pleasant and painful things. And this middle state will sometimes be in pleasures (as will the excess and defect), and sometimes in pains, and sometimes in both. For a person who goes to excess
15 in joy goes to excess in the pleasant, and a person who goes to excess in grief goes to excess in the contrary direction, and this whether the excess is an absolute one or is in relation to some standard, as when someone's feelings are unlike those of most people. The good man, however, has the feelings he ought to have.

Now there is no state that makes a person likely in some instances to accept the excess, and in other instances the defect, of one and the same object. It follows that just as the objects are contrary to one
20 another and to the mean, so too the corresponding states are contrary to each other and to virtue.

It happens, however, that while sometimes all the oppositions are quite obvious, in other cases it may be either the ones on the side of excess, or the ones on the side of defect, that are more obvious. The
25 reason for this contrariety is that the distance from or closeness to the mean is not always of the same degree; sometimes a person will migrate to the mean state more swiftly from the excess and sometimes from the defect. The person who is further from the mean will seem more contrary to it.

In the case of the body, for instance, excess in exercise is healthier
30 and closer to the mean than defect, whereas in diet it is defect that is healthier than excess.

Correspondingly, the states governing the choices that are appropriate in training will be more or less healthy according to the field of choice involved: in the one case it will be the people who are overenergetic, and in the other case those who are more abstemious. The person who is contrary to the mean and to correct reasoning will be
35 in one case the sluggard (rather than both characters) and in the other case the self-indulgent person (not the one who goes hungry). This comes about because our nature from the outset is not in every case equidistant from the mean; we are not sufficiently keen on exercise, and are excessively keen on self-indulgence.

The same is true in the case of the soul. We treat as contrary to
40 the mean the state in whose direction we, and the majority of men, are most likely to err; the other escapes notice as if it did not exist, and because it is rare it is unobserved. Thus, we oppose anger to
1222b gentleness, and the irascible person to the gentle person. Nonetheless,

there is excess also in the direction of being pliable and forgiving, and not getting angry even when thrashed. But people of that kind are few, and most are inclined in the opposite direction: our spirited element is no sycophant.*

So we have now established a catalogue of the states of character in respect of each of the emotions in which there are excesses and defects, and of the contrary states in which people conform to correct reasoning. (Later on, we must inquire what correct reasoning is, and what is the standard we should look to in defining the mean.) From all this it is clear that all the moral virtues and vices have to do with excesses and defects of pleasures and pains, and that pleasures and pains result from the states of character and emotions we have mentioned. Now, the best state in respect of each is the mean. It is clear, therefore, that the virtues will be all or some of these middle states.

Human power and responsibility

6. Let us then take a new starting point for the ensuing inquiry. All substances are by nature sources of a certain sort,* so that each is able to produce many things of its kind, as a human begets other humans, an animal other animals,* and a plant other plants. In addition to this a human being, alone among animals, is a source of conduct, for we would not ascribe conduct to any of the others.*

Among such sources, those that are the first origin of motions are said to be controlling sources, and most strictly those whose effects cannot be other than they are; no doubt God's government is of this kind. But where the sources are unchanging, like the sources of mathematical truth, there is no such thing as control, though the term is used of them by analogy. For there, too, if the source were to change, everything proved from it would change also, while when one consequence is replaced by another, no change takes place, unless by refuting the hypothesis and using its refutation as a proof.* A human being, on the other hand, is a source of a certain kind of change; for conduct is change.

In the other cases, the source is the cause of whatever is the case because of it, or comes about because of it. So we need to understand the way we do this in demonstrations. If the angles of a triangle are equal to two right angles, it is necessary that the angles of a square are equal to four right angles; hence it is obvious that the triangle's equalling two right angles is the cause of the square's equalling four

right angles. If the triangle were to change, the square would necessar-
35 ily change too: if it contained three right angles, the square would
contain six, and if four, the square would contain eight. But if it does
not change, and is the kind of thing it is, then the other must also be
what it is of necessity. That what we are trying to show is necessarily
the case is something evident from the *Analytics*. Here we can say
precisely neither that it is nor that it is not so, except this much: if
40 there is no other cause of the triangle's having this property, this will
be a source as well as a cause of the consequential properties.

So that if some of the things there are admit of being quite other-
1223a wise than they are, their sources must also be of that kind. For a
consequence of what is necessary is itself necessary, whereas what
results from these is capable of turning out in a contrary fashion.
What is in the power of humans themselves* makes up a large portion of this kind of thing, and of things of this kind they themselves
are the sources. So, of the actions of which man is the source and
5 controller—of those at least where he is in control of whether they
occur or not—it is clear that they admit of occurring or not, and
that it is in his power whether they occur or not. But for what is in
his power to do or not to do, he himself is responsible; and if he is
responsible for something, then it is in his power.*

Since virtue and vice and the works that are their expressions are
10 praised or blamed as the case may be (for blame and praise are not
given on account of things that come about by necessity or chance or
nature, but on account of things that we ourselves are responsible for,
since if someone else is responsible for something, it is he who gets
the blame and praise), it is clear that virtue and vice have to do
with matters where the man himself is the responsible source of his
15 actions. We must then ascertain just what are the actions of which he is
the responsible source. Now, we all agree that each man is responsible
for things that are voluntary and in accordance with his own choice, but
that if they are non-voluntary then he is not responsible. It is evident
that whatever he does by choice, he does voluntarily. It is clear, then,
20 that both virtue and vice must concern things that are voluntary.

Voluntariness and its opposite

7. So we must ascertain what the voluntary is, and what the non-
voluntary is, and also what choice is; and because they delimit the
field of virtue and vice, we must first inquire into the voluntary and

the involuntary.* Prima facie there are three things relevant: desire, choice, and thought.* It would seem that one or other of these three is what makes things voluntary or involuntary, voluntary by being in 25 accord with it, involuntary by being contrary to it. But desire itself is of three different kinds: will, temper, and appetite.* So these must be distinguished, and first let us consider accordance with appetite.

It would seem that everything in accordance with appetite is voluntary. For everything involuntary seems to be forced, and what is 30 forced is painful, and so is everything that men do or undergo under coercion; as Evenus says:

Coercion never fails to bring distress.

So, if something is painful, it is forced, and if it is forced it is painful. But everything that is contrary to appetite is painful (for appetite aims at pleasure) and so it is forced and involuntary. The conclusion is that what is in accordance with appetite is voluntary, 35 for these are a pair of contraries.

Again depravity always makes a person less just, and incontinence appears to be a form of depravity.* But the incontinent man is the kind of person to act in conformity to appetite contrary to reason, and it is when he behaves in conformity with it that he acts incontinently. Moreover, unjust action is voluntary. So the incontin- 1223b ent man will act unjustly in acting according to appetite. The conclusion is that he will act voluntarily and that what is in accord with appetite will be voluntary. (It would indeed be odd if those who become incontinent thereby become more just.)

From these considerations, then, it would seem that what is in accordance with appetite is voluntary; but the opposite seems to be the case from the following contrary considerations.

If someone does something voluntarily, he does it because he wills 5 to do it, and what he wills to do he does voluntarily. But nobody wills what he thinks to be bad. But the incontinent man does not do what he wills, for incontinent action is acting contrary to what one thinks is best, under the influence of appetite. So it will follow that the same man is acting voluntarily and involuntarily at the same time, which is impossible. 10

Again, the continent man will act justly, for continence is more of a virtue than incontinence is, and virtue makes people more just. A man acts continently when he acts contrary to appetite but in

conformity to reason. So if acting justly, no less than acting unjustly,
15 is voluntary (for both of these seem to be voluntary, and certainly, if
one is voluntary then the other is), and if acting against appetite is
involuntary, then the same man at the same time will be acting both
voluntarily and involuntarily.*

The same argument holds also in the case of temper. For there
seems to be continence and incontinence of temper no less than of
appetite, and what goes against temper is unpleasant, and one has to
20 force oneself to keep one's temper. So if what is forced is involuntary, then everything that is in accordance with temper will be voluntary. (It is likely that Heraclitus has the strength of temper in
mind when he says that keeping it in check is painful. 'It's hard', he
says, 'to fight with temper: it will gain victory at the cost of life.')

If it is impossible for the same man at the same time to do the same
25 thing voluntarily and involuntarily under the same description, then
the voluntary, rather than what is in accord with appetite or temper, is
what is in accord with volition. A proof of this is that we do many
things voluntarily without either ill temper or appetite.*

It remains, then, to consider whether what is willed and what is
voluntary are the same thing.* This too seems impossible. For it is
30 an assumption of ours that is generally admitted that depravity
makes men more unjust, and incontinence seems to be depravity of
a sort. But the contrary will follow. For no one wills what he thinks
bad, but when he becomes incontinent that is just what he does. If,
then, unjust action is voluntary, and what is voluntary is what is in
conformity to will, when a man becomes incontinent he will no
35 longer be acting unjustly, but will be more just than before he
became incontinent. But this is impossible.

Voluntariness, choice, and compulsion

8. It is clear, therefore, that the voluntary is not the same as acting
in accordance with desire, nor is acting contrary to desire involuntary. The voluntary is not identical with choice, either, as is evident
1224a from what follows. It has been shown that what is in conformity to
one's will is not involuntary; rather, everything that is willed is also
voluntary. (All that has been shown* is that it is possible to do voluntarily something one does not will to do.) But there are many
things that we do because we will to do so, on the spur of the moment;
but nobody makes a choice on the spur of the moment.

If, as we saw, the voluntary must be one of these three—action in 5
accord with desire, with choice, or with thought—and two of these
have been ruled out, the remaining alternative is that voluntary
action is action accompanied by thinking of some sort.*

But first let us carry the discussion further and conclude our
delimitation of the voluntary and involuntary, for it seems that the
presence or absence of force in an action is relevant to our topic. We
say that what is forced is involuntary, and that what is involuntary is 10
forced; so we must first consider what force is and how it is related
to the voluntary and the involuntary.

It appears that force and necessity, and what is forced and what is
necessary,* are contrasted, in the case of conduct, with voluntariness and persuasion. But we speak of force and necessity also in the 15
case of inanimate objects: we say that a stone travels upwards and
fire downwards only by force and necessity. When they travel in
conformity with their own nature and their intrinsic impulse, we do
not say that they are moved by force—but their motion is not called
voluntary either. When they travel contrary to their natural impulse, 20
they move by force, but the opposite condition has no name.

Similarly, with living things, including animals, we see them
being acted on by force, and also acting under force, when their
motion is caused by an external agent against their intrinsic tendency. In inanimate things the initiating source is single; but in
living things it is multiplex, for desire and reason are not always in
harmony. So in the other animals force is a simple matter, as it is in 25
inanimate things, because they do not have a conflict between reason
and desire, but live simply by desire. But in humans both elements
are present, once they have reached the age at which we begin to
assess their conduct. (We do not speak of the conduct of an infant,
any more than of a wild beast, but only of someone who is old enough
to act on reason.)

Now it seems that whatever is forced is painful; no one acting 30
under force is glad to do so. For this reason there is considerable
controversy about the continent and the incontinent man. For each
of them acts under a conflict of internal impulses. The continent
man, they say, drags himself away from appetites for pleasant things,
feeling pain as he does in striving against the opposing desire. 35
The incontinent man, on the other hand, suffers force contrary to
reason; but he seems to feel less pain, because appetite is for what is

pleasant, and he follows gladly. So the incontinent man's condition is closer to voluntariness than to force, because he suffers no pain. Again, there is a contrast between force and necessity on the one 1224b hand and persuasion on the other, and the continent man goes in the direction to which he has been persuaded, not by force but voluntarily. Appetite, on the other hand, which has no share in reason, does not persuade but simply leads.

It has already been said that these people seem, exceptionally, to act both voluntarily and by force, the reason being a certain similarity to the kind of force that we speak of also in connection with 5 inanimate things. However, if one adds in the further element of our definition, the problem is solved. For when it is some external factor that moves or restrains a thing against its internal impulse, we speak of force, and otherwise we do not. But in the continent and incontinent man, the leading impulse is an internal one (since both of the 10 tendencies belong to him); so neither of the two on this account will be acting by force; each, rather, will be acting voluntarily and not under coercion. For we call it coercion when some external source restrains or moves a man against his own impulse—if, for instance, one man grabs another's hand and makes it strike a third party, against both his will and his appetite. However, when the originating factor is internal, there is no force involved.

15 Moreover, both pleasure and pain are present in both cases. The man acting continently feels pain at the moment of acting contrary to appetite, but he rejoices at the pleasure in his hope of future or even immediate benefit to his health. The incontinent man rejoices in the satisfaction his incontinent action brings to his appetite, but 20 he suffers pain from his expectation that he will fare ill.

Thus, there is some reason to say that each of them is acting under force, and that either desire or reason, as the case may be, is making them act involuntarily; for these two are quite separate and come into collision with each other. And so, when people see something like this happening between the parts of the soul, they transfer 25 the notion to the whole soul. In the case of the parts, it is possible to say this; but the soul as a whole acts voluntarily in both the incontinent and the continent man, and neither of them is subjected to force, though an element in them is.

The reason for that is that both parts belong to us by nature. For one of our natural sources of action is reason, which will be present if

development proceeds without being stunted, and another is appetite, 30
which is an attribute present from the moment of birth. Roughly speaking, these are the two marks by which we define what is natural to us; it
is either an attribute of everyone at birth, or something that comes to us
if development proceeds normally, such as grey hair and old age and the
like. So that in a fashion each of the two is acting not according to nature,
but each of them is, strictly speaking, acting according to a natural 35
element, though it is not the same one in each case.

These, then, are the problems concerning the continent and
incontinent person: do one or both of them act under force, so as to
act either non-voluntarily, or simultaneously voluntarily and under
force? If what is enforced is involuntary, are their actions simultaneously voluntary and involuntary? From what has been said it is 1225a
more or less evident how we should tackle these.

There is another way in which men are said to act under force and
coercion, without there being any clash of reason with desire:
namely, when they do something they consider painful and vicious,
but are threatened with flogging, imprisonment, or death if they do 5
not do it. Such acts they say they did under coercion. Or is that
wrong, and do they all do what they do voluntarily, given that it was
in their power not to do it, and endure the suffering?

Alternatively, one might say that some such cases are voluntary and
others not. When it is in the agent's power whether such a situation
should obtain or not, then in every case the agent is acting voluntarily 10
and not under force, even though he is doing what he does not will to
do. When the situation is not under his control, then in a fashion he is
acting under force, but not without qualification. For even if he does
not choose what he actually does, he does choose the thing that is the
purpose of his doing it. Even here, cases differ. If a man were to kill in
order to avoid being caught at blind man's buff, it would be ridiculous 15
to claim that he acted under force and coercion: it has to be a greater
and more painful evil that he will suffer if he does not do the deed.
Thus, he will act under coercion—though not by force or in an
unnatural way—when he does something evil for the sake of a good,
or in order to escape from a greater evil, and does so involuntarily,
these matters not being under his control.*

Hence many regard even erotic love and some kinds of anger 20
and physical condition as involuntary, because they are too strong
for human nature: we extend indulgence, because they are things

capable of doing violence to nature. There is a greater appearance of
acting under force and involuntarily in the case of a man acting to
avoid a severe pain than in acting to avoid slight pain; and, in gen-
25 eral, in acting to avoid pain rather than to secure enjoyment. What
is in a man's power—and it all comes back to this—is what his nature
is able to bear; what it is unable to bear, and what is not the result of
his own natural desire and reasoning, is not in his power. For this
reason, if people are possessed and prophesy, we do not say that it is
in their power to say what they say or to do what they do, even though
what they come out with is a product of thought. Nor do we say that
30 it is a result of their appetite. So there are some thoughts and passions that are not within our power, and neither are the acts that
result from such thoughts and reasonings. As Philolaus* said, some
reasons are stronger than we are.

So, if the relation between voluntariness and involuntariness and
force called for investigation, let that be our settlement of the matter.
35 (The arguments that most obstruct the understanding of voluntariness are those that claim that people can be subject to force and
simultaneously act voluntarily.*)

Concluding definition of voluntariness and involuntariness

9. Now that that discussion has reached a conclusion, and it has
been found that the voluntary is not to be defined by desire or choice,
1225b it remains to define what it is to be in accordance with thought. Now,
voluntariness seems to be contrary to involuntariness, and acting
with knowledge of the person, the instrument, and the effect seems
to be contrary to acting through error about the person, instrument,
and thing, the error being not merely coincidental. (Sometimes a
5 person knows that it is their father but not that the effect will be
lethal rather than salutary, as in the case of Pelias' daughters;* or a
person knows the instrument, knowing he is giving a potion, but
believing it to be a wine or a philtre when it is really hemlock.) What
is done through error, whether of thing, instrument, or person, is
involuntary; the opposite, therefore, is voluntary.

Whatever a man does that is in his power not to do, and does it
not in error and of his own volition, he must needs do voluntarily;
this is what voluntariness is. What he does in error, and because of
10 the error, he does involuntarily. But since knowledge and understanding are of two kinds, one being the possession and the other

the use of knowledge, the person who has it but does not use it could in some cases justly be described as in error, but not so in other cases, as where the failure to make use of the knowledge is due to negligence. Likewise, a person might also be blamed for not having the knowledge, if he does not have it though it was easy and necessary to attain and the failure to do so was due to negligence or pleasure or pain. So let the definition have these points added to it.

Deliberate choice

10. That, then, is how to settle the distinction between the voluntary and the involuntary. Let us next say something about choice,* first setting out in our discussion various problems about it. For one might be in doubt about the genus to which it belongs, and where to locate it, and one might wonder whether what is chosen is or is not the same as what is voluntary. In particular, it is said by some people, and on investigation it would seem to be correct, that choice is one of two things, namely, belief or desire, since both of these appear in its company.

Well, it is obvious that it is not desire, for if so, it would be either volition or appetite or temper, for no one has a desire without experiencing one or other of these. Now, temper and appetite are found also in beasts, but choice is not. Further, in the case of those that have both of these, many choices are made without either temper or appetite, and when these passions are felt, there will be no choice but rather resistance. Again, appetite and temper are always accompanied by pain, but we make many choices in the absence of pain. Nor is volition the same thing as choice, either. For men want some things that they know are impossible, for instance to be king of all mankind or to be immortal; but nobody knowingly chooses what is impossible, nor, in general, things that, though possible, he does not believe to be in his own power to do or not to do. So this much is obvious, that whatever is chosen must be something in one's power.

Similarly, it is clear that choice is not belief, nor any kind of thinking. For we have just seen that what is chosen is in one's power, but we have many beliefs about things that are not in our power, such that the diagonal of a square is incommensurable with the side. Again, choice is not true or false. Choice is not even a belief about practicalities within our power, a belief, say, that something should or should not be done.

This holds of volition no less than of belief: no one chooses the end, only what conduces to the end. I mean, for instance, that no one chooses to be healthy, but rather, for the sake of his health, to go for a walk or to sit down. Again, no one chooses to be happy, but
10 rather, with a view to happiness, to go into commerce or embark on a venture. In general, one who makes a choice makes it clear what he is choosing and what he is choosing it for: the 'what for' is the thing for whose sake he is making the choice, and the 'what' is the object chosen for the sake of something else. It is the end that his volition especially concerns, and his belief is that he should be healthy and
15 do well. So it is obvious from these considerations that choice is something other than belief or volition. For volition and belief are especially concerned with the end; not so choice.

It is clear, then, that choice is neither volition nor belief nor any kind of judgement. How, then, does it differ from them, and what is its relation to the voluntary? The answer will make clear what choice
20 actually is. Among the things that can either be or not be, there are some about which deliberation is possible, and some about which it is not. For some are capable of either being or not being, but to bring them about is not within our power: some of them come about by nature and some through other causes. No one, unless much mis-
25 taken, would try to deliberate about such things. But there are some things that admit not only of being and not being, but also of human deliberation: these are the things that are in our power to do or not to do. Hence we do not deliberate about the affairs of India, nor
30 about how to square the circle—the former are not in our power and the latter just cannot be done; it is the things that are in our power that are the objects of choice and conduct. Indeed, we do not delib-erate even about all the things that are in our power. This makes it clear that choice is not simply a matter of belief.

For this reason someone might wonder why doctors deliberate
35 about matters within the purview of their science but scribes do not. The reason is that there are two kinds of mistake: we either fail in working things out, or fail in attention when we are putting things into effect. In medicine both kinds of mistake are possible, but in the
1226b case of what the scribes do, mistake is possible only in attention and action, and if they reflect on that, they will go on for ever.*

Since, then, choice is not belief or volition, either separately or together (for no one makes a choice on a sudden, but on a sudden one can think that one should act and people can form a volition), it must be a product of both: for both are present when a person makes a choice.

But what kind of product? We must investigate. Its very name already tells us something. Choice is a matter of picking—not random picking, but picking one thing in preference to another, and that is not possible without examination and deliberation. So choice is the product of deliberative belief.

No one deliberates about the end—that stands there for everybody—but about the things that lead towards it, whether it is this or that which is conducive to it, or when that has been decided, how to procure it. We all deliberate thus until we can trace back to ourselves the factor that originates the process. No one makes a choice without preparatory deliberation about what is better and what is worse—deliberation about which of the things capable of being or not being are in our power and are conducive to the end. Hence, it is clear that choice is a deliberative desire for something that is in our power. For we all deliberate about what we choose, though it is not the case that we choose everything we deliberate about.* (I call a desire 'deliberative' when it is originated and caused by deliberation, and the desire arises from the deliberation.)

So choice does not occur in the other animals, nor in humans at every stage or condition of life, because neither does deliberation nor the concept of a reason. However, there is nothing to prevent the multitude from forming a judgement whether something should be done or not, but without the ability to give reasons. The deliberative part of the soul is the part that recognizes a particular kind of cause: for a purpose is one kind of cause, since a cause is the reason why something obtains. We say that the purpose for which something exists or comes to be is its cause; for instance, fetching his chattels is a cause of a man's walking, if that is why he is walking. That is why those who have no fixed aim do not go in for deliberation.

Now, if someone does or refrains from doing something that is in his power to do or not to do, of his own accord and not in error, he acts or refrains voluntarily. Moreover, there are many such things that we do without deliberation or premeditation. From all this it follows that everything chosen is voluntary, though not everything voluntary is chosen, and that whatever is done from choice is voluntary, though not everything voluntary is done from choice. A further thing that is obvious from this is that legislators are right to classify

1227a items as being voluntary, or involuntary, or premeditated; their classifications may not be accurate in detail, but they have got hold of
the truth to a certain extent. We shall say more about these matters
in our inquiry into justice.* What is evident is that choice is not
simply volition, nor simply belief, but belief plus desire when these
follow as a conclusion from deliberation.

5   A man who deliberates always deliberates for some purpose, and
always has an aim in view: in deliberating he is inquiring what is useful
towards that aim. Consequently, no one deliberates about the end
itself: this is the starting point or postulate, like the postulates in the
10 theoretical sciences, about which we spoke briefly at the start of our
discussion, and in greater detail in the *Analytics*. What people inquire
about, whether or not they are practising an art, is what is conducive
to the end; for example, in the case of people deliberating whether to
go to war or not. In advance of this there will the reason for this, that
15 is to say the purpose, such as wealth or pleasure, or whatever of the
kind happens to be the purpose. A man who deliberates, once he has
taken a survey from the point of view of the end, deliberates about
what conduces to bring it within his reach, or what he can himself do
towards the end.

The end is by nature always a good, and one about which people
deliberate in particular, as a doctor may deliberate whether he is to
20 give a drug, or a general where he is to pitch his camp. For them
there is a good, an end, which is the thing that is best in the abstract.
However, contrary to nature, and through perversion, something
that is not the good but only apparent good may be the end. The
reason is as follows. Some of the things there are cannot be employed
except upon the objects that are by nature proper to them, e.g. sight
25 (one cannot see, for instance, what is invisible, nor hear what is
inaudible), but a science can be employed to produce something
other than its proper object. Both health and disease are objects of
the same science but not in the same fashion: the former is its natural object, and the latter unnatural. Likewise, the good is the natural object of volition, but contrary to nature evil too is its object.
30 By nature one wills what is good, but against nature and through
perversion one wills evil.

However, when a thing is corrupted and perverted, it changes not
into some random state, but into the contrary or intervening states.
For it is not possible to go beyond these bounds, just as deception,

too, leads not to some random belief, but to the contrary belief, where there is one, and in particular the belief that is the contrary to the one that would express knowledge. Necessarily, then, deception 35 and choice deviate from the mean to the opposites (both more and less are opposites of the mean). Pleasure and pain are to blame; we are so constituted that the pleasant appears good to the soul, and the more pleasant better, while the painful appears bad and the more 40 painful worse. So from all this, too, it is obvious that virtue is about 1227b pleasures and pains, for they are concerned with the objects of choice, and choice is about good and evil, real and apparent; and, by nature, pleasure and pain are apparent good and evil.

Necessarily, then, since moral virtue is a middle state, always con- 5 cerned with pleasures and pains, and vice consists in excess and defect in the same matters as virtue, it follows that virtue is a moral state expressed in the choice of the mean, relative to ourselves, in those pleasures and pains in respect of which a person's enjoyment 10 or distress indicates his character. (A preference for sweets or for savouries is not sufficient to indicate character.)

Virtue, ends, and means

11. Having given these definitions, we must say what virtue does. Does it make the end correct and the choice faultless (i.e. a choice of the proper end)? Or does it, as some people think, make the reason- ing correct? Not the latter, for what does that is continence, since in 15 continence the reasoning is not corrupted; and continence and virtue are two different things. We must speak about them later, since those who think that it is virtue that is responsible for right reasoning do so for this reason, namely, that that is what continence does, and continence is a matter for praise.*

Let us now proceed to air another problem. A choice may go wrong 20 in being a mistaken choice of means to a correct aim, or a choice of means appropriate to an incorrect aim—or in both ways. Now, does virtue make the aim, or the means to the aim? We maintain that it is the aim, because this is not the result of inference or reasoning, but must be assumed as a starting point.* For a doctor does not inquire 25 whether one ought to be healthy or not, but whether one ought to take a walk or not; nor does a trainer inquire whether one ought to be fit or not, but whether one should take up wrestling or not. Likewise, no other discipline inquires about its end. As in the theoretical

disciplines it is postulates that are the starting points, so in productive
disciplines it is the end that is the starting point and postulate. It goes

30 like this: if this is what being healthy is,* if that is to come about, then
such-and-such must be provided—just as in the other case, if the
angles of a triangle equal two right angles, such-and-such necessarily
follows. The end, therefore, is the starting point of the thinking, and
the conclusion of the thinking is the starting point of the action.

Now, correctness of any kind has as its cause either reasoning or

35 virtue. Hence, the correctness of the end (as opposed to the means),
since it is not due to reasoning, must be due to virtue. The end is the
purpose: for every choice is a choice *of* something *for the sake of*
something else. Now, it is the mean that is the purpose, and what
virtue does is to cause a choice to be made for the sake of the mean.
Choice is not *of* the purpose, but of the things done for the sake of

40 it. Hitting on these, the things that should be done for the sake of
1228a the end, is the task of a different faculty; what virtue causes is the
correctness of the end of the choice.*

This is why we judge a man's character from his choosing, that is to
say, not what he does but for what purpose he does it. Likewise, vice
makes choice be a choice with a contrary purpose. If someone, having

5 it in his power to do noble things and abstain from base things, does
just the contrary, it is evident that he is not a virtuous man. So, too,
vice must be voluntary no less than virtue, for there is no necessity to
behave viciously. That is why vice is blamed and virtue praised; for
disgraceful and evil acts, while blameworthy if voluntary, if they are

10 involuntary are not blamed any more than good acts are praised.

Moreover, when we praise or blame we all look at the choice rather
than the actual deeds, even though the exercise of a virtue is more valuable than the virtue itself. This is because people may perform bad acts
under coercion, but choice cannot be coerced. Again, it is because it is

15 not easy to discern the character of a choice that we are forced to make
judgements of character based on people's deeds. The exercise of virtue
is more valuable, but the choice is more praiseworthy. All this follows
from our assumptions, and also agrees with people's perceptions.

BOOK III · THE MORAL VIRTUES

Courage

1. IN general terms it has been stated that the virtues are middle states,* and that these virtues themselves and their opposing vices are states that find expression in choice. We have listed them; let us now take them in turn and discuss them one by one. First, let us 25 speak about courage.

The almost unanimous opinion is that courage is one of the virtues and that it is fear that is the concern of the courageous man. And in our schedule earlier* we distinguished foolhardiness and fear as contraries, because they are indeed in a manner opposed to each other. It is evident, therefore, that people who are thus charac- 30 terized will similarly be contrasted with each other, that is to say, the coward (who is so called from being more afraid than is right, and less daring than is right) and the foolhardy (who is so called as the kind of person who is less afraid than is right, and more daring than is right). (Hence the name: in Greek the word for 'foolhardy' and 35 the word for 'daring' have the same root.*) So that since courage is the best state of character in relation to feelings of fear and daring, and people should be neither like the foolhardy (for they have a deficiency in one and an excess of the other) nor like cowards (they do the same, but from contrary corners in respect of contrasted feel- 1228b ings: they have a deficiency in daring and an excess of fear) it is evident that the middle condition between foolhardiness and cowardice is courage, for that is what is the best state.

It is held that normally the courageous man is fearless, and the coward is full of fears. The latter fears dangers that are rare and 5 slight as well as those that are frequent and serious, and gets very frightened very quickly. The former, on the contrary, either never feels fear, or if he does, it is slight, reluctant, and rare, and concerns serious dangers. The former endures things that are very frightening, the latter not even mildly frightening things. Well, what kinds of frightening things does the courageous man endure? First, is 10 it things that frighten him or that frighten someone else? If they are things that frighten someone else, then one would not rate his courage as anything remarkable; but if they are things that frighten him, then they must be seriously and frequently frightening.* Now, things that are frightening produce fear in the individual to whom they are frightening: violent fear if very frightening, mild fear if only slightly frightening. It follows, then, that the courageous man 15 feels fears that are violent and frequent, whereas it appeared on the contrary that courage makes a man fearless, a state that implies fearing few things if any, and those slightly and reluctantly.

But perhaps 'frightening', like 'pleasant' and 'good', is used in two different ways. Some things are objectively pleasant or good.* 20 Others are pleasant or good to a particular individual, but objectively they are not so, but rather the contrary, evil and unpleasant— evil like the things that are found expedient by wicked men or pleasant only to the childishness of children. Likewise, some things are objectively frightening, others only frightening to a particular individual. Thus, the things that the coward fears in his cowardice are either not frightening to anyone or only mildly frightening. 25 What we call objectively frightening are the things that are frightening to most people, and to human nature altogether. It is in face of these frightening things that the courageous man feels no fear and displays endurance. They are frightening to him in one way, but not in another: frightening to him as a human being, but not at all so (or only slightly so) to him in his courageousness. These things really 30 are frightening, in that they frighten most people, and that is why this state of character attracts praise, just as a strong man or a healthy man does. It is not that no possible labour can wear out the one, or no possible excess injure the other; they are marked out by the fact that they are not at all, or only slightly, affected by the things 35 that affect many or most people. Sickly people, then, and weak people, and cowards suffer from afflictions that are commonplace but they are more promptly and more severely affected by them than most people are. There are other people* who are left totally or largely unaffected by the things that affect most people.

There remains this problem. To a courageous man is there nothing that is frightening? Is he incapable of fear? Surely there is nothing 1229a to prevent him from feeling fear in the manner we have described. For courage is a way of following reason, and reason tells us to choose what is noble. For this reason a person who endures what is frightening, but not for that reason, is either mad or foolhardy; only

the person who does so for the sake of what is noble counts as courageous. The coward fears what he ought not to fear, the foolhardy 5
dares where he ought not to dare; the courageous man does both as
he ought to, and thus he is a mean, for he is daring and fearful exactly
as reason commands. But reason does not command the endurance
of painful and life-threatening things unless it is noble to do so. The
foolhardy man, then, dares even when reason tells him not to; the
coward does not dare even when reason tells him to. It is the cour- 10
ageous man who dares only when reason tells him to.

There are five kinds of courage, so called because they resemble
courage in being endurance of the same dangers; but the endurance
is for different reasons in the different cases. One is civic courage,
which is based on a sense of shame; another is military courage,
based on experience and on knowledge—not knowledge of dangers
(as Socrates said*), but rather of ways of coping with them. The 15
third rests on inexperience and ignorance: it makes madmen ready
to face anything, and makes children handle snakes. Another kind is
an expression of hope, which makes people face dangers if they have
had a number of lucky escapes, or if they are drunk—for wine is a
great purveyor of hope. Another kind arises from irrational passion: 20
love or rage, for instance. For a man in love is foolhardy rather than
cowardly, and endures many dangers, like the man who killed the
tyrant in Metapontum* and the man of whom they tell stories in
Crete. The case is similar with anger and rage, for rage makes a man
beside himself. That is why wild boars are thought to be brave, even 25
though they are not really; it is only when they are beside themselves that they behave like that, otherwise they are just as unpre-
dictable as foolhardy humans. After all, this effect of rage is
something natural, for rage refuses to accept defeat, which is why
young people make the best fighters. Civic courage, on the other
hand, is the effect of custom. But none of these is true courage, even 30
though they are all useful sources of encouragement in danger.

So far we have spoken only in general terms about what frightens
people, but it will be better to go into greater detail. In general, then,
what is frightening is whatever causes fear, such as things that look
like causing life-threatening pain. People who expect some other 35
kind of pain—a man, say, who foresaw that he was about to suffer
the pains of envy, or jealousy, or disgrace—no doubt experience
pain of some kind and a different kind of emotion, but it is not fear.

It is only pains that are of a kind to take away life whose apparent
1229b approach gives rise to fear. That is why people who are very soft
about some things are nonetheless courageous, and some who are
hard and tough are cowards.

Moreover, it seems pretty much the special characteristic of courage to have a certain attitude to death and its pains. Suppose that
5 someone was capable of reasonable endurance of heat and cold and
other non-dangerous discomforts, but was soft and timid about
death, not for any reason other than because it brings dissolution.
Such a man would be thought cowardly, while a person who was soft
about those discomforts but indifferent about death would be
thought courageous. For we speak of danger only in the case of those
10 frightening things that bring us close to whatever threatens to
destroy us. It is precisely the apparent approach of things that
appear so to threaten that constitutes danger.

The frightening things, then, that we have in mind when we call
a man courageous are, as has been said, those that are capable of
15 causing life-threatening pain. But they must appear close and not
distant, and they must be or appear to be significant on a human
scale. There are some things, of course, that cannot but appear
frightening and terrifying to anyone whatever. Some degrees of heat
20 and cold and other qualities are unbearable to us, with human bodies
conditioned as they are, and it is quite possible that the same is the
case with passions of the soul.

The cowardly and the foolhardy, then, fall into error because of
their characters. To the coward things that are not frightening appear
frightening, and things mildly frightening appear very frightening;
25 to the foolhardy man, on the contrary, frightening things are encouraging, and very frightening things only mildly so. But to the courageous man things seem exactly as they are.

Accordingly, if it is through ignorance that a man faces up to
something frightening—a madman, for instance, who braves a
shower of thunderbolts—that does not make him courageous. Even
if he knows the scale of the danger, a man is not courageous if he is
driven by rage, in the way that the Celts take arms and confront the
30 waves. (Barbarian courage in general involves an element of rage.)
There is a certain pleasure belonging to rage, since it goes along
with a hope of revenge; and some men will endure a lot for the sake
of other pleasures too. However, if it is for the sake of the pleasure of

rage or any other pleasure, or to avoid greater evils, that a man
endures death, he still does not properly count as courageous. If
dying itself were pleasant, intemperate people, in their incontinence, 35
would often have been found dying. As it is, death itself is not pleasant, but some life-threatening activities are, and so many people
through incontinence knowingly bring it on themselves—but none
of them would be thought courageous, however readily they went to
death. Nor is anyone courageous if, as many people do, he seeks 40
death to escape suffering. As Agathon* says:

> The baser sort of men, worn down by toil   1230a
> Fall all in love with death.

So too the poets tell the story of Cheiron, who, though an immortal,
prayed that he might die because his wound was so agonizing.*
    Similarly, all those who face dangers because of experience are
not really courageous; no doubt this is what most military men do. 5
That is the exact opposite of what Socrates thought, when he held
that courage was a form of knowledge. When sailors know how to go
aloft, they are daring not because they know what is frightening, but
because they know how to protect themselves against the dangers. 10
Not everything that makes people fight with greater daring counts
as courage, for in that case strength and wealth would be courage—
if Theognis* is right that poverty can conquer any man.
    Manifestly, some people, because of their experience, do face
emergencies in spite of being cowards. They do so because they
think there is no danger, since they know how to protect themselves.
A sign of this is that when they think they have no protection, and 15
the danger is close at hand, they fail to stand fast.
    Of all these courageous people it is those who stand fast because
of shame who present the most convincing appearance of courage.
Thus, Homer reports Hector* facing the danger of his conflict with
Achilles:

> And shame took hold of Hector.

And   20
> Polydamas will be the first to taunt me.

Such courage is civic courage.
    But true courage is something different from this, and from all
the others, even though it resembles them, as does the courage of

wild beasts which rush in rage to meet the blow. A man should stand
his ground not because he fears disgrace, or is enraged, nor because
25 he does not think he will die, or because he has effective protection,
for in that case he will not think there is anything to be afraid of. But
since every virtue implies choice (in the manner earlier explained: it
makes a man choose everything for the sake of some end, and the
end is what is noble), it is clear that courage being a particular virtue
30 will make a man endure what is frightening for the sake of some end.
Instead of making him do it in error, it will make him judge rightly,
and instead of doing it for the sake of pleasure, he will do it because
it is noble. In a case where it is not noble but insane, he will not face
the danger, for that would be something disgraceful.

We have now explained pretty adequately for our present pur-
35 poses what are the kind of things in respect of which courage is a
mean state, and what it is a mean between, and why, and what is the
effect of things that are frightening.

Temperance and intemperance

2. Next we must try to draw some distinctions concerning temperance* and intemperance. 'Intemperate' has many senses.* A man so
called has, as it were, not been tempered or healed, just as something
1230b that is indiscrete is not discrete. What is indiscrete may be either
incapable of being divided, or, while capable of division, not in fact
divided into discrete parts. It is the same with intemperance: there
are those who by nature cannot accept tempering or chastisement,
and those who can accept, but have not yet received, chastisement
5 for faults in the area where the virtue of temperance is exercised.
Children are an example of the latter: when they are called intemperate it is in respect of a special kind of intemperance. The word is
used in a different sense of those whom it is difficult or altogether
impossible to cure by chastisement.

10 But however many senses 'intemperate' has, it is obvious that its
sphere of activity consists of certain pleasures and pains, and that
intemperate people differ from one another and from other people
by their attitude towards these. (We illustrated earlier how we apply
the term 'intemperance' in an extended sense.) People who through
lack of sensibility are unattracted by these pleasures by some are
15 called 'insensitive' and by others given similar names. However, the
condition is not very familiar or common, because everyone errs

rather in the opposite direction, and susceptibility and sensitivity to these pleasures is inborn in all of us. The prime exemplars of insensitivity are the boors who figure in comic plays and steer clear even of moderate and necessary pleasures.　　　20

Since temperance is all about pleasures, it follows that it is also about desires of a particular kind, and we should find out which these are. The temperate man's temperance is not about any and every desire or pleasure. According to common opinion, it concerns the objects of two of the senses, taste and touch; but in reality it is 25 about the objects of touch only. Temperance is not exercised in respect of the pleasure of looking at beautiful things (without sexual desire) or the pain of looking at ugly things; it is not exercised on the pleasures of listening to beautiful music or the pains of cacophony, nor again on the pleasures and pains of smelling pleasant and foul odours. No one is called intemperate for being sensitive or insensi- 30 tive to sensations of that kind. A man who looks at a beautiful statue, or horse, or human being, or listens to someone singing, without any desire to eat or drink or have sex, but simply wanting to gaze on the beauty and listen to the singing, is no more to be thought intemper- ate than those who were spellbound by the Sirens.　　　35

Temperance and intemperance have to do with the two senses that alone have objects that are felt by, and give pleasure and pain to, animals other than ourselves, namely, taste and touch. With regard to the pleasures of the other senses—harmony and beauty, for instance—they seem to be pretty much totally insensitive. Clearly 1231a the sight of beautiful objects or the hearing of harmonious music has no effect on them worth mentioning—except perhaps in a few prodigious cases.* Nor are they affected by sweet or foul smells, even though all their senses are more acute than ours. When they do 5 take pleasure in smells, it is a coincidental and not an intrinsic enjoy- ment. An example of an intrinsically enjoyable odour is the smell of flowers; by the non-intrinsic kind I mean those that we enjoy through anticipation or memory, like those of food and drink. In such cases our enjoyment derives from a different pleasure, that of eating and 10 drinking. Stratonicus* put it elegantly when he said that some things smell beautiful and others smell delicious. Not all even of the pleas- ures of taste are attractive to the lower animals: not those that are sensed by the tip of the tongue, but only those that are felt in the throat, a sensation that is more like touch than taste. That is why

15 gluttons pray not for a long tongue, but for the gullet of a crane—as did Philoxenus, the son of Eryxis.* So, strictly speaking, the field of intemperance is constituted by the objects of touch, and it is with such pleasures that the intemperate man occupies himself: for the drunkard, the glutton, the lecher, and the gourmet all pursue the
20 sensations we have described, and their vices are the different sub-classes of intemperance. But no one is called intemperate for enjoying the pleasures of sight or hearing or smell: if he does so to excess, we may blame his faults, but we do not despise him. In general, in areas where there is no such thing as continence and incontinence,
25 there is not temperance and intemperance either.*

A man, then, who is of such a character as to fall short in those things that almost everyone must share and enjoy is an insensitive person (or whatever the right term is); the man who exceeds is an intemperate person. While all people by nature enjoy these things and feel desires for them, they are not, nor are they called, intem-
30 perate, for they do not go to excess in rejoicing more than they should when they get them, nor in grieving more than they should when they fail to get them. Nor are they unfeeling, because they do not fall short, but rather go to excess, in feelings of joy and grief.

Since in this area there is excess and defect, it is clear that there is
35 also a mean, and this is the best state, contrasted with each of the others. So if temperance is the best state in respect of the intemperate man's sphere of activity, the mean state with regard to the aforesaid pleasures of the senses will be temperance, a mean between intemperance and insensitivity. The excess will be intemperance,
1231b and the defect is either nameless or signified by the names we have mentioned. The relevant class of pleasures will be more exactly defined when we come later to discuss continence and incontinence.

Gentleness and cruelty

5 3. In the same way we must inquire about gentleness and cruelty. We observe that the sphere of gentleness is the pain that arises from rage: it is having a certain attitude towards this that makes a person gentle. In our chart we made a contrast between irascibility, cruelty, and savagery (all such being forms of the same disposition) and the
10 characteristics of the servile and the milksop. Such are the kind of names we call those who are not moved to rage when they ought to

be, but accept insults cheerfully and are humble in the face of contempt. There are contrasts, too, between being quick to anger and being slow to anger, between being mildly angry and being violently angry, and experiencing for longer or shorter times the pain that we 15 call rage. And since there is here, as we said in other cases, excess and defect (for the cruel man is the one who feels anger too quickly, too violently, too long, at the wrong time, and with the wrong people, and with too many people, while the servile man is just the contrary), it is clear that there is also some character that is at the mid- 20 point of this scale.

Since, then, both these states of character are wrong, it is clear that the state midway between them is correct: such a man gets angry neither too soon nor too late, and he does not get angry with the wrong people or fail to get angry with those people who deserve it. So since the best state of character in respect of these emotions is gentleness, gentleness would be a mean, and a gentle person would 25 be in the middle between a cruel person and a servile person.

Liberality

4. Pride, magnificence, and liberality are also mean states. Liberality is the mean in regard to the getting and spending of wealth. A man who takes more pleasure than he should in every acquisition, and is more pained than he should be by every expenditure, is an illiberal 30 man, while he who has these feelings less than he ought is prodigal, and he that feels both as he ought is liberal. (What I mean by 'as he ought', here and elsewhere, is 'in accordance with correct reasoning'.) And since the two characters first mentioned exhibit excess and defect, and since where there are extremes there is also a mean, and that mean is the best (a particular best for each kind of action), 35 liberality must of necessity be the mean between prodigality and illiberality with regard to the getting and spending of wealth.

We speak in two different senses of wealth and its acquisition, for there are two ways of using a piece of property, such as a shoe or a 1232a cloak: one is its proper use, and the other is its coincidental use— I don't mean coincidental like the use of a shoe as a weight, but rather selling it or hiring it out, which is a use of it as a shoe. Now, a miser is someone who dotes on money, and for him money becomes a matter of possession rather than coincidental use. An illiberal man may be prodigal with respect to the coincidental mode of 5 making money, since what he wants to maximize is the natural pursuit of wealth. The prodigal man goes short of necessities, but the liberal man gives away his surplus.

10   There are also species of these states, excessive or deficient in respect of different parts of their sphere. An illiberal man* may be parsimonious, or he may be niggardly or he may be a profiteer: parsimonious if he will not part with money, niggardly if he gets worried about small sums, and a profiteer if he does not care where his
15   money comes from. If his illiberality amounts to injustice, then he is a fraud and a cheat. Among prodigal people, likewise, we can distinguish between the wastrel who spends without restraint, and the fool who cannot bear the pain of keeping accounts.

Pride

5. As to pride,* we must define its specific nature by the attributes
20   ascribed to the proud man. When two states are close to each other and resemble each other up to a certain point, further differences often escape notice. This happens in other cases no less than in the case of pride. Thus, for instance, contrary characters claim the same quality, with the prodigal claiming to be liberal, the surly person
25   claiming to be friendly, and the foolhardy to be courageous. These characters do indeed share a sphere of activity, and are neighbours up to a point: thus, the courageous man endures dangers, and so does the foolhardy man, but the former does so in one fashion, and the latter in a different fashion, and there is a great difference between the two.

We speak of the proud man, in accordance with the derivation of the corresponding Greek adjective, as having a certain greatness of
30   soul and faculty, and so he seems like the friendly man and the magnificent man. Pride does indeed seem to accompany all the virtues.* For to distinguish between great and small goods is something praiseworthy, and those goods are thought to be great that are the ones pursued by a man whose state of character is the best in respect
35   of these matters, and it is pride that is this best state. Each particular virtue distinguishes correctly between the greater and the lesser in its own area, following the prescriptions that a wise man and his virtue would give. Thus, all the virtues go with this virtue, or it goes with them all.

Again, it seems characteristic of the proud man to be disdainful.
1232b Each virtue makes people disdainful of things irrationally deemed

great: for example, courage makes a man disdainful of dangers, for he thinks that nothing that is disgraceful is great, and that being outnumbered is not always frightening.* So, too, the temperate man disdains great and numerous pleasures, and the liberal man despises wealth. But disdain seems particularly characteristic of the proud man because he cares about few things only, and those, great ones, and he does not care what anybody else thinks. A proud man would pay more attention to what one good man thinks than what a multitude of many ordinary people do, as Antiphon, after his condemnation, said to Agathon, who praised his speech in his defence.* Contempt seems to be a feeling particularly characteristic of the proud person. Of the things about which humans seem most to care, honour and life and riches, he appears to value none except honour. It would indeed grieve him to be dishonoured, and to be ruled by someone unworthy, and obtaining honour is his greatest joy.

This may make him look inconsistent: for to be especially concerned about honour and to disdain the opinion of the multitude* do not seem to go together. Before continuing we must make a distinction. There are two ways in which honour may be great or small: it may be conferred by a multitude of ordinary people, or by those who are worthy of note. Again, it makes a difference what are the grounds on which it is conferred, for its greatness does not depend only on the number and quality of those who confer it, but also on its being honourable. And in truth, public office and other goods are honourable and worthy of pursuit only if they are really great, so that there is no virtue without greatness. Each virtue,* then, as we have said,* makes someone a proud person in respect of those matters that fall within its sphere.

Nevertheless, there is a single virtue of pride, alongside the other virtues, so that the person who possesses this virtue must be called proud in the most proper sense. Among goods, there are some that are honourable, and others identified in our earlier classification; of these, some are truly great and some are small. Some men deserve and claim the former, and it is among these that we must look for the proud man.

We must make a fourfold distinction. A man may deserve great things and think himself worthy of them, or it may be small things that he deserves and thinks himself worthy of; and each of these cases may be reversed: one man may deserve small things and think himself

35 worthy of great and honourable ones, while another may deserve great
things and think himself worthy of small ones. The man who deserves
small things and thinks himself worthy of great things is blameworthy, for he is foolish, and it is no fine thing to be rewarded above
one's deserts. Blameworthy also is the man who, while deserving of
1233a such honours and having them available to him, does not think himself worthy of them. There remains, then, the person opposite to these
two: the man who is worthy of great things, who thinks himself worthy
of them and is of such a character as to believe that he deserves them.
He is the praiseworthy character midway between the other two.

Pride, then, is the best condition of character in relation to the
5 choice and exercise of honour and other honourable goods, and it is
these rather than utilities that we assign as the sphere of the proud
man. From this, and from the fact that it is the mean state that is the
most praiseworthy,* it follows that pride, too, is a middle state. Of
the contraries as shown in our diagram, claiming great things when
10 one does not deserve them is vanity (for it is precisely the people
who think they are worthy of great things when they are not whom
we call vain), while deserving great things while not claiming them
is diffidence (for if a man in possession of deserving qualities does
15 not think himself worthy of anything great, he is diffident). Hence it
follows that pride is a mean* between vanity and diffidence.

The fourth of the characters we distinguished is not proud, but
nor is he altogether blameworthy: he has nothing to do with anything great, since he neither deserves nor claims great things; hence
he is not the opposite of the proud person. To be sure, claiming
20 small things when one deserves small things might look like the
opposite of claiming great things when one deserves great things.
However, such a man is not the opposite of the proud man because
he is not blameworthy, since his character is what reason commands.
Indeed, he is naturally identical with the proud man, since each of
them thinks himself worthy only of what he deserves. He might
even become proud, since he will think himself worthy of what he
25 deserves, unlike the diffident man, who does not, even when they are
available to him, think himself worthy of the honourable goods that
he deserves. What would such a man have done if his deserts had
been slight? Either he would have been vain, claiming great things,
or else he would have claimed even less than he does. No one would
call a person diffident if he were a resident alien who submitted to

authority and claimed no public office, but you would do so if he were a nobleman who thought it a great thing to hold office. 30

Magnificence

6. It is not any casual action or choice that provides the sphere of action of the magnificent man, but only expenditure (unless we are using the word in a transferred sense). Without expenditure there is no such thing as magnificence, for magnificence is splendour in adornment, and adornment does not come from casual expenditure, but from expenditure that goes beyond what is strictly necessary. 35 Hence, a magnificent man is one who as a matter of choice spends great sums on appropriate grandeur while preserving the due mean, and who loves taking the corresponding pleasure. There is no name for the man who spends vast sums in clashing styles, but those whom some people call tasteless and ostentatious have a certain affinity 1233b with him. Imagine a rich man who, when paying for the wedding of his beloved,* thinks it sufficient to make the kind of provision one would offer to mere hangers-on. Such a one is shabby, whereas someone who entertains riff-raff in the style of a wedding breakfast displays something like ostentation, unless he is doing it to acquire 5 celebrity or to gain office. It is the person that entertains suitably and as reason directs who is magnificent; for what is appropriate is what is suitable, and nothing that is unsuitable can be appropriate.*

It must be suitable to the individual case, appropriate to the agent, and to the object, and to the occasion; for instance, what is suitable 10 for the wedding of a servant is different from what is suitable for the wedding of one's beloved. Moreover, it must be appropriate in amount or quality for the agent himself; for instance, people thought that Themistocles' entertainment of spectators at the Olympic games was unsuitable for him as a nouveau riche, though it would have been appropriate for Cimon.* But a person who is indifferent to questions of suitability does not fit into any of the above classes.

So too with liberality: a man may be neither liberal nor illiberal. 15

Other good and bad qualities of character

7. Roughly speaking, each of the other objects of praise or blame in respect of character are excesses or defects or means, but of emotions. The envious man and the malicious man provide examples. For—to take the states of character from which they get

their names—envy is being pained by the good fortune of people
20 who deserve it, while though there is no name for the emotion of the
malicious person,* such a character shows itself by rejoicing at the
misfortunes of those who deserve better. Midway between these is
the person who is righteously indignant, whose attitude was called
by the ancients Nemesis:* he feels pain at undeserved ill and good
25 fortune and rejoices when they are deserved. That is why people
think of Nemesis as a deity.

Modesty is a mean between shamelessness and bashfulness: the
person who cares for nobody's opinion is shameless, the person who
values everyone's is bashful, while the modest person regards only
that of manifestly good people.

Friendliness is a mean between quarrelsomeness and obsequious-
30 ness. The person who falls in readily with every desire of others is
obsequious, the person who repels them all is quarrelsome, while
the friendly person neither falls in with every pleasure nor repels
every pleasure, but falls in with what seems to be best.*

Dignity is a mean between churlishness and servility. A person
35 who leads his life with contempt rather than consideration for others
is churlish, a person who defers to others and is submissive to everyone is servile, while a person of dignity defers in some matters but
not in others, and only to those who are worthy of regard.

The candid and straightforward person, whom some call 'bluff',
is midway between the self-deprecating man and the boaster.
1234a A person who deprecates himself consciously and falsely is self-
deprecating, and one who exaggerates his worth is a boaster. One
who describes himself as he actually is, is a candid person and, in
Homer's expression, solid: altogether, he is a lover of truth while the
other is a lover of falsehood.

Conviviality is also a mean,* and a convivial person is midway
5 between a buffoon and a person who is a humourless boor. In matters of food and drink, there are finicky people and omnivorous
people—those who take next to nothing and do not even like it, and
those who take and enjoy everything that comes. The boor and the
vulgar buffoon stand in just the same relation to each other: the
former finds it hard to take a joke, and the latter accepts everything
10 calmly and cheerfully. Neither is correct: one should accept some
things and not others, and listen to reason: that is what a convivial
man does.

The proof is as before: conviviality of this kind (not that which is so called in an extended sense) is the best state, and it is the mean that is praiseworthy and the extremes that are blameworthy. There are, however, two kinds of conviviality, differing one from the other 15 but both being mean states. One consists in liking a joke, such as a tease, provided it is funny, even if it is against oneself; the other consists in the ability to produce that kind of thing. A man who can produce jokes of the kind that gives pleasure to people of good judgement, even though the laugh is on himself, will be midway 20 between a person who is vulgar and a person who is prim. This definition is better than one that says that the remark must not be painful to the victim, no matter what kind of person he is; rather, it must give pleasure to the person in the mean, for he is the one who judges correctly.

All these means are praiseworthy without being virtues, and their opposites are not vices either, because choice is not involved. They all occur in classifications of emotions, since each of them is a par- 25 ticular emotion. However, since they are natural, they contribute to the natural virtues, for, as will be said later,* each virtue occurs both naturally and otherwise, that is to say, in company with wisdom. Envy, for instance, contributes to injustice (for the actions that 30 express it affect others), righteous indignation contributes to justice, modesty to temperance, and the sincere and the untruthful are respectively sensible and foolish.

The mean is more opposed to the extremes than the extremes are to each other, because it does not occur in combination with 1234b either of them, whereas the extremes often occur together. Sometimes the very same people are foolhardy cowards, or are prodigal in some things and illiberal in others, and in general their badness gets out of bounds. (If it is goodness that gets out of bounds, the result is the mean, for in the mean both extremes are in a manner 5 present.)

The contrariety between the mean and the extremes does not seem to be the same in the case of both extremes: sometimes the contrast is with excess and sometimes with defect. The causes of this are threefold. First, there are the two that we have mentioned before: the rarity of one extreme (as in the case of those insensible to pleasures) and the fact that the error to which we are more prone 10 gives the impression of greater contrariety to the mean. Thirdly, there is the fact that what is more similar seems less contrary; for instance, foolhardiness in relation to courage, and prodigality in relation to liberality.

So now we have said enough about the other praiseworthy virtues, and it is time to speak of justice.

BOOK IV · JUSTICE

JUSTICE: ITS SPHERE AND NATURE: IN WHAT SENSE IT IS A MEAN

The just as the lawful (universal justice)

1. CONCERNING justice and injustice we must inquire what kind 1129a of actions fall within their sphere, what kind of a middle state justice is, and of what things justice is the mean. Let our inquiry take the 5 same course as its predecessors.*

We see that everyone means by justice a state of character such as to make people disposed to do what is just, and to make them act justly and to want what is just; and similarly by injustice a state that makes them act unjustly and want what is unjust. Let so much, then, 10 be laid down as a first approximation. For there is a difference* between sciences and abilities on the one hand, and states of character on the other. One and the same ability or science seems to embrace contraries, whereas a state that is one of a pair of contraries does not do so; health, for instance, is expressed only in healthy 15 activity and not in its contrary: we say that a man's walking is healthy when he walks in the way a healthy man would.

Now often one contrary is made manifest by the other contrary, and often states are recognized from the things that produce them; for if a good condition is obvious, then the bad condition becomes obvious, and the good condition becomes obvious from what con- 20 duces to it, and vice versa. If the good condition is having firm flesh, it must be that the bad condition is having flabby flesh, and that whatever makes flesh firm is conducive to the good condition. And it follows, in general, that if one term is ambiguous, the other will be too; if 'just' is, so will 'unjust' be. 25

Now 'justice' and 'injustice' appear each to be ambiguous, but because the two meanings of each are closely related, the ambiguity passes unnoticed. It is unlike the case where the two meanings are far apart, as when two things actually look quite different, like a lock of hair and the lock on a door.* Let us start, then, by asking in how 30 many senses a man may be called unjust. Both a lawbreaker and a covetous* cheat are regarded as unjust, so clearly both a law-abiding person and a fair-minded person will be just. Hence what is just is what is lawful and fair, and what is unjust is what is unlawful and unfair.

1129b   In so far as injustice is covetousness, it must have goods as its sphere, but not all of them, but only those that are within the scope of good and bad fortune—things that are always good in the abstract, but not for every particular person. These are the things that humans pray for and pursue, but what they should pray is that the things
5   that are good in the abstract may be good for them, and what they should choose is the things that are good for them. The unjust man does not always choose a larger share: faced with things that are in the abstract bad, he chooses a smaller share. However, since a lesser evil is regarded as a kind of good, and it is what is good that is coveted, this, too, can be regarded as covetousness. Such a man is
10   also unfair: this covers both cases and is common to both.

Since, as we saw, a lawbreaker is unjust and a law-abiding person is just, it is clear that whatever is lawful is in a manner just; for whatever is determined by the legislative art is lawful, and we call all such acts just. In every area where the laws make stipulations they aim at
15   the common advantage either of all, or of the best people, or of those in power, or something of the sort; so that in one sense we call just those things that create and preserve happiness and its parts for the political community. And the law commands us to do the deeds of a
20   courageous man (e.g. not to leave one's post, or take flight, or throw away one's weapons) and those of a temperate man (e.g. not to commit adultery or rape) and those of a gentle man (e.g. not to assault or defame anyone). So, too, with other virtues and depravities: law commands some things and forbids others. A well-drafted
25   law does this correctly, while a hastily framed one does the same thing less well.

This justice, then, is complete virtue,* considered not in the abstract but in relation to one's neighbour. This is why justice is often regarded as the greatest of virtues, 'more wonderful than either the morning or the evening star'. As the proverb has it, 'in
30   justice every virtue is compact'.* And it is complete virtue par excellence because it is the actual exercise of complete virtue. And it is complete because a person who possesses it can exercise his virtue not just by himself but also in relation to his neighbour, unlike the

many people who can exercise virtue in their own affairs but not in
their relations with their neighbour. This supports the dictum of 1130a
Bias,* that government will reveal a man; for governing is bound to
involve a relation to one's neighbour and to the community. This,
too, is the reason why justice, alone of the virtues, is thought to be
someone else's good;* for the just man acts in a way advantageous to
someone else, whether a ruler or a comrade. Now, the worst kind of 5
person is the man who exhibits depravity both towards himself and
to his friends, while the best person is the man who exercises virtue
not for himself but for his neighbour—a more difficult task. Justice
of this kind, then, is not a mere part of virtue, but the whole of
virtue; and the injustice that is its contrary is not a part of vice but
the whole of vice. From what we have said it is clear what the differ- 10
ence is between virtue and this kind of justice: they are one and the
same disposition, but the difference is in the actualization of the
disposition. Virtue is the disposition considered in the abstract, and
justice is the disposition considered in relation to one's neighbour.

The just as the fair and equal (particular justice)

2. However, what we are looking for is the justice that is one part of
virtue,* for it is our contention that there is such a thing. The same
goes for the injustice that is one part of vice. 15

How do we show that there is such a thing? A person who is
exhibiting one of the other forms of depravity behaves unjustly but
does not exhibit covetousness—a man who throws away his shield
through cowardice, for instance, or who abuses somebody in a fit of
temper, or who is too mean to offer money to a friend in need. But
when a person acts covetously, he need not be exhibiting any of these 20
vices, let alone all of them, but—since we blame him—he must be
exhibiting wickedness of some kind, and that is injustice. There is,
then, a kind of injustice that is a part of the wider injustice, and a
thing can be unjust as one part of the totality that is unjust in the
sense of unlawful. Again, suppose that one man commits adultery
for the sake of profit* and makes money by it, while another man
does so out of desire even though it costs him money and incurs a 25
penalty. The second man would seem to be intemperate rather than
covetous, while the first is unjust but not intemperate. It is evident,
then, that it is the profit motive that gives rise to the injustice. Again,
all other unjust acts are always ascribed to some particular form of

depravity—adultery, for instance, to intemperance, desertion of a
30 battle comrade to cowardice, and assault to anger—but if a man is a
profiteer, his action is not ascribed to any such depravity but is classified simply as injustice. It is obvious, then, that in addition to the
wider injustice there is a specific injustice. The two share the same
1130b name because their definitions involve the same genus. Both of them
are characterized by their effect on one's neighbour, but the sphere
of one of them is restricted to honour or money or security* (or
whatever would be covered by a single name for all of these things,
if we had one), and its motive is the pleasure provided by profit; the
5 other one has as its sphere whatever falls within the sphere of a virtuous person.

It is clear, then, that there is more than one kind of justice, and
that there is one kind that is distinct from virtue entire; we must try
to understand what it is and what are its qualities.

What is unjust has been divided into what is unlawful and what is
unfair, and what is just into what is lawful and what is fair. The
10 injustice discussed earlier corresponds to what is unlawful. What is
unfair is not the same as what is unlawful, but is related to it as part
to whole, since everything that is unfair is unlawful, but not everything that is unlawful is unfair. Hence, injustice and what is unjust
is not a single thing, but two things differing from each other, parts
in the one case, and wholes in the other. For injustice of this kind is
15 a part of injustice as a whole, and the corresponding justice is part
of justice as a whole. So what we have to discuss is specific justice
and specific injustice, and what is likewise just and unjust. We may
leave aside the justice that answers to the whole of virtue, and the
corresponding injustice, being respectively the exercise of virtue as
20 a whole, or vice as a whole, in regard to other people. It is evident
how one should define what is just and what is unjust in accordance
with this kind of justice and injustice. As a first approximation most
of the things laid down by the laws are things commanded from the
point of view of virtue as a whole; for the law commands us to practise every virtue and forbids us to practise any vice. And those things
25 that are conducive to entire virtue are those legal provisions that
have been enacted to foster education towards the common good.
What, then, of the education of the individual, which makes him,
considered in isolation, a good man: is this within the scope of the
art of politics or of some other art? This must be determined later,

since perhaps being a good man and being a good citizen is not in every case the same thing.

Of particular justice, and that which is correspondingly just, there are two kinds. One kind resides in the distribution, among those who have a share in the constitution, of honour, or money, or whatever else gets divided in such cases where it is possible for one man's share to be equal or unequal to another's. The other kind is what rectifies interactions between individuals.* This, too, comes in two kinds, because there are two kinds of interaction: voluntary and non-voluntary.* Voluntary interactions are such transactions as selling, buying, lending, pledging, borrowing, depositing, and letting—these are called voluntary because they are entered into voluntarily. Non-voluntary interactions may be either clandestine or violent. Clandestine ones include theft, adultery, poisoning, procuring, enticement of slaves, killing by stealth, and false witness. Violent ones include assault, false imprisonment, murder, kidnapping, maiming, defamation, and insult.

Distributive justice, in accordance with geometrical proportion

3. Since an unjust man, and an unjust thing, is unfair or unequal,* it is clear that there is a mean between inequalities. That is what the equal is; for in any kind of action in which there is a more and a less, there is also what is equal. So if what is unjust is unequal, what is just is what is equal. That indeed is what everyone thinks without needing argument. And since equality is a mean, what is just will be a mean of a sort. But equality involves at least two terms. What is just, then, must be a mean, and an equality, and relative to certain things and certain persons. As a mean it will be between two items, one greater and one less; as an equality it will involve two things; as a piece of justice it will concern particular individuals. It follows, then, that what is just involves at least four things: two of them are the interested parties, and two of them are the goods at issue. And the same equality will obtain between the parties and the goods; for the second pair, the goods, stand in the same relation to each other as the first pair do; for if the parties are not equal, they will not have equal shares. Quarrels and complaints arise precisely when equals get unequal shares, or equal shares are awarded to people that are unequal. This is clear from the very expression 'according to desert': for all agree that for a distribution to be just it must be in

accordance with desert, even though not everyone means the same thing by desert.* Democrats identify it with being born free, oligarchs with being wealthy or alternatively of noble stock; aristocrats identify it with virtue.

Justice, then, is a kind of proportion. Proportion is not a property
30 only of the arithmetical numbers in the abstract, but also of number in general;* it is an equality between ratios, and involves at least four
1131b terms. (It is evident that discrete proportion involves four terms, but so, too, does continuous proportion, because it treats one term as two, mentioning it twice. As the length of A is to the length of B, so is the length of B to the length of C: here the length of B has been mentioned twice, and if you put in the length of B twice, the proportion will have four terms.) What is just likewise involves at least four terms,
5 and the ratio between each pair is the same: the same distinction is made between the parties and between the goods.* As A is to B, then, C will be to D, and, by permutation, as A is to C so B will be to D. Thus, one totality matches the other totality and the two are paired by the distribution, and if matters are so combined, the pairing will be a just one. The combination, then, of A with C and of B with D is what
10 is just in distribution, and what is thus just is a mean, and what is unjust violates this proportion; for what is proportional is a mean, and what is just is proportional. (This kind of proportion is called by mathematicians 'geometrical proportion'; for in the case of geometrical proportion the whole stands to the whole as each part stands to
15 its counterpart.) This proportion is not continuous: a single term cannot stand for both a person and a piece of goods.

This, then, is what the just is, namely, what is proportional; the unjust is what violates the proportional. One share becomes too great and the other too small, as happens in practice; the man who acts unjustly* has too much of what is good, and the man who suffers
20 injustice has too little. In the case of evil the reverse happens, for the lesser evil counts as a good in comparison with the greater evil, since a lesser evil is preferable to a greater one, and what is an object of preference is a good, and what is more so is a greater good.

This, then, is one species of what is just.*

Rectificatory justice, in accordance with arithmetical proportion

25 4. The remaining one is the rectificatory kind,* which occurs in both voluntary and involuntary interactions. This form of what is

just is specifically different from the former one. Justice in the distribution of common possessions always follows the proportion described above; the funds of a partnership, too, will be distributed in 30 the same ratio as the contributions of the individual partners. Correspondingly, the injustice contrary to this kind of justice is always a violation of the proportional. In interactions between individuals, however, though justice is a kind of equality, and injustice a 1132a kind of inequality, it is determined not by that kind of proportion, but rather by the arithmetical kind.* For it makes no difference whether a good man has cheated a bad man, or a bad man a good one, nor whether adultery has been committed by a good man or a bad man: the law looks only to the degree of injury, and treats the 5 parties as equal, inquiring only who was the wrongdoer and who was wronged, who caused the harm and who suffered it.

Since this kind of injustice is an inequality, the judge tries to equalize it. When one person has been struck and another struck the blow, or one person has been killed and another did the killing, doing and suffering have been unequally distributed, and the pun- 10 ishment is an attempt* to restore the equality by depriving the wrongdoer of his gain. For in such cases 'gain' is used in an abstract sense, not perhaps always appropriately, as when we speak of the assailant's gain and the victim's loss; it is when the damage has been estimated that the one is called loss and the other gain. Therefore, equality is a mean between greater and less, but gain and loss are 15 respectively greater and less in contrary ways: more of the good and less of evil counts as gain, and the contrary counts as loss, while equality is the mean between them, which is what we are identifying as justice. Rectificatory justice, then, is the mean between loss and gain.

That is why, when people are in dispute, they have recourse to a 20 judge. To go to a judge is to go to justice, for a judge is supposed to be justice personified. People seek out the judge as a mean—in some places, indeed, judges are called mediators—thinking that if they can hit on the mean they will obtain justice. So what is just is a mean, no less than a judge. What a judge does is to restore equality. It is as if a line has been divided into unequal segments, and the 25 judge takes away from the larger segment and adds to the smaller one the amount by which the larger segment exceeds one half. When a whole is divided into two, people say they have got their due when

they receive an equal share; and equality is the mean between greater
and less according to arithmetical proportion. (This is why the
30   Greek word for justice is *dikaion*, because justice is a bisection, for
which the Greek is *dikha*; it is as if the word for justice were *dikhaion*
and as if a judge were called not *dikastes* but *dikhastes*.) For if an
amount is subtracted from one of two equal things and added to the
other, the latter will exceed the former by twice the amount, while if
1132b   it had been merely subtracted and not added, the excess would be
only one such amount. So the greater exceeds the mean by one
amount, and the lesser falls short of the mean by one amount. It is
this that tells us how much must be taken away from the person that
has more and given to the person that has less: the latter must be
given the amount by which the mean exceeds it, while the former
5   must be deprived of the amount by which it exceeds the mean.* Let
the lines AA', BB', CC' be equal to each other,* and let the segment
AE be subtracted from AA', and let the segment CD be added to
CC', so that the whole line DCC' exceeds the line EA' by the segment CD and the segment CF; it will then exceed the line BB' by
the segment CD.

10   These terms, 'loss' and 'gain', come from voluntary exchange; for
to have more than one had before is called gaining, and to have less
than one had at the beginning is called losing. That is how it is in
15   buying and selling and in all cases where the law does not intervene.
But when the parties get neither more nor less but the outcome
restores their belongings, then they each say that they have their due
and have made neither a gain nor a loss. What is just, then, is a mean
between one kind of gain and one kind of loss, namely those that are
non-voluntary;* it consists in having an equal amount before and
20   after the event.

Justice in exchange, reciprocity

5. Some people think that it is reciprocity that is the abstract notion
of justice, as the Pythagoreans maintained: for their abstract definition of justice was 'reciprocation to another'. And people interpret
25   in this sense also the definition of justice given by Rhadamanthus:*

If a man suffered what he did, that would be justice rightly done.

Despite all this, reciprocity fits neither distributive nor rectificatory
justice, for in many cases they are not in accord.* For instance, if a

public official strikes someone, he ought not to be struck in return, whereas if someone strikes a public official, he should not only be struck but also suffer punishment in addition. Further, there is a 30 great difference between voluntary and non-voluntary interactions.

In commercial associations, however, this sort of justice forms a bond: reciprocity not on the basis of simple equality but rather in accordance with proportion. Proportional reciprocation is what holds a city together. There are two alternatives. Men may seek to return evil for evil, and if they cannot do so it feels like slavery. Or they may seek to return good for good, and if they cannot do so 1133a there is no such thing as commerce, and commerce is what binds them together. That is why the temple of the Graces is set in a prominent place, in order to promote give and take, for that is the characteristic of grace. When someone does you a favour, you should do one in return, and next time you should take the initiative by doing a favour yourself.

Proportionate return is achieved by conjoining diametrical oppo- 5 sites. Let A be a builder, B a shoemaker, C a house, and D a shoe. The builder is to take the shoemaker's product, and to give the shoe-maker a share in his own product. If there is first of all proportionate equality, and reciprocation takes place, then what is required will be 10 achieved. If not, the bargain is not equal and the parties are not bound together, for the product of one may well be more valuable than the product of the other, so that equalization is called for. This applies also in the case of other technical skills, for they would disappear if the quantity and quality of the practitioner's activity failed 15 to match the quantity and quality of the improvement produced in the client or patient. For it is not two doctors who come together in an exchange of services, but rather a doctor and a farmer, and in general people of different and unequal kinds; hence the necessity for equalization.

If things are to be exchanged, they must somehow be capable of comparison. That is why money was invented, and it has become a 20 kind of mean. For it is a measure of all things, including excess and defect: it tells us how many shoes are equal to a house or a ration of food. The number of shoes that are worth a house or a ration of food must correspond to the ratio between builder and shoemaker; for if this is not so, there will be no exchange and no coming together, and it will not be so unless the items are in some way equal. All goods,

25 then, as we said before, must be measured by a single measure. The real truth of the matter is that this unit is need: it is that which holds everything together. For if men had no needs, or all had different needs, there would be no exchange at all, or else exchange of a different kind. Money, however, has been invented as a kind of conventional substitute for need. That is why it is called in Greek *nomisma*: because it owes its existence not to nature but to convention (*nomos*). It is in our own power to alter its value or to render it useless.

There will, then, be reciprocity when equalization has been carried out so that the ratio of the shoemaker's product to the farmer's
1133b product is the same as the ratio of shoemaker to farmer.* It is while they are still in possession of their own products that we have to bring them into the equation, not after they have made the exchange* (otherwise one extreme will have both excesses). In this way the equalization can be effected, and so they will become equals and
5 come together. Let A be a farmer, C a ration of food, B a shoemaker, and D his product as equalized. If it had not been possible to effect this equalization, the parties would never have come together.

Need is the one single factor* that holds all together: that is shown by the fact that when two people do not need one another, or one of them has no need of the other, they do not make any exchange. (It is
10 like the case where what you need is something you already have, say wine; you won't exchange that for a licence to export corn.) So equalization is needed. Perhaps we do not need a thing now, but will do so in future: in this case money acts as a kind of surety for us, for by offering money it must be possible for us to get what we want. Of course, money, too, like goods, can change its value, but it tends to
15 be more stable. That is why everything must have a value set on it, for in that case there will always be exchange to bring people together.

Money, then, acting as a measure, makes goods commensurate and equalizes them. Without exchange men would never have come together, and without equality there would never have been exchange, and without commensurability there would never have been equality. Strictly speaking, it is impossible that things so diverse should become commensurable, but we can achieve this suf-
20 ficiently if we focus on need. There must therefore be a unit, laid down by convention (hence the Greek name for money), and it is this that makes everything commensurable, since all things are

measured by money. Let A be a house, B ten minae, C a bed. A is half of B if the house is worth five minae or their equivalent, and the bed C is a tenth of B. How many beds, then, are equal to a house?   25 Five, evidently. Evidently, that was how exchange took place before there was money; for it makes no difference whether a house is exchanged for five beds, or for their value in money.

So we have said what it is for something to be unjust and what it is for something to be just. Once these matters have been determined, it is clear that just action is a mean between acting unjustly   30 and being unjustly treated; for one is having too much and the other is having too little. Justice is a kind of mean, but not in the same way as the other virtues;* it is so because it hits the mean, while injustice   1134a reaches the extremes. Justice is the state that makes a just person do just deeds out of choice, and make just distributions, whether between himself and another, or between third parties. That is to say, he will not allot to himself more of what is desirable and less to his neighbour, nor will he do the reverse in the case of what is harm-   5 ful. Instead, he will deal out equally in accordance with proportion, and similarly between third parties. Injustice, on the contrary, is related to what is unjust, that is to say, to excess and defect of what is beneficial or harmful, in violation of proportion. Thus, injustice is excess and defect because excess and defect are its effects—in   10 one's own case excess of what is in itself beneficial and defect of what is harmful, and in the case of others, much the same, except that the proportion may be violated either way. In the case of unjust action, the too little is being unjustly treated, and the too much is acting unjustly.

Let so much stand as our account of the nature of justice and   15 injustice, and in general of what is just and what is unjust.

Political justice and analogous kinds of justice

6. Now it is possible for someone to act unjustly without being so far an unjust person. What kind of unjust acts, then, make a man a thief or an adulterer or a brigand, that is to say, unjust in respect of a particular kind of injustice? Or is this not the right way to make out the difference? Rather, a man might go to bed with a woman,   20 knowing who she was, but not on the basis of choice but simply out of passion. Such a man acts unjustly, but is not unjust; he is not an adulterer even though he committed adultery. Another example is a man who stole something without actually being a thief; and similarly in other cases.*

Earlier we stated how reciprocity is related to justice; but we must
25 not forget that what we are looking for is not only justice in the abstract, but political justice. This is found among people who are sharing their lives together with the aim of self-sufficiency: men who are free and equal (whether the equality is proportionate or arithmetical*). Among those who are not in this condition there is no political justice, but only a certain semblance of justice. For jus-
30 tice exists only between people who are subject to law, and where there is law there is also injustice, because the law's judgement is what discriminates between what is just and what is unjust. And where there is injustice, people act unjustly towards each other (even though not every unjust action implies injustice): that is, people allot themselves too much of things that are good in the abstract, and too little of things that are bad in the abstract. That is why we do
35 not allow a human being to be a ruler, but enthrone reason instead, because a human being acts in his own interests and turns into a tyrant.

1134b A ruler, on the other hand, is a guardian of justice and therefore of equality also. A ruler, if he is just, is seen to have no more than his share, for he does not allot to himself any greater share of what is good in the abstract, unless such a share is proportional to his merits. It is for others, then, that he labours, and that is why—as we said
5 before—people say that justice is 'someone else's good'. For this reason a ruler must be recompensed, and his reward is honour and prestige; but those who are not satisfied with that turn into tyrants.

What is just for a slave-owner or a father is not the same as justice between citizens, even though it resembles it; because there can be
10 no injustice towards things that are one's own. Now a chattel and a child (if he has not reached a certain age and become independent) are, as it were, part of oneself, and no one chooses to harm himself, which is why there is no injustice towards oneself. In these relationships, then, there is no such thing as political justice, for that, as we saw, takes its rise from law and among men naturally subject to law,
15 namely, those who have an equal share in ruling and being ruled. Justice can be displayed more truly to one's wife than to one's children and chattels: this is household justice, but even that is not the same as political justice.

Natural and legal justice

7. Of political justice one part is natural and the other convention-al.* The natural part is that which has the same force everywhere and is not a matter of positive or negative decision; the conventional part is that which is originally indifferent but is right or wrong 20 as a result of an enactment. Examples are: a prisoner's ransom shall be one mina, a goat shall be sacrificed rather than two sheep. So too are all laws made for particular cases (e.g. the establishment of sacrifice in honour of Brasidas*) and enactments that take the form of decrees.* Some people think that all justice is of this kind, arguing that whatever is natural is invariable and has the same force every- 25 where (in the way that fire burns both here and in Persia) whereas we observe great variation in what is just. This is not really the case, but it is true up to a point. Among the gods no doubt it is altogether false, but with us, although there is a natural element it is, in its entirety, subject to variation—but nonetheless, it is partly natural and partly non-natural.* Among those things that are capable of being other- 30 wise than they are, there is a distinction between what is natural and what is conventional and contractual, even though both are subject to variation; and it is evident which is which. The same distinction applies in other matters too: by nature the right hand is stronger, and yet it is possible that everyone might become ambidextrous.

Things whose justice is established by convention and utility are like units of measurement: measures of wine and corn are not every- 1135a where equal, but larger in wholesale and smaller in retail markets. Likewise, arrangements that are just not by nature but by human devising differ from place to place, since even political constitutions differ, even though there is only one that is everywhere by nature the best.* 5

Each thing that is just by convention is related as a universal to the particulars falling under it: for the things that are done are many, but each kind is one, for it is a universal.

There is a difference between an unjust action and what is unjust, and between a just action and what is just; for something is unjust either by nature or by prescription. Once you do it, it is an unjust 10 action, but before you did it, it was already an unjust thing to do.* Similarly with just action—though there is a difference between acting justly (the general expression) and doing justice (the putting right of some wrong).

Later we must examine each of these in particular, and determine what and how many kinds of them there are and what comes within their sphere.

JUSTICE AND CHOICE

The scale of degrees of wrongdoing

15 8. If what is just and what is unjust is as we have said, then a man acts unjustly or justly if he does the appropriate acts voluntarily. When his action is not voluntary, it is neither unjust nor just save coincidentally, in the sense of doing things that simply happen to be just or unjust. An unjust action, and a just one, is marked off by be-
20 ing voluntary or not; for if it is voluntary it attracts blame and is at the same time an unjust action, but if there is no element of voluntariness then an outcome may be unjust without being an unjust action. By voluntary I mean, as was said earlier,* something within his power that a man does knowingly, making no mistake about the
25 person his action affects, or how it is to take effect, or what will be its upshot. He must know, for instance, whom he is striking, with what, and with what effect. Moreover, the action must not be something done coincidentally, and it must not be forced. If, for instance, one man takes another's hand and strikes a third party, the agent does not act voluntarily, for the act was not in his power. It is possible that the person struck is his father, and that he knew that he was a man
30 and that he was one of the present company, but did not know that he was his father.* A similar distinction may be made about the upshot and about the action in its entirety.

What is done in error, or with awareness but without one's power, or is forced, is non-voluntary. (Many natural processes, it should be
1135b said, are things we do and undergo consciously and yet are neither voluntary nor non-voluntary: examples are growing old or dying.*) In the case of both unjust and just actions there is room for something to be merely coincidental: if a man returns a deposit unwillingly and out of fear, he should not be said to be acting justly or
5 doing what is just except merely coincidentally. Likewise, a man who fails to return a deposit, under compulsion and against his will, must be said to be only coincidentally acting unjustly, and failing to do what is just.

Of our voluntary acts we do some with, and some without, choice;

there is choice when we have deliberated beforehand, and otherwise   10
there is no choice. In interactions between people there are three
kinds of injury: mistake, misadventure, and injustice. Mistakes are
injuries inflicted in error, i.e. when the victim, and the action, and
the means, and the upshot are not what the agent supposed. Perhaps
he did not think he was throwing anything at all, or not this missile,
or not at this person nor with this effect, but either the upshot was
not what he thought—maybe he threw with intent only to prick and   15
not to wound—or else the victim and the missile was other than he
thought. A misadventure is when the injury takes place contrary to
reasonable expectation; if the injury could have been foreseen, but
takes place without malicious intent, it is a mistake. (The difference
between the two is that in mistake the origin of the cause of harm is
internal to the agent, whereas in misadventure it is external.) When
a man acts with awareness, but without deliberation, his act is an   20
injustice. The actions I mean are those that are due to anger or other
passions that are necessary or natural to human beings. When people
do such harmful and wrongful acts, they do act unjustly and their
deeds are unjust, yet this does not mean that they are themselves
unjust or wicked,* since the injury does not originate in depravity.
But when a man inflicts an injury out of choice, then he is an unjust   25
and depraved man.

Hence acts done out of rage are rightly judged as unpremeditated;
the originator of the mischief is not the man enraged but the person
who provoked the rage. Moreover, the matter in dispute is not
whether the event occurred or not, but whether it was justified; for
what occasions rage is apparent injustice. It is not like the case in
business transactions, where the dispute is about what took place,
and one or other of the parties must be depraved (unless they quarrel   30
because they forget what happened). In this case, on the contrary,
they agree about what happened, and the dispute is about whether it
was justified, so that one man thinks he is being treated unjustly and
the other denies it. (Of course a man who has injured another of
malice aforethought cannot but know what he has done.)

But if a man harms another by choice, he acts unjustly; and it is   1136a
unjust acts of this kind, where there is a violation of proportion or
of equality, that make the man that commits them an unjust man.
Similarly, to be a just man you must act justly by choice; if you act
merely voluntarily, then it is only your action that is just.

Not all non-voluntary acts are excusable. Those that people per-
10 form not only in error but also because of the error* are excusable.
There is no excuse, however, for actions that are performed in error,
but not because of the error but because of a passion that is neither
natural nor human.

*Can a man be voluntarily treated unjustly? Is it the distributor or
the recipient that is guilty of injustice in distribution?*

9. Supposing that we have sufficiently defined treating and being
treated unjustly, someone might raise a question which is suggested
by a puzzling passage in Euripides:

> I killed my mother; there's no more to tell.
> With or without your will—and hers as well?*

15 Can one really be willingly treated unjustly, or is all suffering of
injustice involuntary in the way that all doing of injustice is voluntary? And is all suffering one thing or the other, or is it sometimes
voluntary and sometimes non-voluntary? The same question can be
asked about being treated justly. All just action is voluntary, so that
one would expect there to be a similar opposition in either case, and
20 that being treated unjustly and being treated justly should be either
alike voluntary or alike involuntary. But it would seem absurd to say
it is all voluntary, even in the case of being treated justly; for some
people receive just treatment against their will.* Again, one might
raise the question whether everyone who receives injustice is
unjustly treated, or whether suffering is in the same case as doing. In
25 action and passion alike it is possible for justice to be done coincidentally, and similarly (it is plain) for injustice. For to do what is
unjust is not the same as to act unjustly, nor is to suffer injustice the
same as being unjustly treated, and likewise in the case of acting
justly and being justly treated. For it is impossible to be unjustly
treated if no one is acting unjustly or to be justly treated if no one is
30 acting justly.

Suppose that acting unjustly is simply harming somebody voluntarily, and that 'voluntarily' means with knowledge of the victim, the
means, and the manner. Suppose, further, that the incontinent
person voluntarily harms himself: in that case he will be voluntarily
the victim of unjust treatment, and thus it will be possible for a man
1136b to treat himself unjustly. But is it possible to treat oneself unjustly?

This is one of the questions at issue. Again, incontinence may lead to a person's voluntarily accepting harm* inflicted by another who is also acting voluntarily, so that it could be possible for a person to be voluntarily treated unjustly.

Perhaps our definition is inadequate: should we after 'harming with knowledge of the victim, the means, and the manner' add 'against the wish of the victim'? In that case a man may be voluntarily harmed, and voluntarily suffer injustice, but no one is voluntarily treated unjustly, for that is not the will of anybody, not even of the incontinent person. Such a man acts against his own will, for no one wills what he does not think to be good, and what the incontinent does is not what he thinks he ought to be doing.

A person who gives away his property (as Homer says Glaucus did to Diomedes,* 'gold for bronze, a hundred oxen's worth for nine') is not unjustly treated: it is in his power to make the gift, but it is not in his power to be unjustly treated, for which there needs to be someone else to treat him unjustly. It is evident, then, that being unjustly treated is not something voluntary.

Two problems remain of those we intended to discuss. If in a distribution one man gets more than his share, is it the distributor or the recipient who acts unjustly? Is it possible to treat oneself unjustly? If the answer to the first question is that it is the distributor and not the receiver who acts unjustly, then a man who knowingly and voluntarily assigns more to another than to himself will be treating himself unjustly. Indeed, this is what reasonable people seem to do; a decent man is likely to take less than his share. Or are matters more complex? Perhaps such a man is getting more than his share of some other good, such as honour or sheer nobility. The answer to the question is found by applying the distinction we made in the case of unjust action: for the person does not suffer anything contrary to his own will, so that he is not on this account unjustly treated but at most suffers harm.

It is obvious that the distributor acts unjustly, but the man who gets the larger share does not necessarily do so. For it is not the person to whom what is unjust happens who is the wrongdoer, but the person whose role is the voluntary performance of what is unjust, i.e. the originator of the action. In this case it is the distributor not the recipient. But there are many different ways in which we are said to 'do' things, and there are ways in which inanimate objects, or a hand, or a servant obeying an order, may kill someone. In that way, the person taking the larger share does not act unjustly, but 'does' what is unjust.

A judge who makes a distribution in error does not perform an unjust action in terms of conventional justice, nor is his judgment unjust in those terms; but in another sense it is unjust, since conventional justice is something different from primary justice.* A judge 1137a who has knowingly given an unjust judgment is himself grasping too large a share of favour or revenge. A man who has judged unjustly for these motives has an excessive amount no less than if he had himself taken a share of the booty. It makes no difference that what he gets is something different from what he distributes, for if he awards a plot of land in this way, what he gets for himself is not land but money.

5   People think that acting unjustly is something that is in our power, and that therefore it is easy to be just. In fact it is not:* to sleep with one's neighbour's wife, to strike a bystander, to hand over a sum of money is easy and within our power, but to do these things as a matter of character is neither easy nor in our power. Similarly, they 10 think it takes no great expertise to know what is just and what is unjust because it is not difficult to understand matters within the scope of the law (though these are not the things that are just, except coincidentally). However, justice requires actions to be performed, and goods distributed, in a particular manner. To know what this is, is a task more difficult than knowing what is good for health, though even there matters are not simple. While it is easy to be acquainted 15 with honey and wine and hellebore and cautery and surgery, it takes being a doctor to know whose health would benefit from these treatments, and how and when.

This makes people think that acting unjustly is no less characteristic of a just man than acting justly is, because he is not less but more capable of performing each of these actions. A just man is 20 quite able to sleep with another man's wife* or to strike a bystander, and a courageous man is able to throw away his shield and turn and run in either direction. But, except coincidentally, cowardly and unjust behaviour consists not just in doing these things, but in doing them as an expression of character, just as being a doctor and curing patients is a matter not just of whether or not one performs surgery 25 or administers drugs, but rather of the manner in which one does these things.

What is the sphere of justice? It is interactions between people who have a share in things that are good in the abstract, and who can have too much or too little of them. For some beings (for gods, perhaps) there cannot be too much of a good thing, and for others, who are incurably bad,* not even the smallest amount is beneficial and any amount is harmful. For the rest, they are beneficial up to a point: for that reason justice is something particularly human.   30

Equity, a corrective of legal justice

10. Our next topic is equity and the equitable:* what is the relation between equity and justice, and how is what is equitable related to what is just? For on investigation they seem not to be altogether identical, and yet not to differ in kind. Sometimes we praise what is   35 equitable, and the corresponding person, and we use the adjective as   1137b a synonym for 'good' in other areas also, thus indicating by using the word that a thing is better. Yet, on consideration, it seems odd if the equitable can diverge from the just and yet be praiseworthy. For if the two are different, then either what is just is not good, or what is equitable is not good; whereas if they are both good, they are one and the same thing.   5

As a first approximation, those are the considerations that raise a problem about what is equitable: they are all in a manner correct and there is no contradiction between them. For what is equitable, though it is better than one kind of justice, is itself something just; it is not a different kind of thing that is superior to justice. The same thing, then, is both just and equitable, and while both are   10 good, being equitable is better. What gives rise to the problem is that while what is equitable is just, it is not what is just according to the law but is a corrective of legal justice. All law, you see, is universal, but there are some things about which a correct universal prescription is not possible. In cases where the prescription has to be universal, but cannot be correct, the law takes the general case,   15 while fully aware of the error. This does not make the law incorrect: the error belongs neither to the law, nor to the legislator, but to the nature of the case, because such, from the outset, is the stuff of human conduct.

When, then, the law speaks universally, and a case arises that falls   20 outside the universal prescription, a case which the legislator has failed to cover through excessively abstract prescription, it is right

to correct the omission and to say what the legislator himself would
have said if he had been present, and would have put into his law
had he known. So equity is just, and is better than one kind of jus-
25 tice—not better than justice *tout court*, but better than the error that
results from excessively abstract formulations. That is the essence
of equity: it is a corrective of law when law is defective through uni-
versality. That is why not everything is regulated by law, because for
some things it is not possible to lay down a law and instead there is
need of a decree. When a thing is indefinite, the corresponding rule
30 must be indefinite, like the leaden rule that is used by Lesbian architects: the rule is not rigid but moulds itself to the shape of the stone.*
That is the way in which decrees adapt themselves to the facts of
the case.

It is now evident, then, what equity is: it is itself just and is superior to one kind of justice. It is obvious also what kind of person the
35 equitable man is: a person who chooses and performs equitable acts.
1138a He is no barrack-room lawyer, but someone who is willing to take
less than his share even when the law is on his side. The corresponding state of character is equitableness, which is a kind of justice and
not a quite different state.

Can a man treat himself unjustly?

11. Whether it is possible to treat oneself unjustly is obvious from
5 what has been said. For one class of just actions are those that
are prescribed by law, no matter what virtue they fall under: for
instance, the law does not prescribe suicide, and what it does not
prescribe it forbids.* Again, when someone, in violation of the law,
voluntarily harms another (not in retaliation), he acts unjustly; by
'voluntarily' is meant with awareness of the identity of the victim
and the means of harming. A person who in a rage voluntarily cuts
10 his own throat is acting against the bidding of reason and doing
something that the law does not permit, and so he is acting unjustly.
But unjustly to whom? To the state, surely, rather than himself. For
he suffers voluntarily, but nobody is voluntarily treated unjustly.
That is why the state exacts a penalty, and why a particular dishon-
our attaches to a man who has done away with himself, as having
done an injustice to the state.

15 Further, there is the case of a person who is unjust through
unjust action, but is not wholly vicious. Such a man cannot treat

himself unjustly, and this is different from the previous case: the unjust but not altogether wicked person is like the coward: somebody who is not wicked all round, so that his unjust behaviour is not an expression of universal wickedness. For in this case treating oneself unjustly would imply the same thing's being subtracted from, and added to, the same thing at the same time, which is impossible (justice and injustice must always involve more than one person). Again, unjust action is voluntary, done out of choice, and involves taking the lead: for a person who has suffered and returns tit for tat is not regarded as acting unjustly. But if a man harms himself he both suffers and does the same things at the same time. Further, if someone could treat himself unjustly, he could be treated unjustly voluntarily. In addition to all this, no one acts unjustly without committing some particular form of unjust act: but no one can commit adultery with his own wife, or burgle his own house, or steal his own property.

Overall, the answer to the question 'can a man treat himself unjustly?' is given by the distinctions we made in response to 'can one voluntarily be treated unjustly?'

It is obvious that both things are bad—being unjustly treated and acting unjustly. For one means having less, and the other having more, than the mean, which is like health in respect of medicine, and fitness in athletic training. However, acting unjustly is worse,* because it involves vice and merits blame—vice which either is or is close to the complete and unqualified kind (remember that not all voluntary action is an expression of an unjust character). Being unjustly treated, on the other hand, does not involve vice and injustice in oneself. In itself, then, being unjustly treated is less bad, but there is no reason why it should not, coincidentally, be a greater evil. But this is of no concern to a professional treatise. Such a work will regard pleurisy as a greater infliction than a stumble; yet that may be coincidentally more serious, if falling down leads to being taken captive or put to death by the enemy.

Though there is no justice between a man and himself, there is a semblance of justice, in an extended sense, between a man and parts of himself; not every kind of justice, but only domestic justice or master–slave justice. That is the kind of relationship between the rational part of the soul and the irrational part. That is why people believe that a man can be unjust to himself, because these parts can experience things that are contrary to their particular desires. That makes people think that there is a relationship of justice between them parallel to that between ruler and ruled.

Let this be taken as our determination of justice and the other, i.e. other moral, virtues.

BOOK V · INTELLECTUAL VIRTUE

Intellectual virtue and the divisions of the intellect

1. RECALL that we said earlier* that one must choose the mean and not the excess or the defect, and that the mean is what is prescribed by correct reasoning. It is this we should now make precise. 20 For in all the states of character we have discussed, as in other matters, there is a target at which a reasoner aims as he varies the intensity of his efforts, and there is a standard determining the means that we say are between excess and defect, being in accordance with correct reasoning. This is a true statement, but it is not at all en- 25 lightening, because in all other endeavours involving expertise it is equally true to say that we should not strive or relax too much or too little, but a middling amount and in accordance with correct reasoning. But if this was all someone was told, he would be none the wiser; he would not know what sort of treatments to give to the 30 body if someone said, 'those that medicine prescribes, in the manner that a physician would apply them'. So, in the case also of the states of the soul, stating this truth is not enough, but we must work out what correct reasoning is, and what is the standard that determines it.*

We made a distinction among the virtues of the soul and said that ɩ some were virtues of character and others of the intellect. We have 1139a discussed the virtues of character; now let us state our position about the others, after a preliminary observation about the soul. It was said earlier* that there are two parts of the soul, one that involves reason and the other non-rational; now we have to draw a similar distinction within the part that involves reason. Let us assume that 5 there are two parts that involve reason, one that enables us to contemplate the kinds of things whose originating principles are incapable of variation, and another by which we contemplate the things that are variable; for where objects differ in kind, the parts of the soul corresponding to each of the two will also differ in kind, since 10 it is a certain likeness and kinship that gives rise to knowledge. Let us call one of these the scientific faculty, and the other the calculative faculty, for deliberation and calculation are the same thing, but no one deliberates about things that cannot be otherwise. Hence,

15 the calculative faculty is one portion of the part that involves reason. We must, then, work out what is the best state of each of these two faculties, for that will be the virtue of each, and the virtue of a thing is relative to its proper task.

Truth and right desire

2. There are three things in the soul that control conduct and truth:* sensation, intellect, and desire. Of these, sensation does not originate 20 conduct; this is evident from the fact that brutes have sensation but do not exhibit conduct. What affirmation and negation are in thinking, pursuit and avoidance are in desire:* so that since moral virtue is a state that finds expression in choice, and choice is deliberative desire, it follows that if the choice is to be good, both the reasoning must be true and the desire must be right, and the latter must pursue 25 just what the former asserts.* This is the kind of thought and the kind of truth that is practical. In the case of thought that is neither practical nor productive, doing well or badly consists in being true or false, since truth is the task of every faculty of thought; but in the case of the faculty of practical thought it is truth in accord- 30 ance with right desire.* The origin of conduct—its efficient, not its final, cause—is choice; and the origin of choice is desire plus goal-directed reasoning. Hence, there is no choice without intelligence and thought or without a moral state of character: for good conduct and its opposite cannot exist without both thought and character. Thought on its own sets nothing in motion, but only thought that is 1139b practical and aims at an end. This kind of thought governs productive thought also; for whoever produces something produces it for the sake of an end. The product itself is not an end in an unqualified sense, but an end only in a particular relation and of a particular craftsman. A deed done, however, *is* an end in an unqualified sense: for good conduct is an end, and that is what desire aims at. Hence choice is intelligence qualified by desire, or desire 5 qualified by thought;* and to be the originator of this is what it is to be human.

Nothing that is in the past is an object of choice; no one, for instance, chooses to have sacked Troy, for no one deliberates about the past, but only about what is future and capable of being otherwise, and the past is not capable of not having taken place. So Agathon* was right:

> From God there is withheld one power alone: 10
> The power to make undone what has been done.

The task of both intellectual parts, then, is truth. It follows that the virtues of the two parts will be the states that will make them achieve the maximum of truth.

Scientific knowledge of the necessary and eternal

3. Let us take a more elevated view, and start a fresh discussion of these matters. There are, let us say, five distinct states in which the soul attains truth by affirmation or denial, namely, art, knowledge,   15 wisdom, understanding, and intelligence.* (Judgement and opinion are excluded from the list because they admit of mistake.)

Now what knowledge is, if we are to use the word strictly* and not be misled by its replicas, is obvious from what follows. We all suppose that what we know is not capable of being otherwise; for when   20 things are capable of being otherwise, we cannot tell whether they are the case or not once they pass from view. Whatever is known, therefore, is necessary.* Therefore it is eternal, for things that are unqualifiedly necessary are all eternal, and what is eternal neither comes to be nor passes away. Again, every kind of knowledge is teachable, and what can be known can be learnt. But all teaching, as   25 we claim in the *Analytics* also, starts from something already known and works by induction or deduction. Deduction proceeds from universals, while induction provides the point of origin for the universal as well. There are, you see, principles that originate deduction that are not themselves a product of deduction; they are given, then,   30 by induction.* Knowledge, then, is a capability to prove things, and it has other defining characteristics,* which we list in the *Analytics*. A person knows something when he has a certain kind of belief and when he is aware of the principles that support it; for if they are not better known to him than the conclusion, then it is only coinciden-   35 tally that he has knowledge.

Let this, then, be our definition of knowledge.

Art—knowing how to make things

4. In the realm of what can be otherwise there are some things that are   1140a made and some things that are done: making and doing differ from each other, so that a reasoned capability to do things is something

different from a reasoned capability to make things. (On this topic
we can rely on our popular writings.) Neither of these, indeed, is a
5 species of the other, for doing is not a kind of making, nor making a
kind of doing. Building is a particular art, that is to say, a reasoned
productive capability, and there is no art that is not a reasoned productive capability, nor such a capability that is not an art: hence art
10 can be identified with correctly reasoned productive capability.*
Every art has as its scope the realm of becoming: that is to say, the
practice and theory of bringing into being something that is capable
of either being or not being, whose origin is in the producer and not
in the product. For things that exist or come into existence either by
necessity or by nature are not within the scope of art, since they have
15 their origin within themselves. And because making is different from
doing, art is a matter of making, not doing. In a manner, the scope of
art is the same as the scope of chance: Agathon well says, 'Art is in
love with chance, and chance in love with art.' Art, then, as has been
20 said, is a correctly reasoned productive capability, and its opposite,
incompetence, is an incorrectly reasoned capability; both have as
their scope what is capable of being otherwise.

Wisdom—knowledge concerned with the ends of human life

5. Concerning wisdom,* we may grasp its nature if we consider
25 whom we call wise. Well, it seems characteristic of a wise man to be
able to deliberate well about what is good and advantageous to himself, not what is specifically good, for example, health or strength,
but rather what conduces to the good life as a whole. Evidence for
this is the fact that we call men wise on particular topics when they
calculate rightly with respect to some specific good end that is not
30 the object of any art. So in general a man with a gift for deliberation
is a wise man. Now, no one deliberates about things that cannot be
otherwise, or that are impossible for him to do. Given, then, that
knowledge involves proof, and matters whose sources are contingent
35 do not admit of proof (since all such things are capable of being
1140b otherwise) and one cannot deliberate about things that are necessary, wisdom will not be identical either with knowledge or with
art—not with knowledge, because conduct concerns things that
can be otherwise, and not with art, because doing and making are
different in kind. The remaining alternative is that it is a reasoned
5 and correct capacity for action in the sphere of human good and ill.

For in the case of production the goal is something distinct, but it would not be so in the case of conduct; for good conduct is itself the goal. That is why we think of Pericles and his like as wise, because they can see what things are good for themselves and for human beings in general; that is how we think of people who are capable of managing households and governing cities.

The Greek word for temperance is *swphrosune*: this suggests that it is a preservative of wisdom* (*swzousa tēn phronēsin*). What it preserves is the kind of judgement just described. Pleasure and pain corrupt and distort, but they do not distort every kind of judgement—e.g. that the angles of a triangle are, or are not, equal to two right angles—but only judgements in the sphere of conduct. For the originating principles in this sphere are the ends of action, and one who is corrupted by pleasure or pain fails outright to see these; he does not see that he should make every choice and perform every action for the sake of *this*, and because of *that*. This is because vice corrupts the springs of action.

It follows that wisdom is a reasoned and correct capacity for action in the sphere of things that are good for humans. Note this: you can be good at an art, but you cannot be good at wisdom. Again, in art, a person whose mistakes are deliberate is preferable* to one whose mistakes are not; not so in the case of wisdom any more than with the other virtues. It is clear, then, that wisdom is a virtue and not an art. Since there are two parts of the soul that include reason, it will be the virtue of one of them, namely, the faculty of belief (for belief concerns the contingent, and so does wisdom). But it is something more than just a reasoned state; evidence of this is the fact that a state of that sort may be forgotten, but wisdom cannot be.

Intelligence—awareness of the first principles of science

6. Knowledge is a judgement about what is universal and necessary, and there are first principles for all kinds of knowledge, and for the conclusions of every proof (for knowledge involves reasoning). This being so, the originating principle of the objects of knowledge cannot itself be a piece of knowledge or of art or of wisdom; for anything that is known is capable of proof, and the sphere of art and wisdom is what is capable of being otherwise. Nor are these principles objects of philosophical understanding, for philosophers like, at least in some cases, to be able to prove things. Well, the states of

mind by which we attain truth and exclude error about necessary
5 and contingent things are knowledge, wisdom, understanding, and
intelligence; so if three of them (namely, wisdom, knowledge, and
understanding) cannot provide the first principles, it must be intelligence that provides them.*

Understanding, intelligence, and science

7. What is understanding?* In the case of the arts, we consider that
10 the most proficient exponents of them understand their business
very well: thus, Phidias understood well how to work in stone, and
Polyclitus in bronze; in this case 'understanding' means no more
than technical expertise. But we think that there are people who
possess a form of understanding that is general rather than specific.
As Homer says in the *Margites*:*

15   Neither digger nor ploughman was he made by the gods,
         Nor given any other kind of understanding.

So it is clear that understanding must be the most elevated of the
forms of knowledge. The person possessing it—the philosopher—
not only must know what follows from first principles, but must also
have a true grasp of the principles themselves. So philosophical
understanding will be a combination of intelligence and knowledge*—we might say, a knowledge of the highest objects deriving
20 from their head and source.*

   We say this because it would be odd to think that political science
or wisdom is the most excellent form of knowledge, given that man
is not the best of the inhabitants of the universe. What is healthy
and good for human beings is not the same as what is healthy and
good for fishes, while what is white and what is straight is always the
same. It follows that everyone would agree that what is understood
is the same in each case, whereas what is wise differs; for someone is
25 called wise if he considers well his own interests, and people entrust
such things to him. For this reason people call even some of the
animals wise, namely, those that appear to have a power of foresight
with regard to their own lives. It is evident that philosophical
understanding is not the same as political science; for if you call
concern with what is beneficial to yourself philosophy, then there
30 will be many different philosophies. There will not be a single one
concerned with the good of all animals, but a different one for

each—just as there is not a single art of medicine for all existing beings.

It makes no difference if you say that man is the best of all animals, because there are other things that have a far diviner nature 1141b than humans have—most conspicuously, the elements that constitute the heavens.* From what has been said it is clear that philosophical understanding is a combination of intelligence and knowledge about those things that are highest by nature. That is why Anaxagoras and Thales and their like are called philosophers rather than wise men, when we see them mistaken about what is to their 5 own advantage. We say that what they know is remarkable, and wonderful, and difficult, and divine—but, because they are not in quest of human goods, quite useless.*

Wisdom, on the other hand, has as its sphere things that are human and that admit of deliberation; for we say that the task of a wise man is to deliberate well, and no one deliberates about things 10 that cannot be otherwise, or that do not serve some end that is a good achievable by action. A person who is a good deliberator *sans phrase* is a person who by reasoning is able to hit upon what, among goods achievable by action, is the best for human beings. Wisdom is concerned not only with universals, but recognition of particulars is 15 also necessary; for wisdom is concerned with conduct, and particulars are the sphere of conduct. That is why some people who lack knowledge, especially those who have experience, are more effective than those who have it. For if a man knew that light meats are easily digestible and so healthy, but did not know which meats were light, he would not produce health. A person who knows that fowl is light 20 and healthy* is more likely to do so.

Wisdom is concerned with conduct: so we need to have both forms of knowledge, universal and particular—the latter, perhaps, more than the former. And here, too, there will be a kind that has a supervisory role.

Wisdom and political science

8. Political skill and wisdom are the same disposition, but they are different exercises of it.* So far as concerns the city, the commanding wisdom is skill in legislation, while that which deals with par- 25 ticular issues is given the general name 'political skill'. This is concerned with conduct and deliberation, since the ultimate stage is the

enactment of a decree. That is why only those thus occupied are said to be engaged in politics: they are as it were the operatives of the process.

30 It is the wisdom that concerns a person's own self that is regarded as wisdom par excellence and that takes possession of the general term 'wisdom'. Of the other kinds one is household management, another is legislation, and the third is political skill, this last having two branches: deliberative and judicial. Knowing what is to one's own advantage is no doubt a form of knowledge, but it is very differ-
1142a ent from the other kinds, for a man who knows and minds his own business is thought to be wise, while politicians are regarded as busybodies. So Euripides:

> Call me not wise,* who might have lived at ease
> A nameless unit of the military throng
> 5   With no especial share . . .
> For those who must stand out and do the most . . .

For people seek their own good, and think that this is what they ought to do. This opinion, then, has given rise to the view that men like these are wise; and yet perhaps one's own good cannot come about without a household and a city. Moreover, even the manage-
10 ment of one's own affairs is not an obvious matter, but calls for inquiry.

Some evidence for this is provided by the fact that while the young become geometers and mathematicians and acquire understanding in these areas, no one thinks to find wisdom in a young man. The reason is that the sphere of wisdom includes particulars, which are encoun-
15 tered in experience, and a young man has no experience, since that takes time to acquire. (One might also query why a boy may become a mathematician, but not a philosopher or a physicist. Is it because the objects of mathematics are abstract, while the principles of the other disciplines are derived from experience? The young do not really understand the latter, but parrot the terminology; but the essence of
20 mathematical objects is plain enough to them.)

Again, in deliberation error relates either to the universal or to the particular: we may suppose that all heavy liquids are bad, or that this particular liquid is heavy.

That wisdom is not knowledge is obvious: for, as has been said, it is concerned with ultimates, since conduct is particular. It is

something in the opposite corner from intelligence; for intelligence 25
is concerned with terms of which there is no deduction, and wisdom
with ultimates of which there is no scientific knowledge but only
perception—not the perception of the objects of the individual
senses, but the kind of perception whereby we see that the triangle
is the ultimate element of analysis, the final stopping point.* This is
perhaps better called perception rather than wisdom, but it is a dif- 30
ferent kind of perception.

MINOR INTELLECTUAL VIRTUES
CONCERNED WITH CONDUCT

Skill in deliberation

9. There is a difference between inquiry and deliberation: deliberation, that is to say, is a particular kind of inquiry. Skill in deliberation is another item whose nature we need to grasp: is it some kind
of knowledge, or belief, or perspicacity, or something else again?
Well, it is not knowledge, because people do not inquire about what
they already know; it is after all *deliberation* that it is skill in, and a
person who is deliberating inquires and calculates. Nor is it perspi- 1142b
cacity, for that is exercised swiftly without calculation, while deliberation takes time. There is a saying that after deliberation one
should act quickly, but before acting one should deliberate slowly.
Astuteness, too, is different from excellence in deliberation; astute- 5
ness is a species of perspicacity. Nor again is skill in deliberation any
kind of belief. Skill in deliberation is certainly a matter of getting
things right, since bad deliberation produces error; but it is not
matter of right knowledge or right belief. There is no such thing as
right knowledge* (or wrong knowledge, for that matter). Rightness 10
in belief is truth, and, moreover, once something is believed, the
matter is already determined. But again, reasoning is a necessary
condition for skill in deliberation. The remaining alternative is
that skill in deliberation resides in thinking: for while belief is
not inquiry but assertion already formed, mere thinking is not yet
assertion; and a person deliberating, whether well or badly, is still 15
inquiring and calculating.

Skill in deliberating is a particular kind of correctness in deliberating: so we must inquire first what deliberation is and what is its
sphere. Correctness is of various kinds and it is clear that not every

kind constitutes deliberative excellence. An incontinent man, and a bad man, if he is clever,* will by calculation achieve his aim, so that he will have deliberated correctly, but will have procured for himself
20 a great evil. To have deliberated well is regarded as a good thing: for skill in deliberation is precisely correctness in deliberation that achieves what is good. But good itself can be achieved by false reasoning, so that one achieves what one ought, but not by the appropriate means, the middle term of the syllogism having been false. This, too, then, will not be enough to be skill in deliberation, merely
25 achieving what one ought but not by the appropriate means. Again, it is possible for a man to achieve it by long deliberation, while someone else gets there quickly. This, too, falls short of skill in deliberation, which demands correctness about what is beneficial in respect of the end, the manner, and the time. Then again, there can
30 be skill in deliberation *tout court* or with respect to a particular end: skill in deliberation *tout court* concerns the end *tout court*; the other kind concerns the particular end. So if it is characteristic of the wise to have deliberated well, skill in deliberation will be the sort of correctness with regard to what conduces to that end of which wisdom is the true apprehension.*

Judgement, a critical skill

10. Judgement and good judgement,* in the sense in which we
1143a speak of people as being judicious and having good judgement, are not altogether the same as knowledge and belief (if they were, then everyone would be judicious); nor is judgement a particular discipline in the way that medicine is knowledge about what is healthy and geometry knowledge about magnitudes. For judgement is not
5 concerned with things that are everlasting and invariable, nor about any and every changeable thing, but with matters that one might be puzzled over and deliberate about. Hence its sphere is the same as that of wisdom, yet judgement and wisdom are not the same. For wisdom is prescriptive: its job is to tell us what we should do or not
10 do, whereas the job of judgement is simply to offer a verdict. (Judgement is identical with good judgement, and judicious people are those who have good judgement.) Judgement is neither the possession nor the acquisition of wisdom. When we make a practical application of our knowledge of something, our insight* is called a judgement; so, too, when we apply our beliefs within the sphere of

wisdom in delivering a verdict—a sound verdict, for here goodness
and soundness are the same thing—about what other people tell us. 15
This is the origin of the word 'judgement' (the kind that makes
people judicious) from its use in the sphere of insight: for we often
call insight 'judgement'.

Common sense in ethics

11. The gift that is called 'sense', in the way in which we speak of
people being sensible and having common sense, is a matter of sound
discrimination in the sphere of the equitable. An indication of this is 20
that we say that an equitable judge is an especially sensitive person,
and equity is a sensitive judgement in particular cases. Sensitivity is
a discriminative sense that delivers correct verdicts about what is
equitable, a correct verdict being one that delivers truth.

All these dispositions, reasonably enough, converge on the same 25
point: for when we speak of sense and judgement and wisdom and
intelligence, we attribute the possession of sense and intelligence* to
the same people and regard them as having wisdom and judgement.
For all these faculties deal with ultimates and particulars. Being
judicious, sensible, or sensitive is a matter of being a good judge in 30
matters within the sphere of wisdom. What is equitable, you see, is
what is common to all good things in matters that concern others.
All affairs of conduct are particular and ultimate matters, for it is
not only that a wise man must know these things, but judgement and
sense, too, concern affairs of conduct, which are ultimates.

Intelligence, too, is concerned with extremes in both directions: it
is intelligence and not reasoning whose objects are primary terms 1143b
and ultimate particulars. There is one intelligence concerned with
the unchangeable and primary terms in the realm of demonstration,
and another intelligence concerned with the ultimate and contingent element, and the other premiss, in practical reasoning; for
these are the source of our grasp of the end, since universals come
from particulars, and for these you need to have a form of percep- 5
tion which is intelligence.

That is why these attributes are regarded as natural gifts: no one
is a philosopher by nature, but people may owe sense and judgement
and intelligence to nature. Evidence of this is that we think such
things vary with age, and that a particular time of life brings intel- 10
ligence and sense, as in the natural course of things. For this reason

we should pay attention to the unproved assertions and opinions of older, experienced, and wise people no less than to the conclusions of demonstrations, because experience gives them a sharp eye to see clearly.

15 We have stated, then, what wisdom and understanding are, and what is the sphere of each, and how each of them is the virtue of a different part of the soul.*

RELATION OF WISDOM TO UNDERSTANDING

What is the use of wisdom and philosophy?

20 12. One might wonder whether these virtues are of any use. Philosophical understanding does not focus on any of the things that will make a man happy, for it is not concerned with bringing things into being. Wisdom does have that merit, but for what purpose is it necessary? The sphere of wisdom is the things that are just and noble and good for human beings, and these are the character-
25 istic activities of a good man: but if the virtues are states of charac-
ter, mere knowledge of these things will not make us any more likely to do them. The case is the same as with health and physical fitness: mere knowledge of medicine or gymnastics will not make us better able to do what is healthy and fit—in the sense of manifesting, rather than procuring, these physical states. But if you say that wisdom is not a matter of knowing things but aims to make a man good, then
30 wisdom will be no use to those who are already virtuous. Nor will it be useful to those who lack virtue: it will not matter whether they have wisdom themselves as long as they listen to others who do have it. That will be enough for us, as it is in the case of health: we wish to be healthy, but we do not learn medicine. Furthermore, it would seem odd if wisdom, a virtue inferior to philosophical understanding, is to be put in charge of it in the way that an art that has a prod-
uct governs and prescribes everything about it.

35 These, then, are the issues we must discuss: so far we have done no more than set out the problems.

1144a First of all, let us say that these characteristics, even if neither of them produces anything, must be desirable in themselves, because each of them is a virtue of one of the two parts of the soul. Secondly, they are indeed productive: not like medical skill in relation to health, but like health itself.* It is thus that understanding is

productive of happiness: for, being a part of the totality of virtue, its 5
possession and its exercise make a man happy. Again, our task is
achieved only in accordance with wisdom as well as with moral
virtue; for virtue makes the target aimed at correct, and wisdom
makes the means correct.* (The fourth part of the soul, the nutritive
part, has no such virtue; for there is nothing that is in its power to 10
do or not to do.)

What of the objection that wisdom makes us none the more likely
to do what is noble and just? Let us go back a little and start from the
following principle. We note that in some cases men who do
just acts—for instance, those who act as the law ordains either
unwillingly or in error or for some other reason and not because of 15
themselves—are not thereby just men, though indeed they do what
they ought and all that a virtuous man should. Similarly, it seems, in
order to be good you must be in a certain condition when you do
good acts—you must be acting out of choice and for the sake of the
acts themselves.* Virtue makes the choice right, but the things that
need to be done for the sake of it are the province not of virtue but 20
of a different faculty.

We must pause to make these matters clearer. There is a faculty
that is called cleverness: it is the power to hit upon and perform* the
steps that lead to the goal we have set ourselves. If the goal is a noble 25
one, then cleverness is laudable; if not, it is mere smartness: hence
we call both wise and smart* people clever. Wisdom is not the same
as this faculty, but it does not exist without it. It is a kind of eye of
the soul: as is evident and has already been said, it does not achieve 30
its proper condition in the absence of virtue. For those syllogisms*
that contain the originating principles of acts to be done run, 'since
the end, or the highest good, is such and such'—whatever that may
be (for the sake of argument, let it be whatever you please). This is
something that is not obvious except to a good man: for depravity
perverts us and causes us to err about the originating principles of 35
conduct. It is obvious, then, that it is not possible to be wise without
being good.*

Relation of wisdom to various kinds of virtue

13. We must once again inquire about virtue too: for virtue is in a 1144b
similar case. The relationship between natural virtue and virtue
strictly so called is similar to, though not exactly the same as, the

relationship between wisdom and cleverness. For everyone regards each type of character as given us in some sense by nature; for from
5   the moment we are born, we are just and in a way temperate and brave; but we look for something else to count as true goodness, wanting such qualities to be present in a different manner. For these natural characteristics are present in children and in beasts also, but in the absence of intelligence they are evidently harmful. So much
10 seems manifest, that this case is comparable to that of a strong body moving without sight, which may come a great cropper because of being unable to see. But the acquisition of intelligence makes a difference in conduct, and the characteristic will turn into the true virtue it previously only resembled. So that just as in the belief-forming part of the soul there are two types, cleverness and wisdom,
15 so in the moral part there are two types,* natural virtue and true virtue, and the latter cannot occur in the absence of wisdom.*

That is why some people say that the virtues just are forms of wisdom, and why Socrates was partly right and partly wrong in his inquiries: he was wrong to think that all the virtues were nothing
20 but forms of wisdom, but he was right to say that there are no virtues in the absence of wisdom. Evidence for this is the fact that even now everyone when defining virtue, after naming the state of character and its sphere, goes on to say 'in accordance with correct reasoning', and reasoning is correct if it is in accord with wisdom. All men seem in a manner to divine that the kind of state that counts
25 as a virtue is the state in accordance with wisdom. But we must go a little further, for virtue is not just a state in accordance with correct reasoning, but a state accompanied by correct reasoning;* and correct reasoning about these matters is wisdom. Socrates, then, thought that the virtues were types of reasoning—all, indeed, were sciences—whereas we think that they are accompanied by reasoning.
30 It is evident, then, from what has been said that it is not possible to be truly good without wisdom, nor wise without moral virtue. This, too, provides the solution to the argument that seeks to show that the virtues can exist in separation from each other, arguing that one and the same man is not best equipped for each of the virtues, so that he may acquire one before he acquires another. This can be
35 so with regard to the natural virtues, but not in respect of those that
1145a make us call a man simply and truly good. The reason is that if the

single virtue of wisdom is present, all virtues will be present. It is evident that even if wisdom were inactive, we would still have needed it, because it is the virtue of its own part of the soul, and it is clear, too, that no choice will be right without both wisdom and virtue. For the one makes one perform the acts leading to the end, and the other the end.* 5

But again, wisdom is not in authority over philosophical understanding or over the better part of the soul, any more than the science of medicine is in authority over health. It does not make use of it, but provides for its coming into being; the orders it issues are not orders issued to it but orders issued for its sake. The objection is like 10 saying that political skill rules over the gods, because it issues orders about everything in the city.

BOOK VI · CONTINENCE AND INCONTINENCE: PLEASURE

CONTINENCE AND INCONTINENCE

Six varieties of character

15 1. LET us now make a new beginning and state that there are three kinds of objectionable moral condition,* namely vice, incontinence, and brutishness. Two of these have obvious contraries, one of which we call virtue and the other continence. The most appropriate contrast to brutishness would be superhuman virtue, the kind of virtue
20 that belongs to heroes* and gods. Recall that Homer makes Priam say of Hector that he was very good, 'for he seemed the child not of a mortal man but rather of a god'. People say that men become gods by excelling in virtue; if so, virtue of this kind must clearly be the state
25 that is the opposite of the brutish condition. Brute beasts, you see, do not have virtues or vices, and neither do gods; gods have something higher than virtue, and brute beasts have a different kind of badness. A godlike man is hard to find—think of the epithet the Spartans use, when they greatly admire someone, namely, 'divine'—and so, too,
30 the brutish character is hard to find among humans. It is to be met with chiefly among foreigners, but brutish characteristics can also be produced by disease or deformity; and we use the word also to denounce humans who stand out from the rest of the race on account of their viciousness. Later we shall make mention of this condition,
35 and vice we have discussed earlier. Our task now is to discuss incon-
1145b tinence and softness (effeminacy) and continence and toughness; for we must not treat either of these as equivalent to virtue and badness, or as totally different in kind. As in all other cases, we should set out people's perceptions,* examine the problems they raise, and then exhibit the truth of the opinions about these afflictions—of all of
5 them, if possible, but if not, of the most widespread and authoritative. For if the difficulties are resolved, and the reputable opinions are left standing, then the matter has been sufficiently proved.

So: Both continence and toughness are regarded as belonging with good and praiseworthy things, while incontinence and softness

belong with bad and blameworthy things: if a man is continent, then 10
he sticks with his resolutions, and if he is continent he resiles from
them. And an incontinent man, through passion, does what he
knows to be bad, while a continent man, knowing his desires are
bad, is restrained by reason from following them. Everyone agrees
that a man who is temperate is continent and tough; but is a continent man always temperate?* Some say yes and some say no. Is an
intemperate man incontinent, and an incontinent man intemperate, 15
so that the terms can be used indiscriminately? Again, some say yes
and some say no. Can a wise man be incontinent? Some deny this,
while others claim that there are people who are both wise and clever
and incontinent too. Again there are people who are incontinent in
respect of anger, and honour, and profit. These, then, are the things
that people commonly say. 20

Discussion of current opinions about continence and incontinence

2. One might raise the problem what kind of correct judgement* is
present in a person behaving incontinently. Some say he could not
act thus if he possessed actual knowledge. It would be astonishing—
or so Socrates thought—if in the presence of knowledge something
else could get the upper hand of it and 'drag it about like a slave'.
Socrates was opposed to the whole idea,* and claimed that there was 25
no such thing as incontinence. No one, he maintained, can act
against what he judges to be his best interest; such a person must be
a victim of error. Such a view is in contradiction to people's plain
perceptions, and we must investigate the phenomenon, asking what
kind of error is in question if error is indeed the cause. For it is evident that a man who behaves incontinently does not, before he gets 30
into that state, think that that is what he ought to do. Some people
go only part of the way with Socrates: they admit that there is nothing more powerful than knowledge, but they do not agree that no
one acts otherwise than seems best to him. So they say that when the
incontinent man is overcome by pleasures, what is in his mind is not 35
knowledge but belief. Very well then: suppose that it is not knowledge but belief, a weak rather than a strong conviction, as happens 1146a
when people are in two minds. We still have a problem, because we
sympathize with people who abandon such convictions in the face
of powerful desires, but we have no sympathy with depravity or with
any other of the blameworthy states. Shall we say, then, that it is

wisdom that is the countervailing force, this being the strongest of
5 all? This is absurd: it would make one and the same person be both
wise and incontinent, whereas nobody would say that it was the
mark of a wise man voluntarily to do the most base things. Moreover,
it was shown earlier that a wise man is a man of action (taking decisions about ultimate matters) and that, in addition, he possesses the
other virtues.

10 Again, if being continent implies that one has strong and base
desires, a temperate man will not be continent, nor will a continent
man be temperate, for a temperate man's desires will be neither
excessive nor base. But they must be in the case in point; for if the
desires are good, there is something base in a state of character that
stops us following them, so that continence will not always be a good
15 thing. On the other hand, if the desires are weak and not base, continence will be nothing special, and if they are base but weak, it will
be nothing grand.

Suppose that continence makes one steadfast to every belief: in
that case it will be base, if it makes one stick to a false belief. On the
other hand, if incontinence makes one abandon any and every belief,
then there will be a good form of incontinence. Neoptolemus in
Sophocles' Philoctetes* would be an instance: he deserves praise for
20 abandoning what Odysseus persuaded him to do, because he was
distressed by telling a lie.

Again, there is the problem of the sophists' argument. Some
people like to expose other people's paradoxes so that they can, with
luck, appear clever; and their arguments present us with a problem.
25 For our thinking gets tied up when it dislikes a conclusion and does
not wish to stay with it but cannot get away because it is unable to
refute the argument. One such argument leads to the conclusion
that folly plus incontinence adds up to virtue: for incontinence will
make a man behave contrary to what he judges right, while what he
judges is that good things are bad and not to be done. Consequently,
30 he will do what is good and not what is bad.

Again, a person who in his conduct pursues pleasure on principle
might well be regarded as better than someone who does so through
incontinence rather than reasoning: the former will be easier to
cure, since he may be talked into changing his mind. But the incon-
35 tinent man is caught by the popular proverb: if water is choking you,
1146b how will you wash it down? A man who believed in what he was

doing would cease to do it if he was persuaded out of his belief; but this man does it all the same even though he is convinced he should not.

Again, if there is continence and incontinence in every sphere, what is plain incontinence? For no one has all the forms of incontinence, but we say that some people are just plain incontinent.

Solution to the problem about the incontinent man's knowledge

3. These and the like problems arise: some of the claims should be 5 refuted and others left to stand. For the solving of a problem is itself a discovery.

We must inquire first whether people behaving incontinently have knowledge or not, and if so, what kind of knowledge. Next we must consider the sphere of incontinence and continence, that is to say, whether it extends to every kind of pleasure and pain or only 10 certain specific kinds. We must also ask whether being continent is to be identified with being tough or not, and we must ask similar questions about the other matters that are germane to this investigation. The starting point of the inquiry is the question whether the continent and the incontinent person differ from each other by 15 operating in different spheres, or by having different attitudes; I mean whether the incontinent man is incontinent simply by being concerned with certain objects, or just by his attitude, or else by both together. Again we must ask whether any and every object can be the subject matter of continence and incontinence. For plain incontinence does not have a universal sphere but is restricted to the 20 sphere of intemperance. It is characterized not just by its sphere—if it were it would be the same as intemperance—but by the manner in which it is related to it. For the one character is drawn on by a deliberate choice, judging that one should always pursue the present pleasure, while the other does not share the belief, but shares the pursuit.

What of the proposal that those who behave incontinently are acting not against knowledge, but against true belief? This makes no 25 difference to the argument: many people who are in a state of belief are not at all in two minds, but think they have accurate knowledge. Perhaps the idea is that mere believers are more likely than those who know to act against their judgement, because of the weakness of their conviction. We reply that belief will be no different from

knowledge: for some people are no less convinced of what they
30 believe than others are of what they know: Heraclitus shows this.*

But there are two different ways in which we speak of people
knowing something. One man may have knowledge without using
it,* and another may be making actual use of it: both of them are
said to know. Consequently, when someone does what he ought not,
and knows this, it will make a difference whether he is or is not
35 applying this knowledge; the former case seems strange, but not the
1147a latter. Further, since there are two kinds of premiss,* there is nothing to prevent someone's having both premisses and acting against
his knowledge, provided that he is using only the universal premiss
and not the particular; for it is individual acts that get done. And
there are also two kinds of universal term: one is predicable of the
5 agent, the other of the object; e.g. 'dry food is good for every man'
and 'I am a man' or 'such and such food is dry'; but 'this food is
such and such' is a piece of information which he may fail to have,
or fail to use. There will be a huge difference between these ways of
knowing, so that to know in one way would not seem anything odd,
but to know in the other way would be astonishing.

10   There is yet another way,* besides those mentioned, in which we
humans are capable of having knowledge: for within the case of
having knowledge without using it we can discern different ways of
having—one of which is, as it were, halfway between having and not
having, as in the case of a man asleep, or crazy, or drunk. Now this
is just the condition of people under the influence of passions: mani-
15 festly, attacks of rage, desires for sex, and other similar passions alter
our bodily condition and even drive some people crazy. It is clear
that incontinent people should be said to be in a condition similar to
such cases.

The fact that people use words expressive of knowledge is no
indication that they have it: for even those under the influence recite
20 proofs of theorems and verses of Empedocles.* Beginners in a discipline, again, can string words together without knowing what they
mean, when there has not been the time necessary for them to
assimilate it. So we must suppose that the speech of those who are
incontinent is like that of actors on a stage.

Again, one might view the cause from a physiological point of view,*
25 as follows. The one belief is universal, the other is concerned with particular items within the scope of sense-perception. When the two

come together, the soul must thereupon affirm the conclusion, and
if it is a practical matter must immediately act upon it. For instance,
if everything sweet must be tasted and this is sweet (indicating a
particular sweetmeat), a person who is capable of acting and is not   30
prevented must act accordingly. So when there is present a universal
premiss forbidding tasting,* and another saying, 'every sweet thing
is pleasant and this is sweet' (this premiss being operative), and
when desire is present, then it says, 'avoid this' but desire drives on;
because each part of the soul is capable of setting us in motion. So it   35
turns out that incontinent behaviour is in a manner the effect of   1147b
reason and belief,* and one that is not in itself contrary to right
reasoning, but only coincidentally: what opposes right reasoning is
not the belief but the desire. That, too, is why animals are not incontinent, because they make no universal judgements but have only
memory and mental imagery of particulars.   5

The explanation of how the error is dissolved and the incontinent
man regains possession of his knowledge is the same as in the case of
a man drunk or asleep. It is nothing peculiar to this condition and
we must listen to what the physiologists say about it. Now, the last
proposition is an action-guiding belief about a perceptible matter,
and it is that which the man in the grip of passion either does not   10
have, or has only in the sense in which having is not really knowing
but only saying, like a drunken man babbling Empedocles. Because
of this, and because the last term is neither universal nor as scientific
as the universal, what Socrates was trying to maintain actually seems
to be correct:* for it is not as a result of so-called knowledge proper   15
that incontinence occurs, nor is it knowledge proper that is dragged
about by passion, but the perceptual kind.

Let so much suffice about the question whether the person behaving incontinently has knowledge or not, and if so, what kind of
knowledge.

Solution to the problem about the sphere of incontinence

4. The next topic for discussion* is whether all those who are incon-   20
tinent exhibit a particular kind of incontinence, or whether there is
such a thing as plain incontinence, and if so, what is its sphere. What
is obvious is that pleasures and pains provide the sphere of activity
for both continent and tough people on the one hand, and incontinent and soft people on the other.

Among things that produce pleasure, some are necessary, while
25 others, worthwhile in themselves, admit of excess. The necessary
ones are the bodily kind—I mean such as relate to food and the need
for sex, the bodily matters we assigned as the sphere of temperance
and intemperance. By the ones that are not necessary, but worth-
30 while in themselves, I mean such things as victory, honour, wealth,
and other such good and pleasant things. People, then, who go to
excess in such matters, contrary to their own correct reasoning, we
call not incontinent simply, but incontinent with a qualification such
as 'in respect of money, or profit, or honour, or anger', rather than
plain incontinent. This is because they are different from incontinent people and are so called only because of their resemblance. It is
35 like the case of the Olympic victor who bore the name Man:* there
1148a was little difference between his definition and the definition of
man, but nonetheless Man differed from other men. Evidence for
this distinction: incontinence—whether plain or specific—is blamed
not only as a fault but as a kind of vice, whereas none of the others
is so blamed.

What, then, of the people who are incontinent in regard to the
5 bodily enjoyments that we said are the sphere of temperance and
intemperance? Consider a man who pursues excesses of things
pleasant, and shuns the pains of hunger and thirst and heat and cold
and all the objects of touch and taste. If he does so not out of choice,*
but against his choice and judgement, then he is called incontinent,
10 and not with any qualification such as 'in respect of anger', but just
plain incontinent. Evidence of this is that men are called soft with
regard to these pleasures and pains, but not with regard to any of the
others. This is why, leaving out all the others, we group together the
incontinent man with the intemperate man, and the continent man
with the temperate man: it is because in a way the same kind of
15 pleasures and pains provide the sphere for each, even though the
two characters respond differently, the one making a deliberate
choice while the other does not.

Who is more appropriately called intemperate: the man who with
no or only slight desire pursues excessive pleasure and shuns moderate pains, or the man who does so because his desires are fierce?
20 The former, surely: for imagine what he would do if he had vigorous
desires and felt sharp pain at missing the necessary pleasures!

Among desires and pleasures some belong to the class of things that are noble and good (since some pleasant things are by nature worthwhile), others are the opposite, and others are in between, according to our previous distinction, such as wealth and profit and 25 victory and honour. If objects are of the first or the middling sort, then no blame attaches to finding them attractive and desiring and loving them, but only for doing so in a particular fashion which is excessive. Consider people* who contravene reason in yielding to or pursuing one of the things that are naturally noble or good; for instance, those who have an excessive concern with honour, or with 30 their children, and their parents. These are good things, and a concern with them is praiseworthy; yet there can be excess even in them, as when a Niobe fights against the gods, or when the filial Saturos doted on his father to a degree that seemed idiotic.* Since, as we 1148b have said, each of these objects is in itself naturally worthwhile, no depravity attaches to them, even though excesses here are bad and should be avoided. Similarly, there is no room for incontinence, since incontinence not only is something to be avoided but is actually blameworthy. However, because of a resemblance to the condi- 5 tion of the incontinent, people do speak of incontinence in these cases, but with an added epithet—as we call someone whom we would not call plain bad a bad doctor or a bad actor. We do not do so because in such cases we do not have real badness, only something 10 analogous, and in the other cases, too, it is clear nothing is to be taken as incontinence and continence unless its sphere is the same as that of temperance and intemperance. It is because of a certain similarity that we apply the term to anger, and that is why we add a qualification, and call a person 'incontinent in respect of anger' as we say 'incontinent in respect of honour, or of profit'.

Brutish and morbid forms of incontinence

5. Some things are naturally pleasant, and of these some are just 15 plain pleasant, others are pleasant for particular kinds of animals and humans. Other things are not naturally pleasant, and of these some become pleasant through custom or because of some disablement, while others arise from congenital depravity. With respect to each of these there are parallel states of character, one brutish, the other morbid. By brutish states, I mean such things as that of the female human who rips open pregnant women and eats their babies, or the 20 kinds of things those who have gone wild around the Black Sea enjoy,

such as eating raw and human flesh, or taking turns in offering their
children as a dish at a communal banquet, or the stories they tell of
Phalaris.* Besides these brutish states there are morbid ones arising
25 from disease and in some cases madness, like the man who sacrificed
and ate his mother, or the slave who ate his fellow's liver. Other
morbid states result from habit, like pulling out one's hair, biting
one's nails, or eating coal or earth. Another example is male homosexuality. Such practices are due sometimes to nature and sometimes
30 to habituation, as in the case of those who have been sexually abused
since childhood. In cases where nature is responsible, no one would
call such people incontinent, any more than one would call women
incontinent because they are passive rather than active in copulation;
nor would one apply the term to those who are in a morbid condition
1149a because of habituation. For one thing, each of these states is outside
the limits of vice, just as brutishness is. For another thing, whether
or not one yields to these conditions, their presence is not plain
incontinence but only its replica. Similarly, someone who is in the
same condition with respect to fits of rage is not plain incontinent,
but only incontinent in a particular respect.

5   Any excessive stupidity, cowardice, intemperance, or anger is
either brutish or pathological. A man whose nature is to fear just
anything, such as the patter of a mouse's feet, is cowardly in a brutish way; while the man who was terrified of a weasel was just sick.
There are two kinds of stupid people: some are naturally incapable
10 of reason and live by their senses alone, like some distant foreign
tribes; others are morbid cases who suffer from madness or diseases
like epilepsy. Some people may have these traits only at particular
times, and be able to resist them: perhaps, for instance, Phalaris
could have restrained his urge to eat children or enjoy unnatural
15 sex. In other cases people not only have these urges but actually
yield to them. Thus, what is called plain depravity is depravity on a
human scale; other kinds have an epithet attached, such as 'brutish'
or 'pathological'. Similarly, it is clear that there is both brutish and
pathological incontinence, while incontinence plain and simple is
20 what corresponds to human intemperance.

It is clear, then, that the only sphere of incontinence and continence is that of temperance and intemperance, and that in other
spheres there is a different kind of incontinence, so called by extension and not in a plain sense.

Incontinence in respect of anger is less disgraceful than plain incontinence

6. Next let us observe that incontinence of anger is less shameful than incontinence of desires. One reason is that temper does seem to hear what reason says, even though it mishears it, like hasty servants who run out of the room before they have heard all that has been said, and get their orders wrong, or like dogs who bark at a knock on the door without waiting to see if it is a friend. Thus, temper, being hot and speedy by nature, hearing or rather failing to hear an order, rushes to take revenge. When reason or appearance announces an insult or a slight, temper rears up at once, as if reasoning that one must take arms against anything of that sort; whereas desire, if reason or perception says no more than 'pleasant', leaps to enjoy it. Accordingly, temper does in a manner follow reason,* but desire does not. For that reason such incontinence is more shameful, for the person incontinent of anger does in a manner yield to reason, but the other yields not to reason but to desire.

Again, it is more pardonable to yield to natural desires, and to such desires as are common to all men and to the extent that they are common, and anger and bad temper are more natural than desires for what is excessive and unnecessary. Remember the man who excused himself for beating his father by saying, 'Well, he beat his father, and his father beat him,' and (pointing to his child), 'he will beat me when he is a grown man: it runs in the family'. And remember the other man who told his son, who was dragging him out of doors, that he should stop at the threshold, since that was how far he had dragged his own father.*

Again, the more likely people are to plot, the more criminal they are. Now, an ill-tempered man is not a plotter; nor is temper itself, which acts in the open.* Desire, on the other hand, is like the poetical account of Aphrodite as 'guile-weaving daughter of Cyprus' with her embroidered girdle, described by Homer as

Enchantment that makes away with wise men's minds.*

Therefore, this kind of incontinence is more unjust and more shameful than incontinence of anger; it is simple incontinence and even vice of a kind.*

Further, a wanton assailant feels no pain, but one who assaults another in anger does feel pain, while a wanton assailant takes pleasure in his action. Now, the more just it is to be angry at actions, the more unjust they are; it follows that incontinence of desire is more unjust, for there is nothing wanton in anger.

25 It is evident, then, that incontinence of desire is more shameful than incontinence of anger and that continence and incontinence have as their sphere bodily desires and pleasures. But we must grasp certain distinctions among these last. As was said at the beginning, some of them are human and natural, both in kind and in extent, whereas others are brutish, whether due to disabilities or diseases. It 30 is only the first sort that provide the sphere of temperance and intemperance; that is why we call animals neither temperate nor intemperate except by extension, and only if one species of animals stands out altogether from others in wantonness, destructiveness, and voraciousness. Animals do not possess choice or reasoning, but 35 they do depart from the natural norm in the way that madmen do 1150a among humans. Compared with vice, brutishness is a lesser evil but it is a more terrifying one, for in such cases the better part is not just corrupted, as in humans, but totally absent. This is like comparing an inanimate thing with a living one and asking which is worse. The 5 badness of something that has no internal principle of action is always less offensive, and reasoning is such a principle. It is like making a comparison between injustice in the abstract and an unjust man. Each is in a sense worse: for a bad man will do ten thousand times as much evil as a brute.

Softness and toughness, weakness and impetuosity

7. Earlier, we delimited the sphere of intemperance and temper-
10 ance to the pleasures and pains of touch and taste and the corresponding desires and aversions. There are two possible conditions relative to these: a man may be defeated by those that most people can overcome, and he may overcome those by which most people are defeated. If it is pleasures that are in question, the former is incontinent and the latter is continent; if it is a matter of pains, then 15 the former is soft and the latter is tough. Most people are somewhere between the two, with a bias towards the worse ones. Recall that some pleasures are necessary and others are necessary only up to a point, while neither excess nor deficiency is unavoidable. The same is true of desires and pains. It follows that a person who

pursues excessive pleasures* and does so out of choice, for their 20
own sake and not at all for any further consequence, is intemperate.
(Such a person cannot feel regret and is therefore incurable, since
someone who lacks regret cannot be cured.) The person who falls
short in the pursuit of pleasure is the opposite of intemperate; the
person in the mean state is temperate. Similar is the case of the man
who evades bodily pains not because he is defeated by them but as a
matter of choice. Among those who do not make the choice there 25
are two different kinds of people: those who are drawn on by pleasure, and those who flinch from the pain of unsatisfied desire.*
(Suppose someone does something shameful, who is worse: the
man who does it on the basis of zero or slight desire, or the man
whose desires are fierce? Is it worse to beat another when you are not
angry or when you are angry? Surely everyone would think the first
kind of person worse: just imagine what he would have done if he
had been really passionate. That is why an intemperate person is 30
worse than an incontinent one.) Of the conditions mentioned, one
is really a form of softness, while the other is the mark of the intemperate person.

The opposite of the incontinent person is the continent person,
and the opposite of the soft person is the tough person; for toughness is expressed by resistance, and continence by overcoming, and
there is a difference between resisting and overcoming like the dif- 35
ference between not being beaten and actually winning. For that
reason, continence is preferable to toughness. A person who falls 1150b
short in cases where most resist and come through is a soft and
wimpish person, for wimpishness is a kind of softness. Think of a
man who lets his cloak trail on the ground, so as not to be bothered
by the pain of lifting it up; or of a person who behaves like an invalid
and does not realize what a despicable figure he is cutting!

The case is similar with continence and incontinence. If someone 5
is defeated by fierce and excessive pleasures or pains, there is
no reason to be surprised, and provided that he has resisted, his
lapse is pardonable. Think of Theodectes' Philoctetes when he was
bitten by the snake, or Carcinus' Cercyon in the *Alope*; or think of
people who try to keep a straight face but cannot help bursting out 10
laughing, as happened to Xenophantus.* But it is a matter for surprise when someone is overcome, and cannot resist, pleasures or
pains that most people can hold out against—unless this is due to

heredity or disease, like the softness hereditary in the royal family of
15 Scythia, or the softness that differentiates females from males.

Some people are addicted to entertainment: these are generally
regarded as incontinent, but in fact they are soft, because entertainment is a relaxation, an interruption to one's work; and to be
addicted to entertainment is to take this to excess.

There are two kinds of incontinence: impetuosity and weakness.*
20 For some men after deliberating fail, because of passion, to keep to
the conclusions of their deliberation; others because of their failure
to deliberate are driven by their passion. If you tickle someone, then
you cannot be tickled yourself: and in the same way some people
notice and see what is coming and stir themselves and their reasoning faculty beforehand, so that they are not defeated by passion
25 whether pleasant or painful. Mainly, it is quick-tempered and bilious people who suffer from impetuous incontinence: neither of
them wait upon reason, but instead follow appearances, in the one
case because they are hasty, in the other case because of the strength
of their passions.

Intemperance worse than incontinence

8. An intemperate man, as we have said, has no regrets, for he
30 stands by his choice; but every incontinent man does have regrets.
So the situation is not as it was set out in our initial problem:* it is
the intemperate man that is incurable, and the incontinent who is
curable. Depravity is like diseases such as dropsy or consumption,
while incontinence is more like epilepsy, the one being a permanent
35 and the other an intermittent evil. Indeed, incontinence and vice are
wholly different in kind: vice is unaware of itself; not so incontin-
1151a ence.* Among incontinent people those who just have a fling are
better than those who reason out what to do but do not stick to it,
since the latter yield to a weaker passion, and are not caught unpre-
pared. This kind of incontinent person is like people who get drunk
faster, and on little wine, and less than most people.
5 It is evident, in fact, that incontinence is not a vice unless in a qualified sense, because incontinence is in conflict with choice and vice is
in accordance with choice. To be sure, the two states lead to similar
conduct: though incontinent people are not unjust, they do unjust
acts. This recalls Demodocus' comment on the people of Miletus,*
'Milesians are far from stupid, but they do what the stupid do.'

So people who pursue bodily pleasures to excess and contrary to   10
right reasoning fall into two kinds: one does so without conviction,
whereas the other is convinced because he is the kind of person to
pursue them anyway. The former, but not the latter, can easily be
brought to change his mind.* Virtue and vice respectively preserve
and corrupt the first principle, which in matters of conduct is the   15
purpose, just as in mathematics it is the postulates. In neither case is
it reasoning that teaches these principles: here it is virtue, whether it
comes by nature or instruction that teaches us correct beliefs about
first principles. Such a person, then, is temperate, while the opposite is intemperate.

Consider one kind of person whom passion leads to depart from   20
right reasoning. Passion conquers him to the extent that he does not
do what right reasoning tells him to; but it does not conquer him to
the extent that he becomes the kind of person who is convinced that
one should forever pursue the present pleasure. That is what the
incontinent person is: better than the intemperate person, and not
altogether evil, for the best thing in him, his first principle, remains   25
safe and sound.* Opposite to him is another kind of person, the one
who is constant and does not go astray, at least not through passion.
From all this it is evident that one of these states of character is good
and the other bad.

Relation of continence to other states of character

9. Suppose a man abides by any and every reasoning and choice.
Does that make him continent, or must it be a correct choice he abides   30
by? Suppose again that a man abandons any and every choice and any
and every reasoning. Does that make him incontinent, or does the
reasoning have to be not false and the choice correct? That is a problem we set earlier. Perhaps any old choice can provide a coincidental
case of continence or incontinence when someone abides by it or
abandons it, but per se the reasoning must be sound and the choice   35
correct. If someone chooses or pursues A for the sake of B, then per   1151b
se he pursues and chooses B, and A only coincidentally. But when we
speak without qualification, we mean what is per se. So in a manner
the one abides by, and the other abandons, any old belief, but for a
straight case of continence or incontinence it must be a true one.

Some people are constant in their beliefs: we call them 'strong-   5
minded'. They are hard to persuade and later they cannot be got to

change their minds. They have a certain similarity to the continent person, like the similarity between the prodigal person and the liberal person, and between the rash person and the confident person; but they differ in many respects. In the continent person it is pas-
10 sion and desire that fails to effect a change (for in appropriate contexts he is easily persuadable) but in the other case it is reason that fails to effect a change (for these people do form desires and many of them are led on by pleasures). People who are obstinate in this way include the opinionated, the ignorant, and the boorish. The opinionated are motivated by pleasure and pain, because when they win an argument they delight in their victory, and they are pained if
15 their opinions are quashed like a decree that is repealed. Thus, they resemble an incontinent, rather than a continent, person.

Some other people abandon their beliefs, but not through incontinence. An example is Neoptolemus* in Sophocles' *Philoctetes*. Sure, it was pleasure that made him give up, but a noble pleasure, for telling the truth was noble for him, while he had been persuaded by
20 Odysseus to tell a lie. Not everyone who does an action for the sake of pleasure is either intemperate or bad or incontinent; it is only if the pleasure is a shameful one.

There is one kind of person who enjoys bodily things less than he should, and fails to abide by reason. It follows that the continent
25 person is midway between such a person and the incontinent person. While the incontinent fails to abide by reason because of excess enjoyment, a character of this kind fails through insufficient enjoyment. The continent person, however, abides by reason and is not swayed either way. Since continence is a good thing, both the contrary states must be bad, as indeed they seem to be, but because the
30 other extreme is seen rarely* and in few people, that makes men think of continence and incontinence as contraries, just as they think of temperance as the only contrary of intemperance.

Since many words are used in an extended sense, we have come to speak of the 'continence' of the temperate person. Both the continent person and the temperate person are such as never to be
1152a led by bodily pleasures to do anything contrary to reason, but only one and not the other has bad desires. One of them would never feel pleasure contrary to reason, while the other would feel it but not yield to it. The incontinent person and the intemperate person, too, are both like and unlike each other: both of them pursue bodily

pleasures, but the one and not the other thinks this is the right 5
thing to do.

An incontinent man cannot be wise, but he may be clever

10. It is not possible for the same person to be at once both wise and
incontinent, because it was shown earlier that wisdom and moral
virtue go hand in hand. Knowledge alone does not make a person
wise; he has to act on it, which the incontinent person does not do.
The reason why it sometimes looks as if there are people who are 10
both wise and incontinent is that there is nothing to prevent a clever
person from being incontinent, and in our earlier discussions we
pointed out the way in which cleverness differs from wisdom, resembling it in respect of reasoning, but differing in the matter of choice.*
An incontinent person is not like a person who has knowledge and is
bearing it in mind, but like a person who is asleep or drunk. He acts 15
voluntarily, for in a manner he knows what he is doing and why, but
he is not a wicked person, since his choice was good; so he is half-
wicked. He is not unjust, because he has not been a plotter: if he is
one kind of incontinent, he has failed to abide by his deliberations;
if he is the other, bilious, kind he has not deliberated at all. Thus, the
incontinent person is like a city that passes all the decrees it should 20
and has good laws, but never puts them into effect. Recall
Anaxandrides' quip

> The city willed it—but she takes no notice of her laws.*

A wicked person, on the other hand, is like a city that puts its laws
into effect, but laws that themselves are bad.

The sphere of continence and incontinence is the area beyond 25
the condition of most people. The continent man abides by his resolutions more than most people can, and the incontinent man does so
less. The incontinence characteristic of bilious people is easier to
cure than that of the people who deliberate but do not abide by their
resolution. Again, those whose incontinence is due to habituation
are easier to cure than those in whom it is natural, because habit is
easier to change than nature. In fact that is why even habit is hard to 30
change—because it is like nature. Evenus* agrees:

> I tell you it's but lasting practice, friend,
> Yet it becomes men's nature in the end.

We have now said what continence and incontinence are, and tough-
35 ness and softness, and how these states are related to each other.

PLEASURE

Three views hostile to pleasure and the arguments for them

1152b 11. The topics of pleasure and pain* come within the purview of
the political philosopher, for he is the chief craftsman of the end to
which we look when we call a thing good or bad in the abstract.
Moreover, it is essential to consider them, not only because we laid
5 down that pains and pleasures were the sphere of moral virtue and
vice, but also because most people say that happiness involves pleasure. (Thus, the word 'blessed' is related to the word 'bliss'.*)

Now some people think* that no pleasure is a good, either in itself
or coincidentally, since the good and pleasure are not the same;
10 others think that some are, but most are base. Again, there is a third
position, that even if all pleasures are good, it is not possible for the
chief good to be pleasure.

The following are the arguments to the effect that pleasure is not
a good at all. Pleasure is a felt process towards a natural state, and no
process is of the same kind as its end, any more than housebuilding
15 is like a house. A temperate man avoids pleasures. A wise man seeks
not what is pleasant but what is free from pain. Pleasures get in the
way of thought, and the more so the greater the enjoyment: think of
the pleasures of sex—no one could have any thought while engaged
in them. There is no art of pleasure, but every good is the product
of some art. Children and animals pursue pleasures.

20   The arguments that not all pleasures are good are that there are
shameful and objectionable pleasures and that there are harmful
ones, since some things that are pleasant bring disease.

The argument that pleasure is not the chief good is that it is not
an end but a process. These, in rough summary, are the opinions
expressed.

Discussion of the view that pleasure is not a good

25 12. These arguments, however, do not establish that pleasure is not
a good, nor even that it is not the chief good, as is evident from the
following. There are two ways of being good: being good in the
abstract and being good for a particular person. In consequence, a

comparable distinction can be made between natures and dispositions and so between the corresponding changes and processes. Among those that are regarded as bad, some will be bad in the abstract, but not bad for a particular person, but instead worth 30 choosing. Others will not be worthy of choice even by a particular individual except at a particular time and for a particular period, and certainly not in the abstract. Others are not real but only apparent pleasures, namely, those that are accompanied by pain and whose purpose is medicinal, such as those felt by the sick.*

Further, states and activities are two different kinds of good. Thus, the processes that restore us to our natural state* are pleasant only coincidentally, because the activity involved in the correspond- 35 ing desires belongs to the state and nature that has remained unimpaired. This is shown by the fact that there are pleasures, such as the 1153a activities of contemplation,* that involve no pain or desire, since there is no natural impairment involved. What people enjoy while their natures are being replenished is different from what they enjoy when their natures are fully restored. When they are restored, they enjoy things that are pleasant in the abstract, but while being replenished, they enjoy things that are quite contrary, enjoying sharp and bitter tastes that are pleasant neither by nature nor in the abstract. 5 This provides evidence for our account. It shows, moreover, that the pleasures in question are not really pleasures, for as pleasant things differ, so do the pleasures they provide.

What of the claim that there must be something better than pleasure, since (according to some) an end is better than a process? The answer is that pleasures are not processes, nor do they all accompany processes; instead, they are activities and ends. It is not when we are 10 acquiring an ability, but when we are using it,* that pleasure is felt. Moreover, not all processes have an end different from themselves, but only those that are bringing a nature towards completion. Hence, it is not right to say that pleasure is a felt process; one should rather say that it is an activity of a natural state, and substitute 'unim- 15 peded' for 'felt'.* Some people regard it as a process precisely because they think it is the genuine good, and they think that activity is a kind of process; but in fact the two are quite different.

What of the claim that pleasures are bad because some pleasant things bring disease? That is like saying that some healthy things are bad for moneymaking. Both are bad in a single respect, but that does not make them bad. And, indeed, thinking itself can damage one's health.

20 Neither wisdom nor any other state of character is impeded by the pleasure that it offers, but only by alien pleasures—indeed, the pleasures of thinking and learning make us think and learn all the more. There is no reason to be surprised that pleasure is not the product of any art; no other activity either is produced by an art,

25 but rather by the corresponding ability—though of course people regard the arts of the perfumer and the chef as arts of pleasure.

What of the arguments that the temperate man avoids pleasure, that the wise man seeks a painless life, and that children and animals pursue pleasure? A single consideration refutes them all. We have

30 observed in what way all pleasures are good in the abstract, but not good in particular respects. It is the kind that involves pain and desire that animals and children pursue, and that corresponds to the pains the wise man seeks to avoid. It is bodily pleasures that are of this kind, and it is excess in these that makes an intemperate man intemperate. It is these, therefore, that the temperate man shuns—

35 though he does have pleasures of his own.

Discussion of the view that pleasure is not the chief good

1153b **13.** A further point. It is agreed that pain is bad, and to be avoided; some of it is just plain bad, and some of it is bad by getting in the way of some good. Now, the contrary of what is to be avoided, in so far as it is to be avoided and is bad, is good. Necessarily, then, pleas-

5 ure is a good. Speusippus' solution,* that it is like the way a larger thing is contrary both to what is smaller and what is the same size, does not work; for he would hardly say that pleasure was some kind of evil.

If some pleasures are base, that does not prevent the chief good from being a pleasure of a kind, just as it might turn out to be knowledge of a kind, even though certain kinds of knowledge are bad. Given that every disposition has unimpeded exercises, it may be

10 that the unimpeded exercise of all of them, or of one of them,* is what happiness is; and, if so, it is perhaps necessary that this is the thing most worth choosing. This activity is a pleasure. So a certain pleasure might be the best thing of all, even though—if it so be— most pleasures are in the abstract bad.

That is why all people think that a happy life is pleasant, and tie

pleasure up with happiness—reasonably so, for no activity is com- 15
plete if it is impeded, and happiness is something complete. That is
why a happy person needs bodily and external goods, and luck as
well, so as not to suffer impediment to his activities. Some people
say that a man on the rack, or the victim of massive misfortunes, will
be happy provided only that he is good. Whether willingly or not, 20
such people are talking nonsense.* The necessity of fortune makes
some people think good fortune is the same thing as happiness, but
it is not, for an excess of good fortune may get in the way. In that
case perhaps it is not right to call it good fortune, since the scope of
that is determined by reference to happiness.   25

Indeed, the fact that all things, both animals and men, pursue
pleasure is an indication that it is in the way the chief good:

What many people's voice proclaims is never wholly lost.*

But since no single nature or state either is or is regarded as the best
for all, neither do all pursue the same pleasure, even though all 30
pursue pleasure. And yet perhaps they are pursuing not the pleasure
they think or would say they were pursuing, but a universal one: for
all things have something godlike in their nature. But the pleasures
of the body have monopolized the name because they are the ones
we most often come across and the ones all people share; so because 35
they are the only ones people recognize, they think them the only 1154a
ones there are.

It is obvious that if pleasure, and the activity of which it consists,
is not a good, then it will not be the case that the happy man lives a
pleasant life. For if pleasure is not a good, why should he need it,
and what should stop him from living a painful life? For if pleasure
is neither good nor bad, no more is pain; and so why should he avoid 5
it? So, too, the life of the good man will not be pleasanter than that
of others unless his activities are pleasant too.

*Discussion of bodily pleasures and the exaggeration
  of their importance*

14. What of bodily pleasures? There are those who say that while
some pleasures, the noble ones, are very well worth choosing, the
bodily ones, the sphere of intemperance, are certainly not. Those who 10
speak thus must answer the question: why, then, are the contrary
pains bad? Good, after all, is contrary to bad. What of the necessary

pleasures? Are they good only in the sense in which what is not bad is good, or are they genuinely good but only up to a point? In the case of states and processes where there cannot be too much good, there cannot be too much pleasure either; where there can be too much of them, there can be too much of the pleasure too. In the case of bodily goods there can be excess, and it is the pursuit of the excess, and not of the necessary pleasures, that makes a person bad. For everybody enjoys fine foods and wines and sex in one way or another, but not everybody enjoys them in the way they should. With pain, the opposite is the case: one avoids pain altogether and not just excess of pain, for pain is not contrary to excess except for a person in pursuit of excess.*

Now, we should explain not only the truth but also the cause of error, since this helps to produce conviction; for when a plausible account can be given why a falsehood appears true, this reinforces belief in the truth. Accordingly, we must explain why bodily pleasures appear more worth choosing. First, then, it is because they expel pain. Since humans suffer pain in excess, they pursue excessive pleasure, and every kind of bodily pleasure, as a remedy for pain. Because they show up against their opposite, remedial pleasures gain in intensity and that is why people pursue them.

There are two reasons, which have already been identified, why pleasure is not regarded as a good thing. The first is that some pleasures are expressions of a nature that is base, either from birth, as with the brutes, or through habituation, like those of base humans. The second is that some pleasures are remedies for defective natures; and since becoming sound is not as good as being sound, and since these pleasures occur in the course of the removal of the imperfection, they are only coincidentally good.

Another reason is that because of their intensity these pleasures are pursued by those who cannot enjoy other pleasures. (At all events, they go so far as to manufacture thirsts for themselves—an inoffensive practice when these are harmless, but bad when they are harmful.*) For they have nothing else to enjoy, and to many people, because of their nature, a neutral state is painful. A living creature is always under stress, as the physiologists tell us:* even seeing and hearing are painful, they say, but we get used to them. Young people suffer growing pains which make them like drunks, and youth is pleasant. People who are bilious by nature are always in need of relief, since their constitution makes their bodies forever itch in a heightened state of desire, and what drives out pain is pleasure—the contrary pleasure, or any old pleasure if it is sufficiently strong. Thus, they become intemperate and base.

But the pleasures that do not involve pain do not admit of excess:* 15 these are the things pleasant naturally rather than coincidentally. By 'coincidental' pleasures I mean the remedial ones (what makes a thing seem pleasant in these cases is when a cure is effected by the action of the remaining healthy part); by 'natural' I mean those that stimulate the activity of a healthy nature.

No one thing is forever pleasant, because our nature is not simple, 20 but has an alien element within it, inasmuch as we are mortal. So if one element does something, that is unnatural for the other element, and when the two elements are in balance, what is done seems neither painful nor pleasant. If there is any being whose nature is 25 simple, the same action will always be most pleasant to it. That is why God always enjoys one single and simple pleasure, for there is activity not only of movement but also of immobility,* and pleasure belongs rather to rest than to motion. But as the poet says,* 'in all things change is sweet'; this is because of some kind of wickedness, for just as a wicked man is changeable, so a nature needing 30 change is wicked, being neither simple nor good.

So, then, we have discussed continence and incontinence and pleasure and pain, and explained what each is, and how far some of them are good and some bad.

It remains to speak of friendship.

BOOK VII · FRIENDSHIP

The nature of friendship

1234b 1. WHAT is friendship* and what are its characteristics? What kind
of person is a friend? Does the word 'friendship' have a single sense
20 or more than one, and if so how many? How should one treat a
friend, and what are the claims of friendship? These questions about
friendship need to be investigated no less than what is noble and
desirable in people's characters.* For the promotion of friendship is
regarded as the special task of political skill,* and people say that it
25 is on this account that virtue has utility: for people cannot be friends
with one another if they have been wrongfully treated by each other.
Moreover, we all say that our friends are the principal objects of our
just and unjust behaviour. Again, it is held that a man who is a good
man is also a friendly man, friendliness being a state of character. If
you want to take care not to act wrongfully, it is enough to make
friends: for true friends do not wrong one another. But people will
30 not act wrongfully if they are just: therefore, justice and friendship
are either identical or very close to each other.

Furthermore, we consider having a friend to be one of the greatest goods, and friendlessness and solitude to be quite terrible. This
is because it is with friends that we pass our life and to friends that
1235a we willingly offer our company. For we spend our days with our
family or our relations or our comrades, or with our children, our
parents, or our wife. Private right conduct towards our friends
depends on ourselves alone, while our conduct towards others is
determined by law, and does not depend on us.

There are many problems about friendship. In the first place,
there are some that arise from people extending the term and taking
5 in extraneous matters.* Some believe that if A is like B then A is a
friend to B; hence the sayings*

> God ever acts to bring together like and like.
> Jackdaw flocks with jackdaw.
> Thief knows thief, and wolf knows wolf.

10 Natural philosophers build the whole system of nature on the principle that like goes to like. Thus, Empedocles said* that a dog sits on

the tiling because it resembles him. This, then, is the account that
some give of friendship; but others say that it is contraries that make
friends with each other; for what is loved and desired is as dear as a 15
friend, but what is dry desires not dry but wet; hence the sayings*

> Earth is in love with rain.
> In all things change is sweet.

And change is change to a contrary. And like hates like, for

> Potter with potter never can agree.

And animals that live on the same food are each others' enemies.

These beliefs, then, are greatly at variance. According to one 20
group, what is like is friendly and what is contrary is hostile:

> The less is ever hostile to the more
> And hates it from the breaking of the day.*

And, moreover, enemies are far apart from each other, while friendship is held to bring people together. According to the other group, 25
it is contraries that are friends, and Heraclitus criticizes the poet*
for writing

> Perish all strife 'twixt gods and 'twixt men.

There would be no harmony, he says, if there were not high and low
notes, and there would be no animals without the contrariety
between males and females.

These, then, are two views about friendship, and they are too 30
general and too far apart.

There are others that are closer to each other and more akin to
people's perceptions. Some people hold that it is not possible for
bad people to be friends, but only good people. Others think it odd
if mothers are not to love their own children.* Even in beasts we see
that kind of friendship: at least they choose to die for the sake of
their offspring. Others think that utility is all there is to friendship. 35
They offer two facts as evidence. Everybody pursues what is useful
and throws away what is useless, even in his own person (as old
Socrates used to say,* citing spittle, hair, and nails). We get rid of
parts of the body when they are of no use, and finally our whole 1235b
body when it dies. (A corpse, of course, is useless, but people who
have a use for it preserve it, as in Egypt.) Now, these factors seem
to be in conflict with each other: for like is of no use to like, and

contrariety and likeness are at opposite extremes, while contraries
5 are altogether useless to each other, because one contrary destroys
the other.

Again, some people think it is easy to make a friend, while others
think that identifying a real friend is something very rare. You cannot
do it, they say, unless you suffer misfortune, because everyone wants
to be thought a friend of the prosperous. Others warn us not to trust
10 even those who stick by us in misfortune, lest they are deceivers and
pretenders who are offering their company in adversity in the hope of
claiming our friendship when prosperity returns.

The basis of friendship: virtue, utility, or pleasure?

2. We must, then, find an explanation that will best take account of
the views on these topics and will resolve the problems and the contrary positions.* This will come about if the contrary views are
15 shown to be reasonable enough; for such an explanation will be most
in harmony with people's perceptions. In the outcome, if each assertion is true in one sense but untrue in another, both the conflicting
positions will stand fast.

Another problem is whether what we love in a friend is the pleasant or the good. Suppose that what we love is what we desire: this is
20 particularly true of erotic love, the kind where 'none loves but he
who loves for evermore'.* Well, desire is for what is pleasant, so on
this showing what is loved is what is pleasant. On the other hand, if
what we love is what we will, then what is loved is what is good; and
the pleasant and the good are two different things.

Let us, since we need to determine these and related matters,
25 start from the following assumption. An object of wanting or of willing is either a good or an apparent good. That is why what is pleasant
is wanted, for it is an apparent good, since some people think it is
good, while to others it feels good even if they don't think it is good*
(feeling and thinking belong to different parts of the soul). It is evident, however, that both the good and the pleasant are loved.

30 Having clarified that, we must make another assumption. Among
goods, some are good in the abstract, and some are good for a particular individual but not good in the abstract; and the same things
are both good in the abstract and pleasant in the abstract. For things
that are helpful for a healthy body we say are good for the body in
the abstract, but we don't say that of things that help a sick body,

such as drugs and surgery. Similarly, the things that are pleasant for 35
a body in the abstract are the things that are pleasant to a body that
is healthy and wholesome: for instance, looking at things in the light
rather than in the dark, though the opposite is the case for a man
with bad eyes. The wine that is pleasanter is not the one that is pleasant to a man whose palate has been ruined by over-indulgence (some
people would not even pass up wine that is no better than vinegar*)
but the one pleasant to the uncorrupted taste. Likewise with the 1236a
soul: the real pleasures are not those of children or wild animals, but
those of adults: at least, these are what we prefer when we compare
both in memory. As a child and a wild animal is to an adult human,
so is a bad and foolish man to a good and wise one. For them, things 5
are pleasant if they are appropriate to their characters: and those are
things that are good and noble.

Now, things are good in more than one sense, for we call one thing
good because of its essential quality, and another because it is serviceable and useful. Moreover, what is pleasant may be either really
pleasant and really good, or may be pleasant for a particular individual and only apparently good. Hence, just as in the case of inani- 10
mate objects we can choose and love something for each of these
reasons, so, too, in the case of human beings: we love one man for his
character and virtue, another because he is serviceable and useful,
and a third because he is pleasant and gives us pleasure. And a man
becomes a friend when he receives love and returns love, and when
each of the two is fully aware of this. 15

It follows, then, that there are three kinds of friendship. They are
not all so called in virtue of a single thing, nor are they species of a
single genus; yet there is no mere equivocation,* for they are so
called in virtue of their relation to a particular kind of friendship
which is primary. It is like the term 'medical', which we use when
speaking of a mind, a body, an instrument, or an operation, but
which we apply properly to what is primarily so called. The primary
instance is the one whose definition is implicit in all the cases.* For 20
example, a medical instrument is one that a medical man would use;
whereas the definition of the instrument is not implicit in the definition of a medical man. In every case, then, people look for what is
primary, and because the universal is primary they assume also that
the primary is universal, but that is false. Hence, in the case of
friendship, they cannot do justice to all the different perceptions 25

people have. Because a single definition does not fit all, they think the other cases are not friendships, even though they really are, though in a different manner. When the primary friendship does not fit, because they assume that if it were really primary it would be universal, they go on to deny that the others are friendships at all. In 30 fact, there are many kinds of friendship, which was one of the things asserted above when we distinguished three senses of the word. One kind, we said, is based on virtue, another on utility, and a third on pleasure.

Most people's friendships are based on utility: people love one another because they are useful and only in so far as they are useful. 35 As the proverb says:

Glaucus, an ally as long as he stays in the battle, is a friend.

And

The Athenians have given up knowing the Megarians.

Friendships based on pleasure are characteristic of the young, who are sensitive to what is pleasant; accordingly, they are changeable, 1236b for as their characters change as they grow up, so too do their pleasures. But the best people's friendships are based on virtue.

From this it is evident that the primary friendship, the friendship of good people, is mutual exchange of love and choice. To one who loves, the loved one is a friend, and one who returns the love is a 5 friend to the one he loves.* This kind of friendship occurs only among humans, for they alone are conscious of choice, but the other forms occur also in the lower animals. Apparently, indeed, utility is present to a small degree between humans and tame animals and between animals themselves. Recall Herodotus' story of the sandpiper and the crocodile,* and the assemblies and dispersions of birds 10 that are reported by soothsayers.

Bad people may be friends with each other for the sake of utility or pleasure. However, some say that they are not really friends because the primary friendship is absent: a bad man will wrong another bad man, and those who are wronged by each other do not love each other. But it is not true that they do not love. They do not do so with the love 15 of primary friendship, but nothing stops them having the other kinds of friendship. They put up with each other for the sake of pleasure, even though it is doing them harm, behaving in the way incontinent people do. To some who look closely at the matter it seems that those

who love each other for the sake of pleasure are not really friends,
because their friendship, not being of the primary kind, does not share
its stability but is instead unstable. But in fact, as has been said, it is
genuine friendship, derived from, but not identical with, the primary   20
kind. To call that the only kind of friendship is to do violence to
people's perceptions and forces one to utter paradoxes. But it is
impossible to bring all friendships under a single definition. The
upshot is this: in one sense the primary friendship is the only kind of
friendship, but in another sense they all are, not in virtue of some
chance homonymy or accidental relationship, nor yet as belonging to   25
a single species, but rather as related to a single paradigm.

Now, provided that nothing gets in the way, what is good in the
abstract is one and the same thing as what is pleasant in the abstract.
It follows that the true friend, the friend pure and simple, is the
primary friend, and it is he who is worth choosing for his own sake;
he must be such, for if it is for his own sake that you want good
things to happen to him, then he must be someone you want to con-   30
tinue in being.* The true friend, then, is pleasant in the abstract,
and that is why any kind of friend is regarded as pleasant.

But we must make further distinctions, because it is debatable
whether the object of love is what is good for oneself or what is good
in the abstract, and whether or not the exercise of love is itself
accompanied with pleasure, so that the object of love is also some-   35
thing pleasant. The two questions must be answered together. For
things that are not good in the abstract but possibly bad* are to be
avoided, and something that is not good for you is no concern of
yours. What is to be sought is that things that are good in the abstract
should be good for you too. For what is worthwhile is what is good in   1237a
the abstract, but what is worthwhile for you is what is good for you:
and these must be brought to coincide. That is what virtue does; and
the purpose of political skill is to bring this about in cases where it
does not yet exist. Merely being a human being puts one on the way
to this, for the things that are good for men in the abstract are good
by nature. Likewise, a man is further along than a woman, and a   5
gifted man rather than one less gifted. The way forward is via pleasure: what is needed is for noble things to become pleasant. Where
these do not coincide, a person is not perfectly good,* because room
is left for incontinence to arise; for incontinence just is discord in
the passions between what is good and what is pleasant.

10   So since the primary friendship is founded on virtue, such friends will be themselves purely good, and not because they are useful, but in a different manner. For what is good for a particular individual is a different thing from what is good in the abstract. What is the case with states of character applies also to benefit: for what is beneficial in the abstract is not the same as what is beneficial to a particular individual* (in the way that taking exercise differs from taking

15   drugs). The same goes for the state of character that constitutes human virtue, if we assume that a human being is one of the things that are good by nature: the goodness of what is naturally good is good in the abstract, but the goodness of what is not so is good only for that thing.

The case is the same with pleasantness. For here we must pause and inquire whether there is any friendship without pleasure, and

20   how such a friendship differs from others, and on which of the two things the friendship is founded: is a man loved because he is good, even if he is not pleasant, or in any case not for his pleasantness? Given that 'love' has two senses, is it because he is good that the exercise of love seems to involve pleasure? In the realm of knowledge, fresh ideas and information are particularly vivid because of

25   the pleasure they bring, and so, too, it is clear, is the recognition of what is familiar; and the reason is the same in each case.* By nature, at any rate, what is good in the abstract is pleasant in the abstract; and what is good for particular individuals is pleasant to them. It follows straight away that like takes pleasure in like, and that for a human being the pleasantest thing is another human being. This is true even of imperfect beings, and hence it is clearly so with com-

30   plete beings: and a good man is a complete man.

Now, if friendship in action is the mutual, pleasurable choice that two people make of each other's company, it is clear that the primary friendship is nothing other than the reciprocal choice of the things that are good and pleasant in the abstract, and that friendship itself is the state that finds expression in such a choice. For what friend-

35   ship produces is a certain activity, not an external activity, but one in the person loving.

(Contrast our abilities: their activities are always external, operating either in something other than oneself, or in oneself qua other.*) Hence loving is a pleasant feeling, but being loved is not, because while being loved is not an activity of the beloved,* loving is an activity—the expression of friendship. One occurs only in animate things, the other also in inanimate things—because inanimate things 40 can be loved. Friendship in action is treating the loved one as 1237b beloved; a friend is an object of love to his friend qua friend and not qua musician or doctor.

The pleasure of friendship is the pleasure derived from the friend himself in himself; for he is loved for himself and not for being something else. So if it is not because he is good that you take pleasure in him, your friendship will not be of the primary kind. No 5 accidental feature of him should cause more offence than his goodness causes delight. Perhaps a man smells very badly? He gets left alone: he must make do with our benevolence, but not demand our companionship.

This, then, is the primary friendship that everyone recognizes; it is with reference to it that the other kinds are either accepted or contested as friendships, for friendship is thought to be something stable, and only this is stable. A formed judgement is stable, and for 10 a judgement to be correct what leads to it must be neither hasty nor casual. A stable friendship demands trust, and trust comes only with time. A person must be tried and tested, as Theognis says:

> If you would know the mind of man or woman   15
> First try them as you'd try a pair of oxen.

To make a friend takes time; initially there are only would-be friends. This condition is most easily mistaken for friendship, for when people are very anxious to be friends, they render each other all kinds of friendly services and this makes them pass for real friends 20 rather than would-be friends. But it is with friendship as with other things: mere wanting to be healthy does not make people healthy, and neither does wanting to be friends make people friends. Evidence of this is that people who are in this position without having first tested one another are easily set against each other. Though people are not easily set against each other in respect of matters where they 25 have allowed each other to test them, in other matters, where people are anxious to set them against each other, they may well be convinced if evidence is produced.

At the same time it is evident that this kind of friendship does not occur among bad people; for a bad person is distrustful and malignant to all, because he measures other people by himself. For this

30 reason, good people are more easily swindled, unless they have learnt
by trial and error to be chary of trusting. Bad people prefer natural
goods to their friends, and none of them love human beings more than
worldly goods; so none of them are really friends. For in this manner
you never reach the proverbial commonality of friendship: the friend
is an accessory to the goods, and not the goods to the friends.

35   Primary friendship, therefore, is not something that extends to a
large number, since it is difficult to make trial of many people: you
would have to go and live with each of them. Choosing a friend
should not be like choosing a cloak. True, in every case it is the mark
of a sensible person to choose the better of two things: but whereas
you should choose a new and better cloak in place of a worse one
that has been long worn, you should not give up an old friend for a
40 new one whom you do not know to be better. You cannot make a
1238a friend without a trial or in a single day; you need time, and that is
how 'a bushel of salt'* has become proverbial. All the same, if a man
is to become your friend, he must be not only good in the abstract
but good for you. A man is good in the abstract simply by being
5 good, but he is a friend by being good for someone else, and he is
both good in the abstract and good for an individual when these two
coincide, so that what is good in the abstract is likewise good for the
other. Alternatively, a man may not be good in the abstract, but good
for the other by being useful to him. But love itself prevents one
from being a friend to many people at the same time: for it cannot be
10 simultaneously expressed to a large number.

From all this it is evident that it is correct to say that friendship is
something that is stable, just as happiness is something that is self-
sufficient. And it has been rightly said:*

Nature is stable, but not so wealth.

Though it would be far better to say, instead of 'nature', 'virtue'.
15 Other proverbial truths are that time reveals the friend, and that
misfortune does so better than good fortune. It is then that it
becomes clear that the property of friends is common. For only
friends choose a person, rather than the presence or absence of the
natural goods and natural evils that constitute good and bad fortune. Misfortune reveals those who are not real friends but keep our
20 company for utility's sake. It takes time to reveal both kinds of
people: the friendship based on utility is not quick to show itself,

less so than the friendship based on pleasure; but even that, in its pure form, is not immediately obvious.

Human beings are like wines and dishes: the pleasantness of these is immediately obvious, but if it continues too long it becomes unpleasant and no longer sweet; and so it is with humans, too. For a non-relative criterion for pleasantness must take account of its final form and the time it lasts. Most people would agree with this. Their judgement which of two drinks is sweeter is a matter not only of after-effects, but of the actual time of drinking; for something can fail to be pleasant not because of any after-effect, but because its pleasantness is not lasting, even though initially it may take one in.

The primary friendship, therefore, the one from which the others take their name, is, as has been said before, friendship based on virtue and on the pleasure of virtue. The other kinds of friendship are to be found among children and animals and bad people. Hence the sayings:*

Men like to be with others of their age.

And

Pleasure glues bad men to each other.

Bad men may be pleasant to each other not because they are bad or middling but because they are both, say, musical, and one is a musician and the other a lover of music. All men have some good in them and the way they are good makes them fit in with one another. Again, they may be mutually useful and beneficial, not in the abstract, but with regard to some purpose of theirs which in itself renders them neither bad nor middling.*

It is also possible for a good man and a bad man to be friends if one is useful to the other for a particular purpose. A bad man may be useful to a good man for some temporary purpose of his, and a good man may be useful to an incontinent man for some temporary purpose of his, and to a bad man for some purpose of nature. In such a case a good man will want outright for his friend the things that are good outright, and will want conditionally for him the things that are conditionally good for him, in the way that poverty and disease might profit him; he will want these things for his friend for the sake of the outright goods, in the way in which he might want to drink medicine, not in itself but for its effect.

Further, a good man and a bad man may be friends in the ways in which people who are not good may be friends: the bad man may be pleasant to the good but not for his badness but as sharing some interest, as it might be in music. Or they may be friends on the basis of the minimum common goodness that makes some people willing to keep company with a good man to the extent that they accord with one another; for there is something good in all of us.

Friendship and equality

15 3. There are, then, these three kinds of friendship, and in all of the three the word 'friendship' in a manner implies equality; for even those whose friendship is based on virtue are friends with each other on the basis of a kind of equality of virtue.

Another variety of friendship is based on superiority—the kind of superiority that the virtue of a divinity has to that of a human. This is a different kind of friendship, as in general that between 20 ruler and subject. Recall that justice in such a case is also different, being a matter of proportional rather than arithmetical equality.* Within this class falls the friendship between father and son, and that between benefactor and beneficiary. Here, too, there are further varieties: the friendship between father and son is not the same as that between husband and wife, for the latter is between 25 ruler and subject,* and the former between benefactor and beneficiary. In these cases there is an absence, or a modified form, of the reciprocation of love. It would be ridiculous to reproach God for not returning love in the same way as he is loved, and similarly for a subject to reproach his ruler.* The role of a ruler is to receive, not to give, love, or at least to give it in another way. And there is 30 no difference between the pleasure that a man of independent means feels in his possessions or his children and the pleasure felt by someone newly acquiring such things after a period of deprivation.

The same is true for friendships based on utility and those based on pleasure; some are on a footing of equality, others on one of superiority. Because of this, those who think they are on equal terms 35 complain if their partners are not equally useful or generous. The same goes for pleasure, as is clear in love affairs where this is frequently a cause of falling out: one lover does not realize that for the other a different degree of passion is proportionate.* As Eunicus* says:

You speak like a beloved, not a lover.

Such people think that the proportion is the same* for each.

Friendships between unequals

4. To recapitulate: there are three kinds of friendship, one based on 1239a
virtue, one on utility, and one on pleasure, and these are subdivided
into those on a footing of equality and those on one of superiority.
Though both these latter kinds are friendships, it is only equal partners that are friends: it would be absurd for an adult man to be a 5
friend of a child, even though he loves and is loved. There are cases
where it is right for the superior partner to be loved, but where if he
loves in return he will be reproached for loving an unworthy object.
The right measure of love depends on the worth of the friends and a
particular kind of equality. Some cases deserve less love because of
inferiority in age, others because one partner is superior in virtue or 10
birth or some other attribute. Whether the friendship is one of utility
or pleasure or virtue, it is right* for the superior to love less or not at
all. Where the superiority is small, disputes predictably occur. (In
some cases a small difference is of no account, as in the weighing of
timber as opposed to the weighing of gold.) However, people are not
good at judging what counts as small, because one's own good, being 15
close, appears large, while another's good, being distant, appears
small. When the difference is excessive, even the inferior partners do
not claim that it is right for them to be loved back, or loved back to the
same degree. Suppose someone claimed that about God! It is evident,
then, that people are friends when they are on equal terms, and that it 20
is possible to return love without being friends.

It is clear why people seek the friendship of superiority rather than
that of equality, because it offers the advantages both of being loved
and of being superior. Hence some people value a flatterer more than
a friend, because he makes the person flattered appear to enjoy both 25
advantages. Ambitious people are particularly like this, because being
admired implies superiority. There are two kinds of people: some
naturally aspire to friendship and others aspire to honour. A person of
the first kind enjoys loving more than being loved; a person of the
second kind prefers being loved.* What is really loved by a person
who enjoys being admired and loved is the superiority, whereas for the 30
person who aspires to friendship the pleasure is in the loving itself.
For pleasure is necessarily inherent in the active exercise of love,*

whereas being loved is an accidental property; you may fail to notice that you are being loved, but you cannot help noticing that you are loving. Loving, rather than being loved, is the measure of friendship;
35 being loved is a matter of the merits of the beloved. For evidence of this, consider whether a friend would prefer to know, or be known by, the person he loves, assuming that it is impossible to have both. To know, surely, as women do when they give up their children for adoption, like Andromache in Antiphon's tragedy.* The desire to be known, indeed, seems something selfish, aimed at getting rather than giving,
40 whereas one desires to know in order to give practical effect to one's
1239b love. That is why we praise people who go on loving those who are dead: for they know, but are not known.

So, then, it has now been stated that there are several modes of friendship, and how many modes there are, namely three, and what the differences are between giving and getting love, and between
5 friendships of equality and friendships of superiority.

Friendship and likeness

5. At the beginning it was said that the vocabulary of friendship is also used more universally by people who extend their consideration more widely, some saying that like is loved by like, others saying the opposite. Accordingly, we must discuss these relationships and compare them to the kinds of friendship we have discussed.
10 Likeness may be in reference to what is pleasant, or to what is good. Goodness is simple, but badness is polymorphous: for a good man is always the same and does not change character, whereas a bad and foolish man is not the same in the evening as he was in the morning. Hence, unless they do a deal with each other, bad men are
15 not friends but fall out, an unstable friendship being no friendship at all. So this is the link between likeness and friendship, because what is good is like itself. But there is also a link with pleasantness: if two people are alike, they share the same pleasures, and everything is naturally pleasant to itself. That is why members of the same family find one another's voices and characters and company especially pleasant, and the same is true of the other animals. In this way
20 cially pleasant, and the same is true of the other animals. In this way it is possible even for bad men to love each other.

Pleasure glues bad men to each other.

On the score of utility, however, it is the contrary that is friends with

the contrary. For what is like X is useless to X, and therefore master 25
needs slave and slave needs master and husband and wife need one
another. A contrary is pleasant and desirable because it is useful—
not as a constituent of the end, but as contributing towards it. When
a thing has got what it desires, it has attained its end, and no longer
has any appetite for its contrary: the hot does not want the cold nor
the dry the wet.*

Yet in a manner love of the contrary is love of the good: the two 30
are drawn to each other through the mean. They have an affinity like
the matching parts of a tally, and when they come together they
form a single intermediate entity. It is only coincidentally that it is
love of the contrary: in itself it is love of the mean. The contraries
desire not each other but the mean. When people who are too cold
are heated, they are restored to the mean, and so too when people 35
who are too hot are cooled, and similarly in other cases. Otherwise
they are always in a state of desire, because they are not in the mean
states. But a person who is at the mean point enjoys natural pleasures free from desire, whereas others enjoy anything that takes them
away from their natural state.* This kind of relation, indeed, is 40
found even between inanimate things; it is when it is between living 1240a
things that it is love. Accordingly, sometimes people delight in those
who are unlike themselves—the sober in the witty, and the energetic
in the idle—for they are brought by each other into the mean state.
Coincidentally, then, as said, contraries love each other, but on
account of the good.

It has been explained, then, how many kinds of friendship there 5
are, and the different ways in which those who love and those who
are loved are called friends, both where this really is friendship and
where it is not.

Self-love

6. The question whether a man is or is not his own friend calls for
serious inquiry. Some think that everyone is his own best friend, and
they use this friendship as a standard* by which to judge their 10
friendships with their other friends. From the point of view of
theory and of the accepted attributes of friends, the two kinds of
love seem to be in some respects contrary, and in others similar.
Self-love is not friendship pure and simple, but it is analogous to it.
For loving and being loved require two separate partners. So the 15

issue of whether a man is his own friend resembles the question
15 whether the incontinent and continent man acts voluntarily or
involuntarily: it is a matter, we said, of how the parts of the soul are
related to each other.* There is a similar answer to all such questions: whether a man is his own friend or foe, whether a man can
wrong himself, and so on. For all these relationships involve two
separate elements, and in so far as the soul is bipartite, the answer to
the questions is yes, but in so far as the parts are not separate, the
20 answer is no.

It is a man's attitude to himself that determines the other modes
of love that we have regularly used for classifying in our discussions.* For a person is regarded as a friend if he wills for someone
things that are good (or that he thinks are good), not for his own sake
25 but for the other's. Put in another way, if you want someone else's
existence for his sake and not for your own, you would be regarded
as his special friend even though you do not confer on him any benefit, let alone existence. Put in yet another way, you are a friend of
someone if you choose to live with someone merely for the sake of
their company and not for any other reason. (This is like the way
30 that fathers, though they are concerned about their children's existence, prefer the company of others.) These cases all clash with each
other: for some people think they are not loved, unless their friend
wishes them either to prosper, or to exist, or to share his life.

Shall we say that to share the grief of one who grieves is a form of
love? Not if it is for some further reason, in the way that slaves grieve
when their masters grieve, because their grief makes them grumpy.
But it is love when the grief is shared for the griever's sake, as when
35 mothers grieve with their children and birds share each other's
pain.* What a friend really wants is not just that he should feel pain
along with his friend, but that he should feel the very same pain—
being thirsty when his friend is thirsty, for instance—if that is possible, and if not, something as close as possible. The same principle
1240b applies to joy: the mark of a friend is to rejoice for no other reason
than that his partner is rejoicing.

Again, there are sayings about friendship such as that friendship
is equality and that true friends share a single soul. All these can be
applied to the single individual, for that is the manner in which a
man wishes good for himself. No one does himself a good turn for
5 some ulterior motive or to gain favour; nor does he boast of what he

has done for himself, for someone who makes a show of his love
wants not so much to love as to seem to love. Wishing the other to go
on existing, and wanting to share his life and his joy and his grief,
and sharing a single soul, and being unable to live without each
other but rather to die together—these are characteristics of the   10
single individual and he is, as it were, his own companion.

All these things apply to the good man in relation to himself; but
in a wicked man they conflict, as they do in the incontinent. That is
why it is thought to be possible for a man to be his own enemy, even
though as one and indivisible he is the object of his own desire. Such
indeed is a good man whose friendship is based on virtue, but not so   15
the depraved man, since he is not one but many, and in the course of
a single day a different person with no bottom. Thus, even a man's
self-love is reducible to love of the good; for it is because he is in a
manner like himself, and the same as himself, and good for himself
that makes him the object of his own love and desire. That is what a
person is like by nature, but the wicked man is contrary to nature. A 20
good man does not reproach himself: he does not reproach his present self, like an incontinent man, nor his earlier self, like a penitent,
nor his later self, like a man who makes a false promise. (To speak
generally, if we must take note of the sophists' distinctions, he stands
in the same relation to himself as Coriscus and good Coriscus: the   25
two of them clearly add up to only the same amount of goodness.)
When people reproach themselves, they assassinate their own characters; yet everyone thinks himself good.

A person who is good outright seeks to be his own friend, because,
as we said, there are two elements in him that are by nature con-
genial to each other and that cannot be put asunder. In the case of
human beings, each individual is thought to be a friend to himself,   30
but not in the case of the other animals. A horse does not seem good
to itself,* and so is not a friend to itself. Neither are children friends
to themselves until they are capable of choice, for it is only then that
mind and desire can speak with different voices. Love of oneself
resembles love of one's kindred: neither bond is in one's power to   35
break. Even if there is a quarrel, kinsmen remain kinsmen and the
individual remains a single unit as long as he lives.

From what has been said it is clear what are the different senses of
'love' and that all kinds of friendship can be referred to the primary
kind.

Friendship, concord, and goodwill

1241a 7. It is relevant to our inquiry to consider concord and goodwill. Some people think that these two are the same thing, and others think that they cannot exist without each other. Goodwill is neither altogether distinct from friendship nor yet identical with it. When friendship is divided into three kinds, goodwill is not found either in
5 the friendship of utility or the friendship for pleasure. If you will good to another because it is useful to you to do so, it is your interest, not his, that is the motive of your wish; whereas goodwill, like real friendship, focuses on its object rather than on the person who exhibits it. And if goodwill were found in friendship for pleasure, it would be felt also towards inanimate objects. So it is clear that the
10 sphere of goodwill is friendship that is founded on character; but goodwill shows itself merely in willing good, whereas friendship goes on to do what it wishes. Goodwill is the beginning of friendship: every friend has goodwill, but not everyone who has goodwill is a friend. For one who has only goodwill is like a novice: so goodwill is the beginning of friendship but not friendship itself.
15   . . .* For friends are thought to be in concord, and those in concord are regarded as friends. But not any kind of concord amounts to friendship, but rather concord about things that the parties can put into practice and that conduce to their common life. Nor is it only concord in thinking or in wanting, for it is possible to think and to desire contrary things,* as in the discord in the incontinent person.
20 The concord has to be both in choice and in desire. Concord is something restricted to good people: bad people, when they agree in choice and desire, only harm each other. It seems that concord, like friendship, has more than one meaning: whereas the primary and natural form of it is good and not attributable to bad men, there is another
25 sense in which there may be concord between bad people when their choice and desire are fixed on the same objects. But their wants must concern matters where it is possible for both of them to get what they want. If what they want is something that cannot be shared, then they will quarrel, but people who are in concord do not quarrel.
30 Concord, then, is when two parties make the same choice of who is to rule and who is to be ruled, not each choosing themselves, but each choosing the same person. Concord is friendship in citizenship.*
     So much for concord and goodwill.

Benefactors and beneficiaries

8. People query why benefactors love beneficiaries more than beneficiaries love benefactors, while the contrary would be thought more
just. One might suppose that it comes about for reasons of utility
and self-interest; for the one is in credit and the other in debt. But 1241b
that is not all there is to it: there is also something natural about it.
An activity is more desirable than its product, and here we have a
relationship between an activity and its product, the beneficiary
being, as it were, the product of the benefactor. That is why even
animals have an instinct that leads them to produce offspring and
look after them. And in fact parents—mothers more than fathers— 5
love their children more than they are loved by them, and the children in turn love their children more than they love their parents,
because being the active agent is what is best. And mothers love
their children more than fathers do, because they are more likely to
regard the children as more their own work. For people judge work
by its cost, and the mother suffers more, in childbirth.

Let such be our determination on the topic of friendship towards 10
oneself and friendship among a group.

Friendship, justice, and partnerships

9. Justice is regarded as a kind of equality, and friendship, too,
involves equality if there is any truth in the saying 'Amity is equality'. All constitutions exhibit particular forms of justice, for a constitution is a partnership and every partnership is founded on justice. Accordingly, there are as many kinds of justice and of partnership 15
as there are of friendship; these are neighbours to each other and the
differences between them are minute. There is a common relationship that links soul and body, craftsman and tool, and master and
slave. Between these pairs there is no partnership, because they are
not two different things: the first term in each is unified, but the
second belongs to the first and has no unity of its own.* Goodness is 20
not shared between the two items, but all the goodness belongs to
the one for the sake of which the pair exists. For the body is the con-
natural tool of the soul, a slave is, as it were, a part and detachable
tool of his master, and a tool is a sort of inanimate slave.*

The other partnerships are a subset of civic partnerships; for
instance, fraternities, religious orders, or business associations. 25

Within individual households* all the forms of constitution can be found, both the genuine and the corrupt forms; in this respect constitutions resemble musical modes.* Paternal authority is monar-
30 chical, husband and wife together are an aristocracy,* and the siblings form a republic. The corrupt forms of these are tyranny, oligarchy, and democracy. So those are all the different forms of justice.

But remember that there are two sorts of equality: arithmetical and proportional. Accordingly, there will be corresponding sorts of justice, friendship, and partnership.

35 Republican partnership is based on arithmetical equality, and so, too, is friendship between comrades, both being measured by the same standard. The best aristocratic and monarchical arrangements are based on proportional equality, for what is just is not the same for superior and inferior, but should be in proportion. Such is the love of a father for a child, and matters are similar in the case of partnerships.

Civic friendship

1242a 10. The list of friendships includes those between kinsfolk, comrades, partners, and also what is called 'civic friendship'. Friendship between kinsfolk comes in several kinds, one between siblings, another between father and sons; it may be proportional, as in the
5 paternal case, or arithmetical, like that of brothers. (The latter is similar to friendship between comrades: in each case seniority gives certain privileges.) Civic friendship, more than any other, is based on utility, for it is the lack of self-sufficiency that brings people together, even if they would have come together simply for the sake
10 of company. Civic friendship—plus its corrupt forms—are the only ones that are not merely friendships, but partnerships between friends. Other kinds of friendship are based on superiority. The justice on which a friendship of utility is based is justice par excellence, because it is civic justice.

It is quite different when a saw is at the service of a skill: a tool and a skilful soul do not have a common purpose, they are brought together for the sake of the person who makes use of them. A tool
15 does, of course, come in for some attention, which it deserves because of the work it does. That is the whole point of its existence. The essence of a gimlet is twofold, and the more important part of

it is its activity, the boring of holes. In this class come also body and slave, as was said before.

To inquire, therefore, how one should treat a friend is to inquire about a certain kind of justice. Indeed, all justice is about relations 20 towards a friend. For justice concerns individuals who are partners, and a friend is a partner either in one's family or in one's way of life. For human beings are not just political animals, but also domestic animals; they are not like other animals who copulate in season with any chance female or male. No, humans are not solitary animals, but 25 gregarious in a special way, forming partnerships with their natural kinsfolk. Accordingly, even if there were no such thing as the state, there would be partnership and justice of a sort. A household is a kind of friendship.

The relationship of master and slave is the same as that of craft and tools, and of soul and body: such relationships are not friendships or forms of justice, but something analogous, in the way that 30 health is not justice but analogous to it. The friendship of man and wife is one of utility, a partnership; that of father and son is like that between god and man and between benefactor and beneficiary, and the same as that in general of natural ruler to natural subject. That between siblings is the most comradely, being based on* equality— 35

> Never was I called by bastard's name,
> All recognized a single sire of both—
> No less than Zeus my king.*

That is the language of men seeking equality. It is first in the household, then, that the origins and springs are found of friendship, of 40 political institutions, and of justice.   1242b

Recall that there are three kinds of friendship, based on virtue, on utility, and on pleasure, and that there are two varieties of each kind, one on a basis of superiority and the other on a basis of equality. The justice appropriate to each of them is clear from the debates. In the 5 variety based on superiority the claim is based on proportion but it takes two different forms. The superior's claim is based on proportion, but an inverse proportion. Let me explain. The services rendered by the inferior should be in the same ratio to those of the superior as the status of the superior is to the status of the inferior. For the superior is the ruler, and the inferior is the subject. If this is not possible, the superior claims at least an arithmetically equal 10

contribution. (This is the way things turn out in other partnerships where shares are allotted sometimes in accord with arithmetical equality and sometimes in proportion. For if the parties contributed sums of money that were arithmetically equal, they take an arithmetically equal share; but if their contributions were not equal they
15 take a proportion.) The inferior party, by contrast, inverts the proportion and brings together the opposite points of a diagonal.* As a result of this, the superior would seem to come off worse, and the friendship and the partnership looks more like an act of charity. So, equality must be achieved, and true proportion maintained, by some other means. This other means is honour, which is due to a natural
20 ruler or god in relation to a subject. But the profit and the honour have to be made equal.

The friendship that is based on equality is civic friendship. Civic friendship is based on utility, and citizens of one state are friends with citizens of another to the extent that their states are friends.
25 'The Athenians no longer recognize the Megarians,' nor do citizens when they cease to be useful to each other; their friendship is based on ready money. Here too, however, there is a ruler–ruled relationship—not a natural or a monarchical one, but a rotating one, not for conferring benefit in the way that God does, but for the equal shar-
30 ing of benefits and burdens. It is thus that civic friendship aims at equality. But there are two kinds of utility friendships: the legal and the moral. Civic friendship looks to equality and to the object in the way that buyers and sellers do; hence the saying 'fair wages make good friends'.* So when it is based on a contract, a friendship is
35 civic and legal; but when they leave the recompense to each other, it is a moral friendship between comrades. Hence this is the kind of friendship in which recrimination is most likely, the reason being that it is unnatural, for friendships based on utility are not the same
40 as those based on virtue. These people want to have things both
1243a ways: they associate for the sake of utility but as if they were decent people; they represent their friendship as a moral rather than a legal one, as if they were trusting each other.

For in general, of the three kinds of friendship, there are more recriminations in utility friendships than in others.* Virtue is not given to complaint, and friends for pleasure, once they have got and given what they wanted, break off the relationship. But utility
5 friends, if their relations are comradely rather than legal, do not

dissolve the partnership at once. The legal form of friendship, however, is free from recrimination. Discharging a legal obligation is
simply a matter of money (that is how the equality is measured),
whereas discharging a moral obligation depends on voluntary con-
sent. Hence in some places there is a law prohibiting members of a
friendly association from taking each other to court to enforce a voluntary contract: rightly so, for it is not natural for good men to go to   10
law and such associates enter into contracts as good and trustworthy
people. And indeed in such a friendship recriminations on either side
are dubious: what grounds of complaint can either have when their
trust rested not on the law but on the other's moral character?

A further problem is how here to determine what is just. Should   15
one look at the objective amount or quality of service rendered, or
its value to the recipient? It may turn out to be a case of what
Theognis says:*

> To thee, o goddess, this is small, but great to me.

Or it may turn out to be the opposite, as in the saying 'this is a trifle
to you but death to me'. Hence arise recriminations. One party   20
claims recompense for having done a great service to a friend in
need, or something of the sort, holding forth thus about the value of
the benefit to the recipient, while saying nothing about what it meant
to himself. The other party, on the contrary, speaks of what it cost
the donor, and not about its value to himself.

Sometimes the position is reversed: the beneficiary turns round   25
and says how little he got out of the exchange while the donor insists
on how much it cost him. Suppose that A, at considerable risk, has
done B only a drachma's worth of benefit: A will talk about the mag-
nitude of the risk, and B about the paltry sum of money. The same
kind of dispute occurs in connection with the repayment of finan-
cial debts, when there has not been a specific proviso in the contract:
one party claims the value of the money at the time of lending, and   30
the other the value at the time of repayment.*

Civic friendship, then, looks at the contract and the object; moral
friendship looks at the purpose of the agreement, and this is a truer
and more friendly justice. What gives rise to quarrels is that moral
friendship is something nobler, but utility friendship is more neces-   35
sary. People begin as moral friends, friends on the basis of virtue,
but when there is a conflict of private interest, it becomes clear that

that is not what they were. For most people pursue what is noble
1243b only when they have plenty to spare, and the same is the case with
the nobler kind of friendship.

It is clear, then, how such cases are to be distinguished. If they are
moral friends, then we must look at their purposes to see if they are
equal, and if so, no further claim can be made by the one upon the
other. If they are civic friends for utility's sake, we must ask what
would have been an advantageous agreement for them. But suppose
5 that when a return is due one thinks their friendship is of one kind,
and the other thinks it is of another: what is then to be done? Noble
speeches will not make a friendship noble, and something similar
goes for the other case. However, since they made no contract but
only a gentleman's agreement, someone will have to judge between
them, and neither of them must cheat by false pretences. Each will
have to put up with his luck.

Moral friendship is a matter of the parties' purpose. This is evi-
10 dent because if a person having received great benefits is unable to
repay them, he acts honourably if he pays what he can. After all,
even God is content with getting sacrifices that are only as good as
our powers. But a seller will not be satisfied if someone says he
cannot pay more—nor will a moneylender.

Friendships that are not on a straightforward footing leave room
15 for many recriminations, and it is not easy to see what is just, because
it is not easy to measure by a single standard things that are not
straightforward. That is what happens in love affairs: A pursues B
for the pleasure of living together, while B perhaps just regards A as
useful. When A ceases to love, B changes also, and then they calcu-
20 late the quid pro quo and quarrel as Pytho and Pammenes did.*
Teacher and pupil quarrel in this way (for there is no common measure between knowledge and things), and so did the doctor Prodicus*
with a patient who wanted a discount. There is a similar story about
a king and a harpist: the king kept company with the harpist for
pleasure, and the harpist kept company with the king for utility.
25 When the time came for payment, the king said the friendship was
one of pleasure, and that just as the harpist had given him pleasure
by his singing, so he, by simply promising payment, had given the
harpist pleasure.*

But here, too, it is clear how we must decide: we must measure by
a single standard, but a ratio rather than a number. We must measure

by a proportion, in the way that a civic partnership is measured. How 30
can a cobbler do business with a farmer, unless their products are
equalized by proportion? In cases where exchanges are not of like for
like, measurement must be by proportion. Suppose A complains that
he has given wisdom and B that he has given money. What is the ratio
between wisdom and riches, and how is one gift to be compared to the
other? For if B has given half of the less valuable object, and A not 35
even a small part of the more valuable one, it is clear that A is cheating.* But here, too, there may be a fundamental dispute if one says
that they came together for utility's sake, and the other says no, they
did not, it was on the basis of some other kind of friendship.

Special problems about friendship

11. There is a problem about the good man who is a friend loved for 1244a
his virtue. Is it to him that we should offer service and assistance, or
should we rather offer it to a person who makes a return* and is in a
position of power? This is the same problem as whether benefit is
owed more to a friend or to a man of virtue. If one's friend is also
virtuous, then perhaps it is not very difficult, provided one does not 5
pay too much attention to one factor and too little to the other,
greatly encouraging the friendship but doing little for the virtue.
But in the other case, many problems arise: for instance, if A was a
friend but will not be a friend in the future, while B will be, but is
not yet, a friend; or if A became a friend but is one no longer, and B
is a friend at present but not in the past or the future. But it is the
original problem that is most difficult. Perhaps Euripides' verses* 10
have a point:

> If words you offer, words will be your just reward,
> But he who gave a deed shall be with deeds repaid.

It is not the case that everything is owed to one's father; there are
other things that are owed to one's mother, even though the father is
more important. Not even Zeus gets all the sacrifices, and he receives
not all, but only some, forms of honour. Perhaps, then, there are 15
some things that should be done for the useful friend and others for
the virtuous friend. For instance, if someone provides you with food
and necessities, that does not mean that you are bound to offer him
your company; and on the other hand you are not bound to offer
your companion the things that were given you not by him but by

your useful friend. Those who behave like this,* giving everything
to their loved one when they ought not, are good for nothing.

20 The various criteria of friendship set out in our discussions all
belong to friendship in some manner, but not to the same kind of
friendship. Wanting what is good for someone is a criterion for
friendship that does not single out any particular kind: it applies to
a useful friend, to a benefactor, and indeed to a friend of any kind. It
is a mark of one kind of friendship to want the friend to go on living,
and of another kind that one wants one's friend's company. When a
friendship is on the basis of pleasure, one wants to share the grief
25 and the joy. All these criteria apply to one or other kind of friendship, but none of them to some uniform pattern of friendship. That
is why there are many such criteria, each of which is wrongly thought
to belong to some monolithic friendship. But no criterion does—
not even choosing that the friend should go on living. For a superior
person who is a benefactor has his eye more on the preservation of
his benefactions; and as for the person who gave you your own existence, you must want him to go on living but you will prefer the
30 company of your pleasant friends.*

Some friends wrong one another, loving possessions more than
their owners; it is for their sake that they love the owner, as being so
much the more useful. (It is like the way people choose a wine because
it is pleasant, and wealth because it is useful.) Naturally, the owner is
annoyed, as having been chosen for the sake of an inferior object;
35 while they complain because they now want him as a virtuous friend,
when earlier they were looking for a pleasant or a useful one.

Friendship and self-sufficiency

1244b **12.** We must also consider self-sufficiency and friendship, and the
interrelationship of their properties. One might wonder whether, if
someone is totally self-sufficient, he will have any friends, since it is
in time of need that one looks for a friend, and a good man is self-
sufficient* beyond all others. If a man who possesses virtue is happy,
5 what need would he have of friends? A man who is self-sufficient
does not need friends for utility, or for amusement, or for company:
his own company is all he needs. This is most evident in the case of
God: since he lacks nothing, he will not need a friend, and since he
does not need one, he will not have one. Consequently, the happiest
10 human being will have very little need of a friend, except to the

extent that self-sufficiency is not possible. Necessarily, then, the man with the best life will have fewest friends, and they will grow ever fewer. He will not be eager to make friends, and will disdain not only friends for utility but also friends for company. But even this makes it seem obvious that friendship is not for the sake of utility or benefit, but that the only real friendship is based on virtue. For when we are not in need, we all seek others to share our enjoyment; we look for beneficiaries rather than benefactors, and we can judge them better when we are self-sufficient rather than when we are in need. What we need most of all are friends who are worthy of our company.

But we need to consider in regard to this problem whether our view may be only partly right, and may have been misleading because of the comparison.* The matter will become clear if we ascertain what life is, as activity and as end. It is evident that it is perception and knowledge, and consequently sharing life is sharing perception and sharing knowledge. For every individual self-perception and self-knowledge is the most desirable of all things, and that is why an appetite for life is inborn in each of us, for living must be regarded as a kind of knowing. If, therefore, one abstracted and treated knowledge as absolute and independent and did not attach it to oneself (but this is misleading in the way it is written in the text,* though the matter need not be misleading), in that case there would be no difference between knowing oneself and knowing another instead of oneself, and likewise no difference between another living instead of oneself: whereas patently to perceive oneself and to be aware of oneself is more desirable.

Two of the things in the text have to be put together: life is desirable, but so is goodness, and consequently it is desirable that such a nature should belong to one and the same person.* It is possible to set out a series of corresponding items* in such a way that in each pair one member is classified as desirable, and something that is known or perceived, generally speaking, exists by sharing in the nature of the determinate. It follows that wanting to perceive oneself is wanting oneself to have certain attributes. We possess them, however, not in ourselves but by sharing in them by means of knowledge and perception: when one perceives, one is oneself perceived in the manner and respect of the initial perception, and when one knows, one is similarly known. From all this it follows that one

10 always desires to live because one always desires to know, and because one wishes to be oneself the object known.

To choose to live in the company of others might, then, from a certain point of view, seem foolish. Consider first what men have in common with other animals, like eating together and drinking together: if you leave aside speech, what difference does it make whether these things are done in proximity or at a distance? But
15 even in the case of speech, sharing merely casual chatter is a matter of indifference; and as for sharing information, that is not possible for people who are self-sufficient. That is because to receive information implies a deficiency in oneself, and to impart information implies a deficiency in one's friend, and it is parity that constitutes
20 friendship. Nonetheless, it is surely obvious that we all find it pleasanter to share with our friends to the best of our ability the good things that fall to the lot of each of us: in one case bodily pleasure, in another artistic contemplation, in a third philosophy. We need to be near to our friends—there is a proverb 'friends afar a burden are'—so in this shared activity we must stay close together. It is in this that sexual love resembles friendship, for the lover wants to
25 share the life of the loved one, though not as ideally he ought, but in a sensuous way.

The text, then, in discussing the problem, asserts the former conclusion, but the facts are as we saw later, so that it is clear that there is something misleading in the discussion of the question.* We must look for the truth in what follows. A friend, as the proverb says, is a
30 second Hercules—another self. Humanity is scattered and hard to bring together. By nature a friend is what is most akin to his friend, but one friend is alike in body and another alike in soul, and one friend in one part of body or soul, and another in another. But nonetheless, being a friend amounts to being a separate self.* Perceiving
35 a friend, then, must be in a manner perceiving oneself, and in a manner knowing oneself. To share even common pleasures and ordinary life with a friend is obviously pleasant (for it is always accompanied by consciousness of him); but it is even more pleasant
1245b to share the more divine pleasures. This is because it is always pleasanter to see oneself enjoying a superior good, which may be now an emotion, now an action, and now something different from either. If one should live well,* and one's friend likewise, and if living together involves working together, their sharing will be above all in the

things that make up the end of life. Hence we should study together and we should feast together, because such encounters are not for the sake of food and necessary pleasures, in the way that entertainments are. But everyone wishes to share with his friends his enjoyment of the end in so far as he can attain it; failing this, people want above all to do good to their friends and have their friends do good to themselves.

It is evident, then, that we should live together, and that this is the dearest wish of everybody, and especially of the person who is happiest and best. However, in the text the contrary conclusion was drawn: but that, too, was reasonable, since it contained a truth. The solution is to be found by an analysis of the comparison, which was in itself correctly stated.* Because God is not of such a nature as to need friends, the same is claimed to be true of one who resembles God. But if one followed this line of argument, one would say that a virtuous man does not think of anything; because that is not what makes God happy, being, as he is, too grand to think of anything else except himself. The reason is that for us well-being involves something other than ourselves, whereas he is his own well-being.

What of our seeking and praying for many friends? What of the saying that a man who has many friends has no friend? Both dicta are correct. Suppose it were possible to live with and share the experiences of many people at the same time: in that case, the more the merrier. However, this is very difficult, so the sharing of experience has to be restricted to a few. Hence, it is difficult not only to get many friends—since they have to be tried and tested—but also to enjoy them when you have them.

Sometimes we want a loved one to be absent from us provided he is happy; at other times we want him to share our own fortune. Wanting to be together is the mark of friendship, and if it is possible both to be together and to be happy, that is everyone's choice. But if it is not possible to prosper together, then we choose as the mother of Heracles might have chosen, preferring him to be a god rather than staying with her as a slave of Eurystheus.* One might make a joke like the one made by the Spartan in the tempest when someone told him to call on the Dioscuri for help.*

We regard it as the mark of a lover to want to keep his loved one from sharing his own troubles, and as a mark of the beloved to want to share them. Both of these wishes are reasonable, for to a friend nothing should give so much pain as his friend gives pleasure. On the other hand, we feel it is not his own pleasure that he should choose. That is why people keep their friends from sharing in their

1246a troubles, being content to suffer on their own; they do not want to seem to be selfishly choosing their own joy at the cost of the suffering of their friend, though they would of course be less burdened if they were not suffering alone.

Since well-being and companionship are desirable, it is clear that companionship combined with a lesser good is preferable to separ-
5   ation with a greater good. But since the precise value of companionship is unclear, people differ. Some think that the mark of friendship is to share everything, just as the very same food is pleasanter when one dines in company; others reject this, saying that if you took the argument to its limit, it would mean that it was better to experience extreme adversity in company rather than to enjoy solitary good fortune.

10   There is something similar in the case of ill fortune. Sometimes we do not want our friends to be present or to grieve, when they are not going to make anything better; at other times their presence gives us the greatest pleasure. This paradox is quite reasonable, and is explained by what we have said earlier. To see a friend in pain or
15   in a bad state is something we shun in the abstract, just like seeing ourselves in a similar condition. However, just seeing a friend is as pleasant as anything can be (for the reasons given above), and it is pleasant to see him not ailing when one is ailing oneself. Whichever of these is more pleasant sways the balance of wishing him to be present or not.

20   This kind of thing occurs among inferior people, for the same reason: they are anxious that their friends should not prosper, and not be absent,* if they themselves are faring badly. Hence, some suicides kill their loved ones along with themselves, feeling that otherwise they would feel their own sufferings more. In the same way, a man who remembers former prosperity suffers more than if
25   he thought he had always fared badly.

BOOK VIII · VIRTUE, KNOWLEDGE, NOBILITY, AND HAPPINESS

Virtue and knowledge

1. SOMEONE might raise the following question. Is it possible to use any given thing both for its natural purpose and also in other ways—whether qua itself, or coincidentally? Consider the eye as an example: one can use it to see, or to mis-see, by twisting it sideways so that things appear double. Either of these is the use of an eye qua eye, because it is an eye; but it is also possible to use it coincidentally, 30 as it might be to sell it or eat it. The case is similar with knowledge: you can use it correctly and you can use it to err.* When someone makes a deliberate mistake in spelling, he is using knowledge as if it were ignorance, topsy-turvy, in the way that dancing girls sometimes use their hands as their feet and their feet as their hands. 35

Well, then, if all the virtues are forms of knowledge, it would be possible to use justice as injustice: someone who does unjust deeds will be acting from justice, just like a man using his knowledge to display ignorance. If this is impossible, it is obvious that the virtues cannot be forms 1246b of knowledge. Perhaps one cannot actually use knowledge to display ignorance, but only to make mistakes, that is to say, to do the same things as an ignorant person would. Even so, it is not possible, from justice, to do the same acts as would result from injustice.

Again, if wisdom is knowledge and a form of truth, it will lead to 5 the same perversion. In that case it would be possible to act foolishly out of wisdom, and to make the same mistakes as a fool. If there was only one way of using each thing qua itself, people behaving thus would be acting wisely.* In the case of all the other forms of knowledge, there must be a superior one that causes the perversion. But what can divert the one that is superior to all?* There is no knowl- 10 edge or intelligence left to do so. Nor can virtue either, which is something it uses, the virtue of the governing element making use of the virtue of the governed.*

What, then, is it? Recall that some say that incontinence is a vice of the non-rational part of the soul, and that the incontinent man is a kind of intemperate man who still retains his intelligence. Is that

15 correct? Suppose that desire is so strong as to pervert him, and make
him reason in a contrary fashion. If so, it is evident that if there is
virtue in him, but error in his reason, the role of the two will be
reversed.* In that case, it will be possible to use justice unjustly and
wrongly, and wisdom foolishly.

   There will also be opposite possibilities. For it would be odd if
20 depravity turning up in the non-rational part will pervert virtue
in the rational part and turn it into error, while virtue in the non-
rational part, occurring while there is error in the rational part, will
not convert it and make it form wise and correct judgements. (After
all, wisdom in the rational part makes intemperance in the non-
rational part act temperately: that is what continence seems to be.)
25 So it will be possible to act wisely out of ignorance.

   These consequences are very odd: especially behaving wisely out
of ignorance. We never see this in other cases. Intemperance perverts knowledge of medicine or orthography, but the contrary of
intemperance does not convert ignorance into knowledge, because it
30 lacks an extra element. Virtue in total, however, is more powerful
than vice in this way: the just man can do whatever the unjust man
can do, in the way that power ranges wider than impotence.

   So it is clear that in humans wisdom and good dispositions of the
non-rational element go hand in hand. Socrates was right to say that
35 nothing is stronger than wisdom, but wrong to claim that it was a
science. For wisdom is a virtue, not a science; it is a different kind of
cognition.

Luck, good fortune, and happiness

   2. Since not only wisdom and virtue bring about well-doing, but we
1247a say also that the fortunate do well,* on the assumption that fortune
produces well-doing and the same results as knowledge,* we must
inquire whether it is by nature, or otherwise, that one man is fortunate and another unfortunate, and how matters stand on this topic.
That there are some people who are fortunate is a matter of observation.* For people who lack wisdom succeed in many things where
5 luck rules; and also in areas where there is an art, but where there is
also scope for luck, for instance in the case of generalship and steers-
manship. Are people like this as a consequence of some disposition,
or do they achieve their fortunate results not because of any quality
of their own? At the present time people take the following view, that

some people are fortunate by nature, and that nature gives people   10
certain qualities, so that they differ from each other from birth: just
as blue-eyed and black-eyed people differ,* so, too, fortunate people
differ from unfortunate people.

For that they do not succeed by wisdom is evident. For wisdom is
not unreasoning, but can give an account of why it is acting as it
does; but these people would not be able to say why they succeed
(that would be an art). That they succeed is obvious, though they are   15
lacking in wisdom in the very things in which they are fortunate,
and not just in other matters. (There would be nothing strange in
that case: Hippocrates, for instance, was a geometer but in other
matters he was thought silly and foolish, and once on a voyage, they
say, because of his unworldliness he was cheated of much money by   20
the customs men at Byzantium.*) For in navigation it is not the
most skilled who are fortunate, but it is as in dice where one man
throws a blank and another throws a six* in accordance with his
natural good fortune.

Or are people fortunate through being loved, as they say, by a god
so that success is the result of something external? Just as a badly
constructed ship often sails better, not on its own account, but   25
because it has a good helmsman; in this way the fortunate man has a
good helmsman in the shape of a spirit. But it would be strange for
a god or a spirit to favour such a man rather than the best and
wisest.* If, then, success must be due to either nature or intelligence, or some kind of guardianship, and two of these are ruled out,   30
then the fortunate must be so by nature.

Nature, however, is the cause of what occurs either universally or
generally, whereas luck is the opposite. Now, if prosperity contrary
to expectation seems to belong to luck—but if someone is fortunate,
he is so by luck—the cause would not seem to be* the kind of thing
that is the cause of what is universally or generally the same. Further,
if a man prospers or fails to prosper because he is the kind of man he   35
is, just as a man sees poorly because he is blue-eyed, then not luck
but nature is the cause. Such a man, then, is not so much fortunate
as gifted by nature. So we shall have to say that those whom we call
fortunate are not so by luck. In that case they are not fortunate at all,
for the fortunate are those whose goods are caused by good luck.*   1247b

If this is so, will luck not exist at all,* or will it exist, but not be a
cause? No, it must both exist and be a cause. It will, then, also be a

cause of good to some people and bad to others. Should it be eliminated altogether, and should it be said that nothing happens by luck,
5 but that we merely say that luck is a cause, when there is some other cause, because we do not see it? (It is for this reason that when they define luck, some people lay down that it is a cause that is opaque to human reasoning, on the assumption that there is a natural factor.) That would set us a different problem.*

Since we see people being fortunate once only, we must ask why we do not see them succeeding again through the same cause and
10 yet again.* For the same cause has the same effect. So this will not be a matter of luck. But when the same event results from antecedents that are indeterminate and indefinite, the result will be good or bad, but there will be no empirical knowledge of it,* as otherwise some fortunate people would have learnt it. Or would all the sci-
15 ences be types of good fortune, as Socrates said?* What, then, prevents such things from happening to somebody often in succession, not because he is the kind of person he is, but like a long run of success in throwing dice?

What follows then?* Are there not impulses in the soul of two kinds: some from reasoning and others from unreasoning appetite? And are these not prior? For if the impulse that comes from the
20 desire of the pleasant, and also the appetite, are by nature, then by nature everything will march towards the good.* If, then, there are some people well endowed by nature (as musical people without professional knowledge of singing are well endowed in that respect) and who without reasoning are impelled in accord with nature, and desire what they ought and when they ought, these persons will suc-
25 ceed even though they lack wisdom and reasoning, just as men will sing well who are incapable of teaching singing. People of this kind are fortunate—people who without reasoning succeed most of the time. It will follow that the fortunate are so by nature.*

Or is there more than one sense of 'good fortune'?* For some actions come from impulse and from people who choose to act, and
30 other actions do not, but quite the contrary. And in those cases if people succeed in things in which they seem to have reasoned badly, we say that they have also been fortunate. So again in these cases, if they wanted a different, or a lesser, good than they have received. In the case of these people it is possible for them to be fortunate through nature, for the impulse and the desire, being for the right thing,

prospered, though the reasoning was futile. In the case of these 35
other people, when reasoning seems not to be correct, but desire
happens to be present as a cause, the desire being rightly directed
comes to the rescue. (And yet, on some occasions, a man reasons
again in this way under the influence of desire and is unfortunate.)
But in the other cases, how can there be good fortune in accordance
with a good endowment of appetite and desire? But then if in this 1248a
case fortune and luck are twofold, is there in the other case just one
and the same fortune or is there more than one?

Since we see some people succeeding against all sciences and
correct reasonings,* it is clear that something else is the cause of
the good fortune. But is this or is it not good fortune, the desiring
of the right thing at the right time in a case where human reasoning 5
is not the cause? For that of which the desire is natural is not altogether without reason, but the reason is distorted by something. So
such a person is thought to be fortunate, because luck is the cause
of things contrary to reason, and that is contrary to reason since it
is contrary to knowledge and the universal. But, as it seems, it is not 10
really the result of luck, but it appears to be so for this reason.
Consequently, this argument does not show that good fortune is by
nature, but that not all those who seem to be fortunate succeed by
luck, but by nature. Nor does it show that luck is nothing, or is not
a cause of anything, but that it is not the cause of all the things it
seems to be. 15

But this further question might be put: is luck the cause of the
very fact of desiring what one should when one should? If so, will it
be the cause of everything? For it will be the cause also of thought
and deliberation. For even if someone deliberated after having
deliberated, he did not deliberate in turn about that; there is a certain starting point. Nor did he think, having thought before think- 20
ing, and so on to infinity.* So intelligence is not the starting point of
thinking, nor is counsel the starting point of deliberation. What else
is there, then, save luck? Thus, everything will be by luck.

Or is there some originating principle with no other principle
external to it which, because it is the kind of thing it is, can produce
this kind of effect? That is what we are looking for: what is the starting point of motion in the soul? The answer is plain: as in the uni- 25
verse, so here, God moves everything by intelligence.* For in a
manner the divine element in us moves everything. Reason is not

the originator of reasoning, but something superior. But what can be superior to knowledge and to intelligence, except God? For virtue is an instrument of intelligence.

30 And for that reason, as I said earlier, people are called fortunate who, lacking reason, succeed in what they attempt. Deliberation is not useful to them. For they have an originating principle of a kind that is superior to intellect and deliberation, while those who have reason, but do not possess this, nor inspiration, have not the same ability. And they attain to a power of divination that is swifter than 35 the reasoning of the wise men and philosophers; indeed, the divination that comes from reasoning should almost be done away with. But some people through experience, and others through habit, have this power of using the divine element in their inquiry: and this sees well both what is and what is to come, even in the case of people whose reason is thus disengaged. Thus, those of a melancholic tem-40 perament also have good dreams. For the originating principle 1248b seems stronger when reason is disengaged, just as blind people remember better, having a more powerful memory when released from fixation on visible objects.

It is obvious that there are two kinds of good fortune.* One of them is divine, which is why the fortunate person seems to succeed through God. This man is the one who is successful in accordance 5 with impulse; the other is successful contrary to impulse, but both are non-rational. And the one kind of good fortune is continuous, and the other non-continuous.

Complete virtue and nobility

3. About each virtue by itself we have already spoken; now, since we have distinguished their natures one by one, we must give a more accurate description of the excellence that arises out of their combin-10 ation, which we now name nobility.* Obviously, anyone who is to receive such a title must possess the particular virtues. In other cases, too, it is impossible for it to be otherwise: no one can be healthy in his whole body if none of its parts is healthy. All the parts, or most of them and the most important, must necessarily be in the 15 same condition as the whole.

The difference between being good and being noble is not merely nominal: they differ essentially. Among all goods, some are ends that are valuable for their own sake; and among these, some are noble, namely, those that are laudable for their own sake. Such things are laudable no less than the actions that proceed from them—justice 20 itself and just actions—and so too are temperate actions since temperance itself is laudable. But health is not laudable, nor is its exercise; neither is the exercise of strength, since strength is not laudable. But though not laudable, they are goods nonetheless. Likewise, this 25 is clear by induction in other cases too.

A good man is a man for whom natural goods are good.* Let me explain. The things for which men compete and which are regarded as the greatest goods—honour and wealth, health and strength, and good fortune and power—are indeed naturally good, but they can be harmful to some people because of their characters. Neither a 30 fool nor an unjust or intemperate person would get any benefit from them, any more than a sick person would benefit from a healthy person's diet or a deformed weakling from the equipment of someone in robust health. A person is a noble person because of possessing those goods that are noble for their own sake, and because of 35 doing noble deeds for their own sake. What things, then, are noble? The virtues and the works of virtue.

There is a certain civic character, such as the Spartans have,* and other similar people might have. It is a character of the following kind. There are some who think one should have virtue, but only for 40 the sake of the natural goods. Such men are good men (for the nat- 1249a ural goods are good for them), but they do not have nobility; for their noble qualities are not acquired for their own sake. The perfectly virtuous acquire them and also make these the object of their purpose— not only these, but things that by nature are not noble but merely good become noble for them; for things become noble when people's 5 motives in doing and choosing them are noble; and that is why to the noble person the natural goods are noble. What is just is noble, and that is what is according to worth; and he is worthy of these things. What is fitting is noble, and these things are fitting for this man: wealth, high birth, and power. To the noble person what is useful is 10 also noble;* but for the many there is not this harmony, for things that are good in the abstract are not good for them, as they are for the good man. To the noble person they are also noble, for he does many noble deeds by means of them. But a person who thinks that one should possess the virtues for the sake of external goods will do noble 15 things only coincidentally. Nobility, then, is complete virtue.

Pleasure has already been discussed:* what kind of thing it is, and in what sense it is a good; and how things that are pleasant in the abstract are noble in the abstract and things that are good in the abstract are also pleasant. But there cannot be pleasure except in action; and so the truly happy man will also have the most pleasant
20 life. This human quest is not an idle one.

The doctor has a standard by reference to which he distinguishes a healthy from an unhealthy body, and the degree to which each activity is advisable and healthy, and beyond which in either direction it ceases to be so. Similarly, in regard to actions and choices of things that by nature are good but not praiseworthy, the good man
1249b should have a standard of possession, choice, and avoidance concerning abundance and scarcity of wealth and other gifts of fortune. Earlier we said, 'in accordance with reasoning'—but this, like saying
5 in matters of diet 'in accordance with medicine and medical reasoning', is true but uninformative.*

Here, as elsewhere, one should conduct one's life with reference to one's superior, and more specifically to the quality of one's superior's activity. A slave, for instance, should look to his master's, and everyone to the superior to whom he is subject. Now, a human being
10 is by nature a compound of superior and inferior, and everyone accordingly should conduct their lives with reference to the superior part of themselves. However, there are two kinds of superior:* there is the way in which medical science is superior, and the way in which health is superior; the latter is the *raison d'être* of the former. It is thus that matters stand in the case of our intellectual faculty. For God is not a superior who issues commands,* but is the purpose of the commands that wisdom issues. But 'purpose' is ambiguous,
15 as has been explained elsewhere; this needs saying, since of course God is not in need of anything. To conclude: whatever choice or possession of natural goods—bodily goods, wealth, friends, and the like—will most conduce to the contemplation of God is the best; this is the finest criterion. But any choice of living that either through excess or through defect hinders the service and contem-
20 plation of God* is bad. This applies to the soul: for the soul the ideal standard is to have the minimum awareness of the irrational part of the soul qua irrational.

That, then, is our statement of what is the standard of nobility and what is the point of the things that are good in the abstract.

EXPLANATORY NOTES

BOOK I

CHAPTER I

1214a 1 *BOOK I*: the first seven chapters of this book form a prologue to the entire treatise, composed in a more literary style than is typical of Aristotle's technical works.

2 *temple of Leto in the shrine at Delos*: in Greek mythology, Leto gave birth to Apollo and Artemis on the island of Delos.

5 *Noblest of all*: the Greek word '*kalon*', which here and elsewhere I translate 'noble', also means 'beautiful'. This does not mean that in ancient Greek thought ethics and aesthetics were the same thing, but it is an indication that the boundary between the two was not as sharp as it became in the Christian era.

15 *and how it is to be attained*: this sentence indicates the structure of what follows. The rest of chapter 1 responds to the theoretical question 'what is happiness and what is its origin?', whereas chapter 2 concerns the practical question 'what goal in life should I pursue?' The two questions are connected, but not identical.

23 *some kind of spirit*: it was believed that a man who saw a nymph became possessed by her—a belief alluded to by Socrates in Plato's *Phaedrus* 238c–d. In English the word 'nymphomaniac' is most unfairly restricted to sexual obsession in females. The word translated 'spirit' is '*daimon*', the word used by Plato for beings intermediate between gods and men, with some of the functions Christians were later to attribute to guardian angels.

30 *in a broad sense*: the Greek word '*epistēmē*' is used by Aristotle sometimes as a very general term covering all kinds of knowledge; sometimes it is restricted to strictly scientific knowledge. This passage hints at the ambiguity of the word.

32 *the greatest good is wisdom*: 'wisdom' here and throughout my translation renders the Greek '*phronēsis*'. Later, in Book V, Aristotle will give the word the restricted meaning of practical knowledge; here, and in general when discussing the opinions of his predecessors, he uses it in a general sense including theoretical knowledge.

32 *others say it is virtue*: the Greek word translated 'virtue', namely '*aretē*', is the abstract noun corresponding to 'good'. Anything that is good has an *aretē* but it sounds archaic in English to speak of the virtues of a good knife or a good strawberry. However, the traditional translation, 'virtue', is to be preferred to the one proposed by some recent commentators, 'excellence', which carries irrelevant overtones of competition.

BOOK I, CHAPTER 2

1214b 7 *should set up for himself*: in place of OCT's '*thesthai*' I read '*dei thesthai*'.

26 *necessary conditions*: controversies about the distinction between components of happiness and its necessary preconditions continue. To this day some commentators wrongly argue that in Aristotle's ethical system the possession of a modicum of worldly goods constitutes an element of the happy life, whereas, as will be seen later, that is no more than a prerequisite for happiness.

BOOK I, CHAPTER 3

1215a 10 *perhaps presumptuous*: the Greek word corresponding to 'blissful' is the one commonly used to describe the happiness of the immortal gods.

BOOK I, CHAPTER 4

23 *as some senior philosophers have thought*: no one quite knows who the senior philosophers are. Speusippus and Xenocrates believed that happiness consisted in virtue—but as Aristotle's contemporaries they are hardly senior enough. Possibly Socrates and Plato are meant—but it seems an odd way to refer to philosophers whom Aristotle frequently quotes by name. Aristotle's own view is that you need to exhibit the character in action—hence the transition to the discussion of different forms of life.

27 *pursued only out of need*: I retain the MSS reading, needlessly excised by OCT.

37 *and the hedonistic life*: Aristotle's list of the three candidates for a happy life is drawn from a Greek tradition that apparently goes back to Pythagoras. It seems an excessively short list. Even though 'philosophy' is to be understood broadly to include scientific research, where are we to place the life of a poet or a musician, or of medical and legal practitioners? Elsewhere Aristotle seems to make room for other types of worthwhile elements in happiness (e.g. I.2, 1214b8, VII.12, 1245a22).

1215b 6 *Anaxagoras of Clazomenae*: Anaxagoras (*c.*500–428) was the first notable Athenian philosopher, a client of the statesman Pericles and an early proponent of big bang cosmology.

BOOK I, CHAPTER 5

18 *totally satisfy one's desire*: it is at first surprising that Aristotle devotes a chapter to popular valuations of life, since he said earlier (1214b35) that we do not have to consider the opinions of the multitude. But he was rejecting only the theoretical opinions of the many about the nature and origin of happiness: what he here treats as data worthy of consideration are the everyday choices and decisions (actual and hypothetical) of the ordinary person. We return to consideration of the philosophers at 1216b2.

1216a 1 *Apis*: Apis was a sacred bull venerated at Memphis.

16 *Sardanapallus or Smindyrides of Sybara*: 'Sardanapallus' is the Greek name for Ashur-bani-pal, king of Nineveh 667–647. He and Smindyrides were proverbial examples of luxurious living, and the home of the latter gave us our word 'sybarite'.

37 *investigated further later on*: the different kinds of pleasure are discussed in Book VI, 1152b1–1154b35. The way in which pleasure is woven into happiness is explained in the final book, at 1249a17–21.

38 *discover the nature of each of them*: the inquiry into virtue and wisdom is not a matter of two wholly separate inquiries. The division between virtue and wisdom presupposed in the traditional trichotomy is something Aristotle is going to correct, substituting for it the distinction between moral and intellectual virtues.

1216b 3 *The elder Socrates*: this is of course the famous Socrates, the iconic philosopher of ancient Athens. But who is he being distinguished from? Socrates the younger figures in *Metaphysics* Z.11, 1036a25, as the proponent of a naive view of definition, but is not otherwise known.

8 *you are a just person*: Socrates, like Aristotle, was unhappy with the dichotomy between virtue and wisdom, but for an opposite reason: he thought that the two were identical.

BOOK I, CHAPTER 6

28 *perceptions*: 'perceptions' renders the Greek word '*phainomena*', which, like it, can mean either sense-perceptions or opinions. The context here and in similar passages in Aristotle makes clear that the latter is what he has in mind. The methodological advice presented here is repeated in Book VI (1145b2 ff.). Aristotle has already been acting upon it since the beginning of the *EE*, since the traditional opinions about the three lives are the true but unenlightening statements that are the starting point of the inquiry. However, he makes his use of it explicit only at 1217a20, in connection with the statement that happiness is the greatest and best of human goods.

38 *what is the case, but why it is the case*: unlike OCT, I accept the emendation of '*to ti*' to '*to hoti*'.

BOOK I, CHAPTER 7

1217a 20 *and seek then to gain*: I accept Solomon's emendation of '*epeita*' for '*epi to*'.

27 *some share of the divine in their nature*: commentators are not agreed who, if any, are the beings who by definition have some share of the divine in their nature. Most likely, Aristotle is referring to the ensouled heavenly bodies whose superiority to humans is emphasized at V.7, 1141b2.

30 *different from happiness*: the topic of non-human animals' relationship to pleasure and happiness is resumed at VI.7, 1153b7–25.

33 *including some good things*: I translate the MSS reading, not the emendation accepted by OCT.

BOOK I, CHAPTER 8

1217b 1 *we must inquire what this chief good is*: at this point the *EE* and the *NE* begin to converge in structure, having hitherto followed different courses. The *EE* begins with the concept of happiness, and goes on to discuss the nature of goodness; the *NE* begins with the notion of the supreme good and goes on to consider happiness as the most popular candidate for the title. But both treatises contain a criticism of the Platonic Idea of Good; the one in *NE* I.6, unlike this chapter, begins with an apology for disagreeing with Plato.

3 *that the chief good is Goodness Itself*: I translate '*ariston*' as 'chief good', '*auto to agathon*' as 'Goodness Itself', and '*idea tou agathou*' as Idea of Good'. In the *NE* Aristotle rejects the notion of Goodness Itself; here he accepts it but denies that it is any kind of Platonic Idea. The three opinions about the chief good mentioned here are that it is (1) the Idea of Good, (2) an element common to everything that is good, (3) the end of what is attainable by human action. Aristotle rejects (1) and (2) and accepts (3) (1218b7–11).

8 *the Idea of Good*: the Theory of Ideas, presented in a number of Plato's dialogues, especially the *Phaedo*, the *Meno*, and the *Republic*, offers among other things a theory of predication. Socrates, Simmias, and Cebes are all called 'men': now, when we say 'Socrates is a man', does the word 'man' stand for anything in the way that 'Socrates' stands for 'Socrates'? Plato introduces the Idea of Man as the prime bearer of the name 'Man'. In general, where a common predicate is true of many individuals, Plato will say they are all related to a certain supersensible, unchanging, Idea or Form: where A, B, C are all F, they are related to a single Form of F. Sometimes he will describe the relation as one of imitation: A, B, C all resemble F; sometimes he will talk rather of participation: A, B, C all share in F, they have F in common between them. In Plato's later dialogues (perhaps dating from the time when Aristotle was a member of his Academy) the theory is subjected to searching criticism. Aristotle in his own works repeatedly attacks it, sometimes with contempt. In his ethical treatises the criticism is directed particularly to the Idea of Good, which in the *Republic* is placed at the summit of the ethical universe.

17 *bear a closer resemblance to logic*: the discipline to which Aristotle refers here is dialectic, as described in his *Topics* 101b2. This deals with the exposure of fallacies, ambiguities, and the like, and ranges across many disciplines, not just ethics alone.

23 *in our popular and our philosophical works*: the word translated 'popular' is often just transliterated into English as 'exoteric'. Aristotle is referring to non-technical works to be read outside the Lyceum. No one knows whether any of his surviving works belong in that class.

25 *in as many ways . . . as being:* Aristotle put forward a theory of categories in a work of that name. It involves listing ten different kinds of expression that might appear as predicates in a statement about an individual. We might say of Socrates, for instance, that he was a man, that he was five feet tall, that he was wise, and that he was older than Plato. Aristotle would say that these statements are in the categories, respectively, of substance (or essence), quantity, quality, and relation. Here he applies the theory to the predicate 'good'. Justice is a good quality to have, proportion is goodness in the category of quantity, opportunity is goodness in the category of time, teaching and learning are good things to do. All these goodnesses are radically different kinds of thing. What of goodness in the category of substance? Only God is essentially good, nothing else has goodness as its essence. ('Mind and God' is probably a hendiadys here.)

34 *Nor is there a single science:* apparently it was a Platonist thesis that there was a one–one correspondence between Ideas and sciences (*NE* 1096a30). Against this Aristotle argues that goodnesses of different kinds are studied by different sciences. Scholars have been shocked by the statement here that there is no single science of being. Does not Aristotle devote his *Metaphysics* to first philosophy, the science that studies being qua being? The astonishment is due to a misunderstanding of the nature of this science. It is not the study of a mysterious object called 'being qua being'; rather, it studies being (i.e. all there is) from the point of view of being, that is to say from the point of view of ultimate and universal explanation. There are many sciences of being: thus, biology studies being qua living, physics studies being qua changeable, and metaphysics studies it qua being. Similarly, there are many sciences of the good—even of human good. Medicine studies the good of health and gymnastics the good of fitness. The contents of the *EE* give instruction in the most important science of human good—a science for which Aristotle's most general name is '*politikē*'.

1218a 2 *where things can be ranked as prior and posterior:* for Aristotle, A is prior to B if you can have A without B but you cannot have B without A. Thus, 2 is prior to 3 because you can have two things without having three things, but if you have three things a fortiori you have two. On Platonic theory an Idea is prior to whatever falls under it. Aristotle argues that this will make nonsense of ordinary series: instead of multiplication by two being the first and basic form of multiplication, there will be Pure Multiplication ahead of it in the series.

11 *there is also Goodness itself:* Aristotle is not arguing here that there is no such thing as Goodness itself (there is, and he is going to tell us what it is at 1218b11); he is arguing that 'itself' does not signify the eternity and separability characteristic of Ideas. (Note that I adopt a punctuation of the text different from OCT.)

18 *they start with numbers:* in the dialogues of Plato there is no identification of Ideas with numbers, but several texts of Aristotle (e.g. *Metaphysics* A.7,

991b1–10) suggest that Plato at some stage made such an identification. 'Nowadays' perhaps indicates that the reference here is to some follower of Plato such as Xenocrates, the head of the Academy from 339.

36 *what is written in the text*: this is the first of several references in the *EE* to a text or handout that seems to have accompanied the lectures (cf. II.2, 1220b11, VII.12, 1244b29–45). Attempts to identify the text are pure speculation (including my own earlier suggestion that the references are to the *NE*; see my *Aristotelian Ethics* (Oxford 1978), 225–9).

1218b 15 *something that will have to be explained later*: in Book V Aristotle explains that wisdom is the intellectual virtue that finds expression in the discipline of political science. This has three main parts: one concerns the human as an individual, one as a member of a household, and one as a member of a city (1141b23–1142a11).

BOOK II

BOOK II, CHAPTER I

31 *discuss what follows*: in the first chapter of Book II Aristotle reverses the methodological procedure he commends earlier (1216b34) and later (1220a17). Instead of considering first the unanalysed opinions of others and going on to develop his own analysis, he here offers first a technical proof of his own position, and only later goes on to show how it accords with or clarifies popular opinions.

1219a 1 *has a use or has work to do*: this sentence is packed with Aristotelian technical terms. First we have the triad 'condition' (*diathesis*), 'state' (*hexis*), and 'power' (*dunamis*). The difference between the three terms (not consistently maintained by Aristotle himself) is best illustrated by an example. The ability to hear is a power; acuteness of hearing is a state; a temporary deafness is a condition. Secondly, we have the Greek word '*ergon*', which calls for a variety of renderings; in individual contexts 'work', 'working', 'job', 'function', 'task', 'product', or 'deed' would be the most appropriate. It is impossible to use the same word all the time without producing odd statements such as that the shoe is the function of a shoemaker, or that seeing is the product of the eye. I have tried to use the English word most suitable to the context, but I have tried never to use more than one version in the course of a single argument; if in such a case Aristotle proceeds from a premiss in which one translation would be the most natural to a conclusion in which the other would be more natural, I tend to use a redundant translation such as 'work, or function'. The word is the bane of the translator. We can take consolation from reminding ourselves that the fact that in English we have many different words to perform the tasks for which Greek had only one is a remote consequence of the distinctions Aristotle carefully draws in texts such as the *EE*. Finally, there is another technical term, *chrēsis*, which can mean exercise, operation, or use. In the case of a faculty, 'operation' suits best; with virtue, 'exercise' is the most natural rendering; in the case of a bridle, 'use' is better. In many cases, 'employment' will serve.

23 *the work of a good shoemaker is a good shoe*: I punctuate the Greek differently from OCT, reading '*ei de tis estin aretē skutikē, kai spoudaiou skutews to ergon esti spoudaion hupodema*'.

24 *Let us postulate that the work of the soul is to be alive*: I take '*poiein*' to mean 'postulate'; others translate the passage 'The work of the soul is to make [something] to live'. Unlike OCT, I accept the emendation '*toutou*' for '*tou*'.

30 *things in the soul are either states or activities*: I accept the emendation '*ta en autē*' for '*hautē*'.

1219b 26 *an examination of the soul*: on Aristotle's psychology, see the Introduction, pp. xiv–xv.

28 *each endowed with reason*: 'reason' here translates the pregnant Greek '*logos*', which, besides being the everyday Greek word for a spoken word or a written text, has a number of grander meanings. When used technically in the *EE*, it most commonly means either the reasoning faculty of human beings, or a particular piece of reasoning.

32 *It makes no difference*: Aristotle deliberately sidesteps the question that has often preoccupied modern philosophers and psychologists, namely, whether different human powers are located in spatially distinct parts of the human body.

36 *not a matter of substance*: instead of the OCT, I translate Allan's conjecture '*ousia tou autou*'.

37 *are peculiar to the human soul*: I translate the MSS reading, which the OCT amended to mean 'are not peculiar'.

1220a 19 *as if we knew*: the text here is corrupt and OCT gives up the attempt to emend it. I translate Spengel's emendation '*ei eideiēmen*'. Coriscus often appears as a John Doe figure in the Aristotelian writings. But there was in his circle a real Coriscus, whose son Neleus eventually inherited Aristotle's library.

BOOK II, CHAPTER 2

1220b 1–7 *Now, character . . . is capable of obedience to reason*: the MSS are here particularly corrupt. I follow the OCT reconstruction of the text except that in b3 I follow Allan in reading '*auto*' instead of '{*to*}'.

15 *These are passive experiences*: I retain '*alla paschei*' as in MSS.

BOOK II, CHAPTER 3

38 *in the following table*: having explained that virtue is a middle state between a state of excess and a state of deficiency, Aristotle confusingly goes on to give a list of states in which states of excess figure in the left-hand column, states of deficiency in the middle, and virtues on the right.

1221a 20 *to excess in every possible way*: I accept the emendation '*kai akolastos ho epithumetikos hou mē dei*'.

BOOK II, CHAPTER 5

1222a 10 *relative to ourselves*: does 'relative to ourselves' mean 'relative to human beings' or 'relative to each individual'? A parallel text in the *NE* (1106a30 ff.) makes the latter more likely, but the former is perhaps to be preferred on the basis of a later *EE* passage (1222a37).

1222b 4 *our spirited element is no sycophant*: '*ou kolakikon ho thumos*' is a difficult passage, but OCT is right not to amend it. Aristotle is talking about the spirited element within us, and 'no flatterer' is a meiosis. The phrase may be a quotation from some gnomic writer, which would explain the strangeness of the expression.

BOOK II, CHAPTER 6

16 *sources of a certain sort*: the word '*archē*', here translated 'source', is an Aristotelian term of very wide application. Literally 'beginning'—it is the Greek word corresponding to 'starting point' in the previous line— it is used also of axioms in geometry, and of particular kinds of cause, and of ruling elements of various kinds. The word is often translated 'principle', but to do so regularly in an ethical treatise may cause confusion with moral principles, which are something totally different.

18 *an animal other animals*: I accept Casaubon's elegant emendation '*homoiōs*' instead of OCT '{*on*} *holōs*'.

20 *we would not ascribe conduct to any of the others*: 'conduct' here, as in other similar contexts, renders the Greek word '*praxis*', which elsewhere is used as a very general term for 'action'. But one could not say that animals are incapable of action: remember Henry V's urging his troops at Agincourt to imitate the action of a tiger.

28 *using its refutation as a proof*: in the following paragraph Aristotle explains how a change of axiom will involve a change of theorems; here he notes that an axiom may have many different consequences, but it will be affected by this only if one of the consequences is self-contradictory, in which case the contrary of the axiom will be proved by *reductio ad absurdum*.

1223a 2 *What is in the power of humans themselves*: I retain the MSS reading, whereas OCT deletes '{*ho*}'.

9 *if he is responsible for something, then it is in his power*: the upshot of Aristotle's attempt to place the theory of human action within a general discussion of causation is as follows. Some causes are themselves caused; only those whose causation is uncaused count as sources. Some sources, namely controlling sources, are sources of movement; God is the source of necessary movements, and humans are sources of contingent movements. Among non-controlling sources there are two kinds: substances that generate their kinds, and axioms that give rise to theorems. See my *Aristotle's Theory of the Will* (Oxford 1979), 3–10.

BOOK II, CHAPTER 7

23 *the voluntary and the involuntary*: in his discussion of voluntariness Aristotle employs two pairs of terms: '*hekwn*' and '*akwn*' to express the state of the agent, and '*hekousion*' and '*akousion*' to describe what is done. I use 'voluntary' and 'non-voluntary' to correspond to the latter pair. To correspond to the latter I use 'voluntarily' and 'non-voluntarily' instead of the pair 'willingly' and 'unwillingly' favoured by some translators. In English only what is done voluntarily can be done either willingly or unwillingly. What is not voluntary can be divided into two classes: what is simply not voluntary, not the outcome of any volition of the agent, and what is involuntary, that is to say, in actual conflict with the agent's volition. Aristotle in places seems to run these two classes into one.

24 *desire, choice, and thought*: Aristotle's strategy is to inquire whether there is some mental state such that being in accordance with it makes an act voluntary. Mental states are either cognitive or affective or mixtures of both. In the present chapter he explores the possibility of identifying voluntariness with some affective state, and at the beginning of the following chapter he opts to identify it by its relation to a cognitive state.

27 *will, temper, and appetite*: the three kinds of desire correspond to the three parts of the soul that Plato distinguished in Book IV of the *Republic*: reason, temper, and appetite. It is the third kind of desire to which Aristotle devotes most attention, offering two arguments in favour of its identification as the source of voluntariness, and two arguments against.

37 *incontinence appears to be a form of depravity*: this is the first appearance of the incontinent man, a character who is going to figure prominently throughout the *EE*. He is someone who does what he correctly believes he ought not to do. In Book VI Aristotle will make a careful distinction between him and the vicious man, who does what he ought not to do, without any saving realization of its wrongness.

1223b 17 *both voluntarily and involuntarily*: the two pairs of arguments for and against the identification with appetite are full of premisses that Aristotle elsewhere rejects and straightforward deductive fallacies, as I have spelt out in detail in *Aristotle's Theory of the Will*, 14–21. The explanation of this puzzle is that he is not here setting out his own position, but reviewing arguments of others in accordance with his general policy of setting out the difficulties that arise from the views of the many and the wise on the topic in question.

27–8 *we do many things voluntarily without either ill temper or appetite*: in this brief remark we are at last given Aristotle's own reason for rejecting the suggested identifications.

29 *whether what is willed and what is voluntary are the same thing*: the 'will' involved in what is willed is desire that has its source in the reasoning part of the soul. The argument against regarding it as the source of

voluntariness is that the incontinent man is acting voluntarily, but he is acting against the imperatives issued by his will. Incontinence, in fact, is a form of weakness of will.

BOOK II, CHAPTER 8

1224a 3 *all that has been shown*: I follow Barnes in altering the positioning of the brackets in the OCT text.

7 *voluntary action is action accompanied by thinking of some sort*: here Aristotle draws his conclusion, that voluntariness is to be defined cognitively. He will spell out later that it is awareness of what one is doing and how, and the circumstances and likely upshot of one's action. But already he realizes that this needs qualification, because an action done in full awareness of all this may yet not be voluntary if it is enforced. So before spelling out his official conclusion, he interpolates a section on force.

13 *what is forced and what is necessary*: it is not clear whether Aristotle draws a sharp distinction between force (*bia*) and necessity (*anagkē*). English law distinguishes between duress and necessity as mitigating circumstances: there is necessity when the constraints arise from natural causes, duress when they are caused by human beings. In translating '*anagkē*' I have used 'coercion' when human agency is involved.

1225a 15–19 *these matters not being under his control*: here Aristotle is probably distinguishing between cases where the existence of duress is the result of the agent's own action, and cases where it is not. An instance of the former would be a case where a person voluntarily joins a terrorist organization, in which he knows he will be forced, under threat, to engage in violence.

33 *Philolaus*: a Pythagorean philosopher contemporary with Socrates.

35–6 *The arguments . . . people can be subject to force and simultaneously act voluntarily*: the text of this cryptic footnote is corrupt, and OCT gives up the attempt to amend it. I follow Dirlmeier and P2 in adding '*logoi*'.

BOOK II, CHAPTER 9

1225b 4 *lethal rather than salutary . . . Pelias' daughters*: after the Golden Fleece expedition Jason and Medea persuaded Pelias' daughters to cut him up so that Medea could rejuvenate him by boiling him.

BOOK II, CHAPTER 10

18 *choice*: the word '*prohairesis*', rendered 'choice', presents special difficulty to the translator. Usually Aristotle takes a common word, like 'knowledge' or 'wisdom', and gives it, in special contexts, a technical meaning. Here, however, he was the first to give the word wide currency, and its usefulness is open to doubt. As Elizabeth Anscombe wrote, 'The notion of "choice" as conceived by Aristotle is a very peculiar one.

If it had been a winner, like some other Aristotelian concepts, would not "prohaeretic" be a word as familiar to us as "practical" is?' (*From Parmenides to Wittgenstein* (Oxford 1981), 71). It is obvious that it is a very solemn kind of choice, made after deliberation, and on the basis of a thought-out plan of life. Carrying out a monastic vow or a New Year's resolution seems to be the closest thing in modern life to making an Aristotelian choice. Perhaps 'resolution' would be a more appropriate translation, or perhaps one should write 'Choice' with a capital C.

1226b 2 *they will go on for ever*: if the scribe makes a mistake in attention, he misreads; if he makes a mistake in action, he mistranscribes. Aristotle's comment seems mistaken: it is not so much that if you reflect you will go on for ever as that you will never get started.

18 *it is not the case that we choose everything we deliberate about*: unlike OCT, I think the MSS reading '*bouleuometha*' makes good sense. Aristotle has in mind the possibility of reaching a dead end in deliberation.

1227a 2 *in our inquiry into justice*: see below, Book IV, 1135b11 ff.

BOOK II, CHAPTER 11

1127b 19 *continence is a matter for praise*: in Book VI Aristotle will lay out clearly the relations between the four different possible states of character: virtue, vice, continence, and incontinence. In virtue the reasoning is right, and the action is right, and there is no wrong desire; in continence the reasoning is right and the action is right, but wrong desire is present; in incontinence the reasoning is right, but wrong desire is present and the action is wrong; in vice the reasoning, the desire, and the action are all wrong.

25 *must be assumed as a starting point*: Allan's emendation '*alla dei hwsper archēn touto hupokeisthai*' seems to me to force itself on us.

30 *if this is what being healthy is*: I read '*ei*' for '*dei*' for reasons given in *The Aristotelian Ethics* (Oxford 1978), 132.

1228a 1 *the correctness of the end of the choice*: the Greek is crabbed here, compressed and difficult. The translation I give can be reconciled with the MSS, but would fit more easily a text in which '*to*' was amended to '*tou*'. The point Aristotle is making is that virtue is the cause of the virtuous mean's being the goal of the choice.

BOOK III

BOOK III, CHAPTER 1

23 *the virtues are middle states*: I accept Fritzsche's emendation '*hai aretai*' for '*te en tais aretais*'.

28 *our schedule earlier*: the schedule is given at II.3, 1221a17–19, above.

36 *in Greek . . . have the same root*: the Greek words are '*thrasus*' and '*thrasos*'.

1228b 10–12 *seriously and frequently frightening*: OCT offers a number of unnecessary modifications to the MSS. I translate the MSS text: '*ei ta hautw, eie autw megala kai polla phobera*'.

19 *objectively pleasant or good*: the word '*haplws*' needs careful treatment. It is used by Aristotle to make a number of different contrasts. When he says that something is good *haplws*, he may be making a contrast with particular circumstances. In such cases 'in the abstract' is the best translation. Sometimes, as here, the contrast may be with relation to a particular person; in that case 'objective' is to be preferred. A quality may be ascribed to someone *haplws* in contrast to particular species of that quality; in which case, 'simple' or 'straight' will serve, or even '*tout court*'. The translation of '*agathon haplws*' as 'absolutely good' is almost never right, since it suggests that something is good come what may, which is the opposite of what Aristotle means.

37 *There are other people*: I cannot make sense of OCT here and translate '*hoi de*' instead of '*kai eti*'.

1229a 15 *as Socrates said*: see Plato's *Laches* 684b.

23 *the man who killed the tyrant in Metapontum*: Plutarch (*Moralia* 760c) tells of an Antileon of Metapontum who assassinated Archelaus of Heraclea in order to rescue his beloved Hipparinus from the tyrant's attentions.

41 *Agathon*: a celebrated Athenian tragic poet who figures as the host in Plato's *Symposium*.

1230a 2 *Cheiron . . . his wound was so agonizing*: Cheiron was a centaur wounded by the arrows of Heracles.

12 *Theognis*: a sixth-century elegiac poet from Megara.

18 *Homer reports Hector*: the first Homeric quotation does not appear in our editions; the second is *Iliad* xxii.100.

BOOK III, CHAPTER 2

38 *temperance*: the Greek word '*swphrosune*' is rendered by some translators as 'moderation', but I prefer the traditional version, 'temperance', in spite of the fact that total abstinence as recommended by temperance societies would be regarded by Aristotle as a vice rather than a virtue.

39 '*Intemperate*' *has many senses*: the Greek for 'intemperate' is '*akolastos*', which is formed from a root meaning 'chastise' with the privative prefix '*a*'.

1231a 4 *in a few prodigious cases*: as when 'Orpheus with his lute made trees | And the mountain-tops that freeze | bow themselves when he did sing.'

11 *Stratonicus*: a musician and comedian of uncertain date, whose stock-in-trade was the kind of joke that New Yorkers like to make about Philadelphia.

16 *Philoxenus, the son of Eryxis*: several gourmands bore the name Philoxenus; one was a poet who seduced the mistress of Dionysius I of Sicily.

25 *there is not temperance and intemperance either*: the punctuation in OCT is bad here, and I have followed Barnes's correction.

BOOK III, CHAPTER 4

1232a 4 *a miser . . . An illiberal man*: it is not clear whether the miser and the illiberal person are distinct characters, or one and the same. In *Politics* I.10, where the same example of the shoe is used, exchange is defined as the natural use of money, and usury the unnatural. But it is not clear, either there or here, whether hoarding, the mere building up of capital, is natural or unnatural.

BOOK III, CHAPTER 5

1231a 19 *pride*: the Greek word translated 'pride' means literally 'great-souled-ness', but that is too clumsy to use. 'Magnanimity' is more elegant, but has a different meaning. The pride in question is of course proper pride.

1232a 31 *accompany all the virtues*: OCT prints a lacuna, which is unnecessary; I accept the emendation '*hoti*' for '*hote*'.

1232b 1 *nothing that is disgraceful . . . is not always frightening*: a difficult passage, amended by editors in various ways. I accept the OCT text, taking it to mean that none of the horrible things that can happen to a courageous man seem great to him. This is a plausible claim; but '*aischron*' does not seem quite the right word to refer to these horrors.

8 *Antiphon . . . speech in his defence*: Antiphon was the planner of the coup that overturned democracy in Athens in 411. When democracy was restored shortly after, he was tried and executed. Thucydides thought his speech in his own defence was the best he knew.

16 *the opinion of the multitude*: with some MSS support, I delete OCT's '*kai*'.

24 *Each virtue*: OCT's deletion of the first '*hekastē*' is unnecessary.

25 *as we have said*: the reference is to the passage immediately preceding.

1233a 8 *that is the most praiseworthy*: following Rackham, I delete '*hautē*'.

16 *pride is a mean*: Aristotle's canonization of pride as a fundamental virtue contrasts with the Christian tradition according to which humility is a virtue and pride one of the greatest sins. St Thomas Aquinas ingeniously argued that Christian humility was not only compatible with, but an actual counterpart of, Aristotelian pride. Both virtues moderate ambition, he says: humility ensures that one's ambitions are based on a just assessment of one's defects, pride ensures that they are based on a just assessment of one's gifts (*Summa Theologiae* IIa IIae q. 161 a. 1 ad 3).

BOOK III, CHAPTER 6

1233b 2 *rich man . . . beloved*: the casual assumption here that a good man will have a male lover for a while and then happily go on to sponsor his wedding breakfast seems odd in itself, and to clash with the later remark in Book VI that intercourse between males is bestial.

9 *nothing that is unsuitable can be appropriate*: OCT gives up the attempt to amend this corrupt text. I translate '*dei de prepon kath 'hekaston einai kai gar tou prattontos kat 'axian kai peri hon*'.

12–13 *Themistocles . . . Cimon*: Cimon was a noble Athenian millionaire of the fifth century with a distinguished military record. Themistocles was the general who commanded the Athenian forces during the Persian invasion of 480. He was of ancient stock, but his mother was not an Athenian.

BOOK III, CHAPTER 7

21 *the emotion of the malicious person*: English, like Greek, lacks a name for this. German, however, has one: *Schadenfreude*.

24 *called by the ancients Nemesis*: not only ancient Greeks but also modern Anglophones speak of people meeting their nemesis when they suffer deserved downfall.

34 *what seems to be best*: OCT's insertion of '*pantwn*' is not necessary.

1234a 4 *Conviviality is also a mean*: the Greek word translated as 'conviviality' is often rendered 'wittiness'. But Aristotle makes clear that the virtue he has in mind can be passive as well as active: the ability to take a joke no less than the ability to make one.

28 *as will be said later*: the later discussion is in V.13, 1144b1–17.

BOOK IV

BOOK IV, CHAPTER 1

1129a 6 *its predecessors*: like the earlier books, Book IV endeavours, by drawing distinctions, to sort out the true from the false in confused popular impressions on its topic.

12 *there is a difference*: this difference has already been adumbrated in *EE* 1218b38.

30 *like a lock of hair and the lock on a door*: to illustrate the kind of ambiguity he has in mind Aristotle uses the Greek word '*kleis*', which can mean a key or a collarbone. The example, if literally translated, would not work in English.

32 *covetous*: the Greek word is '*pleonekthēs*', which means a man who wants more than his fair share; other possible translations are 'greedy' or 'grasping'.

1129b 26 *complete virtue*: the general justice delineated in this chapter includes all the other virtues as parts of itself, but it is more than just the sum of its parts because it involves the actual exercise of these virtues in relation to other people. The notion of complete virtue, and its relation to happiness, was introduced at II.1, 1219a37.

30 *in justice every virtue is compact*: a quotation from Theognis, a sixth-century elegiac poet.

1130a 1 *Bias*: Bias of Priene was one of the revered Seven Sages of the sixth-century Greek world.

   3 *someone else's good*: in the first book of Plato's *Republic* (343c) Thrasymachus argues that only a fool would be just, since justice benefits only other people.

BOOK IV, CHAPTER 2

  14 *the justice that is one part of virtue*: having discussed general justice, whose scope is as wide as the laws and all the virtues, Aristotle now turns to particular justice, which is concerned specifically with fairness and equality.

  24 *one who commits adultery for the sake of profit*: we do not know whom Aristotle had in mind, but there is no difficulty in calling to mind men in our own time who have had affairs with wealthy women and lived on the proceeds.

1130b 2 *honour or money or security*: this list makes clear that particular justice is concerned not only with property, but also with other goods that are in short supply and are objects of competition, as described later, at VIII.3, 1248b27.

1131a 1 *interactions between individuals*: having distinguished particular justice from general justice, Aristotle now further distinguishes two forms of particular justice: distributive justice and rectificatory justice. Rectificatory justice itself comes in two kinds, one of which corresponds to English civil law and the other to English criminal law. Distributive justice is discussed in chapter 3, and rectificatory justice in chapter 4.

   4 *voluntary and non-voluntary*: voluntary interactions (e.g. contracts) are transactions between two willing parties; non-voluntary interactions (e.g. theft) are those in which the victim has no part.

BOOK IV, CHAPTER 3

  10 *unfair or unequal*: a single Greek word, '*ison*', corresponds both to 'fair' and to 'equal'. In what follows, Aristotle is mainly thinking of equality, but by introducing a contrast between two different kinds of proportion he succeeds in making the distinction between the two concepts that we can make more simply by saying that inequality is not necessarily unfair.

  27 *not everyone means the same thing by desert*: Aristotle illustrates his general point by reference to the distribution of political rights and offices, where the criterion of distribution will depend on the nature of the constitution, whether it is democratic, aristocratic, or oligarchic, as he explains in *Politics* IV.7–8.

  30 *of number in general*: in a proportion involving four terms, A is to B as C is to D. Aristotle distinguishes between arithmetical and geometrical proportion. In arithmetical proportion the difference between A and B is the same as that between C and D: as in the series 2,4,8,10. In geometrical proportion B is the same multiple of A as D is of C: as in the

series 3,6,8,16. A particular case of proportion is continuous proportion, as in the series 2,4,6 and in the series 2,4,8; Aristotle tells us to treat this as if it were a four-term proportion, 2,4, 4,6, or 2,4, 4,8.

1131b 5 *the same distinction . . . between the parties and between the goods*: suppose that A has invested £100 and B has invested £50 in an enterprise that has made a profit of £15. Then in a just distribution A's dividend C will be £10 and B's dividend D will be £5 and we shall have A:B = C:D, and A:C = B:D and also A+C = B+D.

19 *the man who acts unjustly*: Aristotle here seems to assume that it is the distributor of the dividend who has allotted himself too much. Later he considers the case where the distributor and the beneficiary are distinct (1135a1–3).

24 *one species of what is just*: this was named in the Aristotelian tradition 'distributive justice'.

BOOK IV, CHAPTER 4

25 *the rectificatory kind*: Aristotle's rectificatory justice includes both the award of compensation such as would be made in a civil court, and the infliction of punishment as in a criminal court. In this chapter he makes it look as if the purpose of both judgments is simply a restoration of the status quo; later he will qualify this in the case of punishment (1132b30).

1132a 2 *the arithmetical kind*: there are still four terms to the proportion: wrongdoer–gain–victim–loss, but no numerical value has to be attached to the terms corresponding to the parties in order to take account of their social status, previous record, etc. All is to be settled in terms of 'loss' and 'gain'.

10 *the punishment is an attempt*: the same Greek word corresponds both to 'punishment' and to 'loss' or 'deprivation'.

1132b 5 *the amount by which it exceeds the mean*: if we have a six-inch line AB, the mean or midpoint C will be three inches from A. In the illustration, the wrongdoer A has taken the equivalent of four inches, leaving only two inches to B and so the line is now divided at D and AD is twice the length of DB.

The judge awards to B an amount equivalent to CD, restoring the original division.

6 *Let the lines AA′, BB′, CC′ be equal to each other*: here Aristotle uses a more complicated example to make the point he has made in the previous passage, which is more simply illustrated by the single line shown above.

19 *those that are non-voluntary*: there can be non-voluntary loss even in voluntary transactions, e.g. when a loan is not repaid.

BOOK IV, CHAPTER 5

25 *Rhadamanthus*: one of the three judges of the dead in the Underworld.

28 *they are not in accord*: here Aristotle is rejecting the *lex talionis*, an eye for an eye, a tooth for a tooth. He goes on in the next paragraph to give a welcome to a different kind of reciprocity, which is the basis of commercial transactions. His theory of geometrical proportion, hitherto applied to distribution, is now applied to exchange.

1133a 33 *the ratio of shoemaker to farmer*: how is this to be ascertained? The text does not make this totally clear. In commenting on the passage, Aquinas says that the proportion between farmer and shoemaker is to be settled by the labour and expense each incurs in the production of his product. This idea was later taken up by Karl Marx and incorporated in his labour theory of value.

1133b 3 *not after they have made the exchange*: it is obvious that a price should be fixed before goods are exchanged with each other or for cash, but the reason Aristotle offers is obscure.

7 *Need is the one single factor*: the word translated 'need' could also be translated 'demand', and commentators disagree about which is more appropriate. The translation 'demand' would make Aristotle an early advocate for the free market economy; but the need which is the ultimate driver of exchange is something more fundamental. Only when people have satisfied their real needs do they begin to demand luxuries.

33 *not in the same way as the other virtues*: like the other virtues, justice hits the mean, but while the other virtues are flanked by two different vices, one for excess and one for defect, justice is flanked on either side by the single vice of injustice.

BOOK IV, CHAPTER 6

1134a 17–23 *Now it is possible . . . similarly in other cases*: the paragraph seems out of place and would fit better in chapter 8. It is in any case surprising. Perhaps a case can be made for saying that a single one-night stand does not make a man an adulterer, but that is not the view that would be taken in most divorce courts. And would Aristotle say that only a serial killer is really a murderer?

28 *proportionate or arithmetical*: arithmetical in a democracy, proportionate under other kinds of constitution.

BOOK IV, CHAPTER 7

1134b 18 *one part is natural and the other conventional*: Aristotle's distinction between natural and conventional justice corresponds to the distinction made popular by his followers between natural and positive law.

23 *Brasidas*: a Spartan general in the Peloponnesian War.

24 *form of decrees*: the distinction between laws and decrees corresponds roughly to our distinction between statutes on the one hand, and statutory instruments and ordinances on the other.

30 *partly natural and partly non-natural*: the examples given above appear to be instances of non-natural variation: but what are examples of natural variation? Did Aristotle perhaps think, as Montesquieu did, that different constitutions suit different climates?

1135a 5 *by nature the best*: in *Politics* IV.7–8 Aristotle tells us that this is aristocracy, in the sense of a constitution where rule is in the hands of a group of men specially qualified by their talents and virtues.

11 *already an unjust thing to do*: this may seem to commit Aristotle to an ontology of unperformed actions, or Platonic Ideas; but no more than someone who says, 'You mustn't do that—it is terribly unjust.'

BOOK IV, CHAPTER 8

23 *as was said earlier*: this definition echoes the one in II.9, 1225b5–10. This chapter fulfils the promise of later discussion made in the treatment of the voluntary at II.10, 1227a2.

30 *was his father*: Aristotle obviously has in mind the murder by Oedipus of his father, Laius, as dramatized in Sophocles' *Oedipus Rex*, discussed in detail in the *Poetics*.

1135b 2 *growing old or dying*: growing old is in our power to do, but not in our power not to do, and hence it is not voluntary.

24 *this does not mean that they are themselves unjust or wicked*: Aristotle lays down unacceptably strict conditions for vice, just as he has excessively demanding standards for virtue. In each case the problem is caused by his overemphasis on the concept of *prohairesis*, or choice. Most people, if his criteria are applied rigorously, are neither virtuous nor vicious; they will fall into one of the intermediate categories to be described in Book VI.

1136a 10 *not only in error but also because of the error*: what is the difference between these two cases? According to Aquinas, the test is whether, when you find out the truth, you are or are not sorry about what you have done.

BOOK IV, CHAPTER 9

13 *I killed my mother . . . well?*: the distich is from a lost play which told the story of Alcmaeon, who killed his mother to avenge his father's death.

23 *some people receive just treatment against their will*: e.g. those who are justly punished.

1136b 1 *voluntarily accepting harm*: Aquinas' example of passion allowing injustice to oneself is an infatuated man allowing a whore to rob him.

10 *Glaucus did to Diomedes*: Glaucus swapped his gold armour for Diomedes' bronze armour (*Iliad* vi.236).

34 *primary justice*: this is the same as the natural justice of chapter 7.

1137a 6 *In fact it is not*: once again, Aristotle is setting the bar for the vice of injustice ridiculously high.

20 *quite able to sleep with another man's wife*: Aristotle should here have made use of his distinction between virtues and two-way skills such as arts and sciences; instead he brings in the difference between the presence and absence of choice.

38 *who are incurably bad*: who are these non-human beings? We do not know, but Christian commentators could identify them with the fallen angels that we meet in *Paradise Lost*.

BOOK IV, CHAPTER 10

31 *equity and the equitable*: the topic of this chapter interrupts the discussion in chapters 9 and 11 of the relationship between justice and voluntariness. But Aristotle's distinction between what is just and what is equitable cast a long shadow: in England, for instance, in the centuries-long distinction between the common law courts and the courts of equity.

1137b 31 *moulds itself to the shape of the stone*: the purpose of this malleable rule was presumably to match two irregular stones to each other.

BOOK IV, CHAPTER 11

1138a 7 *what it does not prescribe it forbids*: this statement is very puzzling: the law does not command us to breathe or sleep, so does it forbid both? Some commentators have amended the text; others have supposed that Aristotle is referring only to killing.

32 *acting unjustly is worse*: Democritus was the first to say that it is worse to do injustice than to suffer injustice. This may seem like a truism, but it conflicts with a number of influential ethical systems that encourage one to judge actions only by their consequences and not by the identity of their agents.

BOOK V

BOOK V, CHAPTER 1

1138b 18 *we said earlier*: 1222a9 and 1222b7, where a promise is made to inquire later in more detail what is involved in correct reasoning. Now, as earlier (I.6, 1216b32–3), Aristotle follows his method of starting with what is true but obscure, and trying to clarify it.

34 *what correct reasoning is, and what is the standard that determines it*: the answer to the first question is given in this book: it is the output of wisdom (*phronēsis*). The answer to the second question is not given until the final book, at 1249a1 ff.

1139a 3 *It was said earlier*: in Book II, 1219b31–40 and 1220a10, we were introduced to two non-rational parts of the soul: the nutritive part and the part that listens to reason. From 1219b28 we gather that his second non-rational part can also be called a rational part in so far as it obeys reason's commands. It is this part that is the locus of the moral virtues. Now we turn to the superior rational part, the one that gives the commands, and we learn that it, too, is bipartite, having a scientific part and a calculative part. The superior part of the soul is the home of the intellectual virtues, and each of its two parts has its proper virtue, as we learn in subsequent chapters.

BOOK V, CHAPTER 2

17 *control conduct and truth*: Aristotle presents his account of the sources of human conduct in the terminology of the theory of agency of Book II chapter 6, where, too, the point was made that only humans are capable of conduct (1222b19).

21 *What affirmation and negation are in thinking, pursuit and avoidance are in desire*: the parallel between the cognitive and affective operations of the mind is that asserting is saying 'yes' to a statement, pursuit is saying 'yes' to a proposal or course of action. Correctness in assertion is truth, correctness in desire is rightness.

25 *the latter must pursue just what the former asserts*: the assertion that is the conclusion of the reasoning and the pursuit that is the upshot of the desire are one and the same thing, namely, the choice.

30 *it is truth in accordance with right desire*: 'it' here means the good functioning of practical reason. Correct reasoning about what is here and now the courageous thing to do, carried out in the mind of a man who has no desire to be courageous, would be an example of truth without right desire.

1139b 4 *intelligence qualified by desire, or desire qualified by thought*: Aquinas points out that the second alternative is more accurate, since choices are described as good or bad rather than as true or false (see II.10, 1226a4).

9 *Agathon*: we have met Agathon before at Book III, 1229b40 and 1232b8, and we will meet him again at 1140a19.

BOOK V, CHAPTER 3

16 *art, knowledge, wisdom, understanding, and intelligence*: unlike other translators, I try to render Aristotle's intellectual virtues by one-word translations. This means that some of my terms are not an exact fit to their Greek equivalents, as will be explained in due course. Aristotle's consideration of intellectual virtues begins with a list of seven candidates for the status. Two, judgement and belief, are immediately eliminated because they may be false, whereas truth is the task of the intellectual powers. Later, Aristotle will go on to eliminate art and to show that the remaining three candidates can be reduced to two.

19 *if we are to use the word strictly*: the Greek word '*epistēmē*' is the noun from the commonest Greek word for 'know'. Aristotle often uses it in this general sense, but here, and in other treatises, he gives it a strict sense as meaning systematic and scientific knowledge.

22 *Whatever is known . . . is necessary*: why does Aristotle rule out scientific knowledge of contingent truths? Possibly there lurks in the background

the epistemological fallacy, that is, the argument from 'Necessarily, if p is known, p is true' to 'If p is known, p is necessarily true'.

31 *they are given . . . by induction*: induction, for Aristotle, is the grasping of a universal truth by the consideration of individual examples. It is an operation of the intelligence, as stated in chapter 6 below.

32 *other defining characteristics*: the premisses of the proof must be themselves known, and better known, than the conclusion, if the conclusion is to count as knowledge.

BOOK V, CHAPTER 4

1140a 10 *art can be identified with correctly reasoned productive capability*: Aristotle's word *technē* covers arts such as architecture, crafts such as shoemaking, and skills such as oratory. For many centuries the English word 'art' had a similar broad coverage, and I retain this traditional translation even though in certain contexts it sounds archaic. Arts are *reasoned* capacities in the sense that they can be taught orally and there can be textbooks of them: they are not like keeping one's balance on a bicycle.

BOOK V, CHAPTER 5

24 *wisdom*: the Greek word '*phronēsis*' is often translated 'practical wisdom', but the adjective is superfluous: wisdom is always concerned with life rather than with theory. The definition of wisdom and its relationship to the other virtues, intellectual and moral, is the principal theme of Book V.

1140b 12 *a preservative of wisdom*: Aristotle seems to get carried away by his implausible etymology. Earlier he has explained that what preserves sound judgements about the good life is not the virtue of temperance, but rather continence, which is a different thing (1227b12–16). He clears up the relationship between the two states in Book VI; and he can respond that the sound judgement that is preserved by continence does not amount to wisdom, because wisdom and virtue must go hand in hand (see 1144a36, below).

24 *in art, a person whose mistakes are deliberate is preferable*: for instance, a tennis coach may show his skill by demonstrating to a pupil how *not* to volley. It is because art can be exhibited by wrong performance that art is not a virtue, and drops out of Aristotle's shortlist.

BOOK V, CHAPTER 6

1141a 8 *it must be intelligence that provides them*: 'intelligence' is the best translation of '*nous*' because, like the Greek word, it can mean both the general intellectual faculty, and a particular form of excellence.

BOOK V, CHAPTER 7

9 *What is understanding?*: of all the names of the intellectual virtues, '*sophia*' is the hardest to translate. The traditional 'wisdom' will not do, as

explained above (note to 1140a24). In many contexts 'philosophy' will do, if we remember that during the Aristotelian centuries philosophy included science, so that physics, for instance, was called 'natural philosophy'. But philosophy is most often thought of as a discipline rather than an intellectual state of mind. Hence I opt for 'understanding'; universal understanding is, after all, what philosophy, both ancient and modern, aims at.

14 *As Homer says in the Margites*: the *Margites* was a comic poem about a moron, often attributed to Homer; it survives only in fragments.

19 *a combination of intelligence and knowledge*: it is thus that Aristotle reduces the intellectual virtues to a shortlist of two: wisdom and understanding.

20 *deriving from their head and source*: literally 'having a head on it'.

1141b 2 *the elements that constitute the heavens*: the ensouled heavenly bodies, whose movements are invariable.

4 *quite useless*: Anaxagoras has already twice been cited as holding an unworldly view of happiness (Book I, 1215b6, 1216a11), while Thales was supposed to have fallen into a well while gazing at the heavens.

20 *light and healthy*: there is no need to delete 'light' as OCT does. Note that Aristotle here treats knowledge of the more specific ('fowl') as on a par with knowledge of the individual.

BOOK V, CHAPTER 8

24 *they are different exercises of it*: literally 'their being is not the same'— an expression Aristotle often uses to contrast an actuality with its corresponding potentiality. In I.5, 1216b19, political science appears as a productive science whose output is law and order.

1142a 2 *Call me not wise*: the quotation is from a speech of Odysseus in the lost tragedy *Philoctetes*.

25–8 *It is something in the opposite corner from intelligence . . . final stopping point*: both intelligence and wisdom differ from knowledge by being concerned with things outside the scope of reasoning, but intelligence is concerned with the axioms that precede reasoning, and wisdom is concerned with the practical application that follows on reason.

BOOK V, CHAPTER 9

1142b 10 *There is no such thing as right knowledge*: since knowledge is always of what is true, there is no scope for distinguishing between knowledge that is right and knowledge that is wrong.

19 *if he is clever*: I am adopting Ross's emendation 'ei deinos'.

34 *that end of which wisdom is the true apprehension*: it is also possible to translate the sentence so that what wisdom truly apprehends is the means, rather than the end; but that would conflict with the general build-up of the chapter.

BOOK V, CHAPTER 10

35 *Judgement and good judgement*: it is not easy to decide how to translate the Greek word '*sunesis*'. The key passage for its interpretation is 1143a8: wisdom tells us what we have to do; this virtue tells us whether what has been done is good or bad—whether in our own case or in that of others (1143a15).

1143a 12 *our insight*: the Greek word thus rendered can mean 'learn' as well as 'understand'.

BOOK V, CHAPTER 11

26 *sense and intelligence*: whereas previously intelligence was treated as part of understanding, and contrasted with wisdom, it now appears as a part of wisdom. This is explained in the following paragraph: besides the intelligence that was contrasted with wisdom as being prior to reasoning, there is an intelligence that is identical with the perceptive element in the application of wisdom in the particular case (1142b25).

1143b 16 *each of them is the virtue of a different part of the soul*: if Aristotle ends up with just two intellectual virtues, he must be counting skill in deliberation, judgement, common sense, and one form of intelligence as parts of wisdom, just as he counted knowledge and the other form of intelligence as parts of understanding (1141a19).

BOOK V, CHAPTER 12

1144a 4 *like health itself*: the possession of health finds expression in healthy activities, and the possession of understanding finds expression in the intellectual activities that constitute happiness.

8 *virtue makes the target aimed at correct, and wisdom makes the means correct*: this does not mean that wisdom is not concerned with the target: it is precisely its grasp of the nature of the target that enables it to choose the correct means.

19 *out of choice and for the sake of the acts themselves*: once again, as in Book IV, Aristotle is setting unrealistically strict conditions for virtue, based on his concept of choice.

24 *hit upon and perform*: I am rejecting the OCT's emendation of the text from '*autou*' to '*autwn*'.

28 *and smart*: I accept Rowe's emendation '*tous panourgous*'.

31 *those syllogisms*: the beginning of this sentence is often mistranslated as 'those syllogisms that deal with acts to be done', and the corresponding Greek is used to foist on Aristotle the term 'practical syllogism'. See my *Aristotle's Theory of the Will*, 111–12.

1144b 1 *it is not possible to be wise without being good*: if we are to make this consistent with Aristotle's earlier remarks, we have to take 'good' as meaning 'at least continent'.

BOOK V, CHAPTER 13

15 *in the moral part there are two types*: the elaboration of the distinction between natural and moral virtues fulfils the promise made earlier at III.7, 1234a28.

17 *the latter cannot occur in the absence of wisdom*: 'no virtue without wisdom' is less in need of qualification than 'no wisdom without virtue', but it is the latter that is now used to show that if one virtue is present, all are.

27 *accompanied by correct reasoning*: Aristotle is responding to the claim that it would be enough to depend on others for moral guidance.

1145a 5 *the other the end*: this cryptically concise sentence is full of ambiguities. The most likely interpretation is that wisdom is a correct appreciation of the end, while virtue makes one carry out (and not just identify) the means to the end.

BOOK VI

BOOK VI, CHAPTER 1

16 *three kinds of objectionable moral condition*: the earlier books offered a simple threefold structure of classification in which each virtue is flanked by two contrasting vices. We now learn that matters are really much more complicated. There is a six-point scale, which runs, in ascending order, brutishness–vice–incontinence–continence–virtue–heroism. Each of these conditions is discussed in detail in Book VI, but the emphasis is on continence and incontinence.

20 *the kind of virtue that belongs to heroes*: to this day, candidates for canonization in the Roman Catholic Church must be shown to have exercised 'heroic virtue'.

1145b 3 *set out people's perceptions*: not sense-perceptions, but perceptions in the comparatively recent sense of opinions—the things that appear to people to be true. The methodology described here is the one announced in Book I, 1216b26–35, and these early chapters of Book VI offer the most substantial implementation of it.

14 *is a continent man always temperate?*: the phenomena of continence and incontinence can occur within the sphere of any virtue, but Aristotle initially focuses on the sphere of temperance (which is the sphere of incontinence par excellence, 1146b29) and only later considers other spheres.

BOOK VI, CHAPTER 2

21 *what kind of correct judgement*: knowledge, true belief, and the conclusions of correct practical reasoning are different forms of correct judgement: the distinction between these items will shortly be brought into play (1145b33, 1146a4).

25 *Socrates was opposed to the whole idea*: in Plato's *Protagoras* (from which the phrase 'drag it about like a slave' is a quotation, 352b) Socrates defends the view that one cannot act against one's judgement of what is best to do, and therefore any wrong choice must be based on erroneous belief.

1146a 19 *Neoptolemus in Sophocles' Philoctetes*: in the play Philoctetes has the magic bow of Heracles. If Troy is to fall, it is essential to get possession of it, and so Odysseus orders Neoptolemus to obtain it by trickery, but this goes against Neoptolemus' conscience, and so he reneges on an earlier promise to do so.

BOOK VI, CHAPTER 3

1146b 30 *Heraclitus shows this*: it is not clear whether this sixth-century philosopher is being quoted in support of the account of dogmatism, or as an instance of it.

32 *have knowledge without using it*: this is a distinction often made by Aristotle and it is easy to think of examples. I know the order of the kings and queens of England, and I know how to sing the *Marseillaise*, but I am not at the moment making use of either of these pieces of knowledge. But what is having and not using a piece of ethical knowledge? If it is merely not acting upon it, then the distinction merely restates and in no way explains the phenomenon of incontinence. What Aristotle means, I think, is that an item of knowledge is operative if it thrusts towards action, e.g. when from a universal premiss particular consequences are drawn that are closer to practical implementation. See my *Aristotle's Theory of the Will*, 161.

1147a 1 *there are two kinds of premiss*: Aristotle here distinguishes them as universal and particular. Universal practical premisses take the form 'an agent of such and such a kind should do an action of such and such a kind' or 'a thing of such and such a kind is good for an agent of such and such a kind'; e.g. 'dry food is good for every man'. Particular premisses set out the practically relevant features of the current situation, such as 'cabbage is dry and here is some cabbage'.

10 *yet another way*: in the normal case of having and not using, the non-use is the result of the agent's own choice. But in the case of sleep, drunkenness, and madness the person is actually unable to make use of the knowledge. Comparing incontinence to such states makes it appear like the result of some irresistible impulse. Compare what Aristotle has said about passion and compulsion in Book II, 1225a19–35. Such passages are difficult to reconcile with Aristotle's insistence that the incontinent person acts voluntarily.

20 *verses of Empedocles*: this passage is meant to counter the objection that the incontinent must be actually using his knowledge, because while he is sinning he mutters, 'I shouldn't be doing this, you know.' The Presocratic philosopher Empedocles, best known for ending his life by

jumping into the volcano of Etna, was the author of particularly difficult philosophical verses.

24 *from a physiological point of view*: in his *De Motu Animalium* Aristotle gives a quasi-mechanistic account of how the different parts of the soul set the body in motion. This is alluded to at 1147a35.

30 *a universal premiss forbidding tasting*: it is a pity that Aristotle does not spell out this premiss, but it is clearly the premiss of temperance, concerned with the avoidance of excessive gustatory pleasure. The particular premisses of the reasoning are 'every sweet thing is pleasant, and this is sweet', and these, in conjunction with the universal, yield the concluding imperative 'don't taste this'. In the incontinent man this last utterance is mere babble (1147b12).

1147b 1 *the effect of reason and belief*: the reasoning that leads to the belief that this is pleasant, because it is sweet.

15 *Socrates... actually seems to be correct*: the belief that leads to incontinence is the belief about the delight of this particular sweetmeat, which is not knowledge by Aristotle's standards, and what is dragged about is the conclusion 'don't taste this'.

BOOK VI, CHAPTER 4

20 *The next topic for discussion*: here Aristotle addresses the fifth of the common sayings that he set up for discussion in chapter 1.

35 *bore the name Man*: an Olympic victor in 456 BC was called Anthropos.

1148a 6 *not out of choice*: i.e. not like the intemperate man, whose maxim is 'always pursue the present pleasure' (1146b24).

28 *Consider people*: I use this noncommittal phrase because it is not clear whether Aristotle thinks these people are to be blamed or to escape blame.

33 *Niobe ... Saturos ... idiotic*: Niobe had a dozen or more children, and boasted that she was more prolific than Leto, who had given birth only to Apollo and Artemis. In revenge for this insult to his mother, Apollo killed all Niobe's children. Saturos was, most likely, a fourth-century king of the Bosporus who deified his father.

BOOK VI, CHAPTER 5

1148b 24 *the stories they tell of Phalaris*: Phalaris was a sixth-century Sicilian tyrant who roasted his enemies alive in a brazen bull. Aristotle here and below at 1149a14 adds further details to the story.

BOOK VI, CHAPTER 6

1149b 1 *does in a manner follow reason*: the maxim 'one must take arms against anything of that sort' has the appropriate form for the universal premiss of a practical syllogism.

13 *dragged his own father*: the point of introducing these stock comedy stories is presumably to show that a propensity to anger is natural because it is often inherited.

15 *acts in the open*: earlier, Aristotle maintained that the impulse to anger depends more on reason than the impulse to lust; here he says that the execution of anger does not involve calculation in the way that the execution of lust may.

18 *Enchantment . . . wise men's minds*: *Iliad* xiv.214, 217.

20 *vice of a kind*: but not real vice, as pointed out in the first chapter, 1145a35 ff., and again below at 1151a5.

BOOK VI, CHAPTER 7

1150a 20 *pursues excessive pleasures*: in translation I omit a phrase marked by OCT as corrupt.

26 *flinch from the pain of unsatisfied desire*: cf. Oscar Wilde's remark 'the only way to get rid of temptation is to yield to it'.

1150b 9 *Theodectes . . . Carcinus . . . Xenophantus*: Theodectes was a contemporary of Aristotle who wrote fifty (lost) plays, much admired by Alexander. Carcinus, author of 160 (lost) plays, is often quoted favourably by Aristotle. Xenophantus was a young musician in the court of Alexander who outlived Aristotle by some forty years.

19 *impetuosity and weakness*: in terms of the structure of the practical syllogism outlined in chapter 3 we can say that the impetuous person never completes his reasoning—he hears the word 'pleasure' and leaps to enjoyment (1149a35)—while the weak person completes his reasoning but does not act on it because desire drives him on (1146b34).

BOOK VI, CHAPTER 8

31 *our initial problem*: at 1146a31.

36 *vice is unaware of itself; not so incontinence*: the bad man believes what he is doing is the right thing for him to do; the incontinent man knows he is doing what he ought not to do—though this knowledge, according to 1147a14, is, as it were, stupefied at the moment of action.

1151a 8 *Demodocus' comment on the people of Miletus*: not much is known about the poet Demodocus, except that he came from an island adjacent to Miletus.

14 *can easily be brought to change his mind*: the repentant incontinent does not really change his mind, since he already had sound convictions; what he does is to begin to act upon them.

25 *his first principle, remains safe and sound*: this shows how we are to qualify the statement in V.12, 1144a34, that the end is not apparent except to the good man.

BOOK VI, CHAPTER 9

1151b 18 *Neoptolemus*: we have met him before, at 1146a19; see note there.

30 *the other extreme is seen rarely*: the continent insensitive man is someone who knows he ought to have a certain amount of sex, but dislikes it, and has intercourse out of a sense of duty, as it were with gritted teeth.

BOOK VI, CHAPTER 10

1152a 13 *resembling it in respect of reasoning, but differing in the matter of choice*: earlier Aristotle pointed out that a clever person differed from a wise person because his cleverness might be used to effect a vicious choice; here he shows that an incontinent person differs from a wise person because either (if he is impetuous) he has made no choice or (if weak) he has failed to put his choice into effect.

22 *Anaxandrides . . . takes no notice of her laws*: Anaxandrides was a comedy poet contemporary with Aristophanes, whose speciality was comedies about rape.

31 *Evenus*: a fifth-century sophist.

BOOK VI, CHAPTER 11

1152b 1 *The topics of pleasure and pain*: in Book I (1216b28 ff.) Aristotle said that it needed to be investigated whether bodily pleasures are constituents of happiness, and whether there are other pleasures that make a happy life a pleasant life. He promised a later discussion, and he now fulfils his promise. The answer he gives to the first question is that bodily pleasures are necessary to prevent the obstruction of virtuous activity (1153b18) and that the pursuit of the right amount of them is itself an exercise of virtue (1154b15–18). The answer to the second question is that intellectual pleasures are prime constituents of happiness (1153a1).

7 *the word 'blessed' is related to the word 'bliss'*: Aristotle links the Greek word *makarios* to the Greek word for 'rejoice', *chairein*.

8 *some people think*: Aristotle follows his usual method of sorting out the true from the false in the opinions of other people. He identifies three groups: those who think no pleasure is good, those who think that only a minority of pleasures are good, and those who think that all pleasures are good but none of them is the chief good. His own position will differ from all of these: a certain kind of pleasure is indeed identical with the chief good.

BOOK VI, CHAPTER 12

33 *those felt by the sick*: if something tastes delicious to a person only because he is sick, then it is not really delicious.

34 *processes that restore us to our natural state*: e.g. eating and drinking. The theory expressed in the following lines is that such pleasures are not activities of the empty belly or dehydrated system, but of the bodily organs that remain sound. It is not clear how this theory is supposed to apply to the pleasures of sex.

1153a 1 *the activities of contemplation*: there is no need to delete 'activities' as OCT does.

   11 *It is not when we are acquiring an ability, but when we are using it*: the text is cryptic, simply 'not when acquiring but using'; but 'ability' must be added in order to make sense.

   15 *substitute 'unimpeded' for 'felt'*: so Aristotle's definition of pleasure is 'the unimpeded activity of a natural state'. But it is clear from the subsequent discussion that it is only states whose activities are conscious that he has in mind. The unimpeded activity of the digestive system would not count as a pleasure in itself.

BOOK VI, CHAPTER 13

1153b 5 *Speusippus' solution*: Speusippus was Plato's nephew and succeeded him as head of the Academy. The position that Aristotle attributes to him is that the badness of pain does not prove that pleasure is good, any more than the fact that Tweedledum is not shorter than Tweedledee proves that he is taller than him: they may be the same size. Hence the ideal state might be one that is neither pleasant nor painful. It is not clear how this commits Speusippus, as Aristotle maintains, to saying that pleasure is intrinsically evil.

   11 *of all of them, or of one of them*: here, as earlier, Aristotle leaves open which, and how many, pleasurable activities are intrinsic to happiness. In the final book of the *EE* he will say that happiness consists of the activities of all the virtues. This contrasts with the position of *NE* X, where it is identified with contemplation, the activity of the virtue of understanding.

   21 *such people are talking nonsense*: Aristotle may have Plato in mind (see *Crito* 48b8–9; *Republic* 353e10–354a4).

1153a 28 *What . . . is never wholly lost*: the reference is to Hesiod, *Works and Days* 763–4.

BOOK VI, CHAPTER 14

1154a 21 *except for a person in pursuit of excess*: if you suffer because you are refused a tenth portion of cheesecake, Aristotle will not count this as real pain.

1154b 3 *bad when they are harmful*: it is not clear from the text whether eating salted potato crisps while drinking cocktails falls into the inoffensive or harmful category.

   7 *as the physiologists tell us*: nobody knows who these physiologists were, or what precisely they said about such topics as growing pains.

   15 *pleasures that do not involve pain do not admit of excess*: these are the pleasures that are highest in Aristotle's categorization of pleasures. From chapters 10 to 14 we learn that there are five kinds of pleasure, on a scale of increasing goodness. At the bottom there are the pleasures

of the sick, which are not really pleasures at all (1153b33 and 1154a32). Next up the scale are the coincidental pleasures of food and drink and sex as enjoyed by the gourmand and the lecher (1152b35 ff., 1154a17, a35–63). Above these are the aesthetic pleasures of the senses, divided into two classes: those of the inferior senses of touch and taste, and the pleasures of the superior senses of sight, hearing, and smell (1153a26). Finally, there are the pain-free pleasures of the mind mentioned here and at 1153a1 and 20.

26 *activity . . . of immobility*: in *Metaphysics* Λ.7 Aristotle argues that God, though unchanging, must be capable of thought. He then devotes the rest of the chapter to the question 'what does God think of?'

29 *as the poet says*: Euripides, in his *Orestes*, line 234.

BOOK VII

BOOK VII, CHAPTER I

1234b 18 *What is friendship*: the Greek word '*philia*' means both 'friendship' and 'love'. So, too, the verb '*philein*' can mean either 'love' or 'be friends with'. In English I use whichever rendering seems most appropriate to the particular context. Aristotle also has words for particular kinds of love, such as '*erōs*' for erotic love.

22 *what is noble and desirable in people's characters*: i.e. the moral virtues, including justice, the subjects of earlier books.

24 *the special task of political skill*: politics and friendship are closely linked also in Aristotle's *Politics*, as when he says that a state is a community of families and other associations that 'are created by friendship, for to choose to live together is friendship' (1280b38–9).

1235a 5 *extending the term and taking in extraneous matters*: i.e. using it about non-human, and indeed non-living, creatures.

6 *hence the sayings*: the first is from the *Odyssey* xvii.218; the authors of the other two are unknown.

11 *Empedocles said*: Empedocles of Agrigentum (*fl.* 490 BC) built up an elaborate physical system based on a number of cosmic principles, one of which was the attraction of like to like.

16 *hence the sayings*: the first two are from Euripides, the third from Hesiod.

23 *The less . . . from the breaking of the day*: Euripides again, *Phoenissae* 539–40.

26 *Heraclitus criticizes the poet*: Heraclitus takes issue with Homer, *Iliad* xviii.107.

33 *mothers are not to love their own children*: Aristotle is not denying that mothers can be good, but is pointing out that even middling mothers love their children.

37 *as old Socrates used to say*: so Xenophon tells us, *Memorabilia* I.2, 53–4.

BOOK VII, CHAPTER 2

1235b 14 *resolve the problems and the contrary positions*: a reiteration of the methodological principle first enunciated in Book I at 1216b26–35.

21 '. . . *loves for evermore*': Euripides, *Trojan Women* 1051.

28 *to others it feels good even if they don't think it is good*: i.e. to the incontinent.

39 *would not even pass up wine that is no better than vinegar*: I suggest we read '*oute*' and '*parengcheirousin*' for '*paregcheousin*'.

1236a 17 *there is no mere equivocation*: as when a barrier and a wisp of hair share the name 'lock' (cf. 1129a30). In this passage Aristotle sets forward a doctrine of analogy that was to be very influential throughout the Middle Ages. A medical instrument (e.g. a stethoscope) is not at all like a medical textbook, and stethoscopes and books are not species of a genus in the way that cats and tigers are; yet we are not making a mere pun when we call them both 'medical'. Medical things are described by the same adjective, Aristotle tells us, because they all have a relationship—a different relationship in different cases—to a medical man, the person who uses them both. The meanings of the different analogous terms have a single focus on what medieval Aristotelians called the 'prime analogate'; modern commentators in a case like this speak of 'focal meaning'.

20 *in all the cases*: unlike OCT, I accept Bonitz's emendation of '*pasin*' for '*hēmin*'.

1236b 3 *To one who loves . . . is a friend to the one he loves*: A by loving B makes him his friend; B by returning the love makes A his friend.

9 *Recall Herodotus' story . . . crocodile*: 'the sandpiper is of service to the crocodile and lives in the greatest amity with him; for when the crocodile comes ashore and lies with his mouth wide open, the bird hops in and swallows the leeches. The crocodile enjoys this, and so never hurts the bird' (*Histories* ii.68).

30 *good things to happen to him . . . continue in being*: OCT gives up the attempt to amend this corrupt passage, but we can make sense of it if we accept the emendation of '*hōi*' (Spengel) instead of '*hōs*'.

37 *but possibly bad*: unlike OCT, I accept Jackson's suggestion that we read '*kaka an pōs tuchē*'.

1237a 8 *not perfectly good*: in the perfectly good person, as described in the final book of the *EE*, goodness and pleasure come together. It is in the noble activities of the good man that the highest pleasure is to be found, and that pleasure, goodness, and nobility coincide. It is the task of ethics to bring about this coincidence.

14 *beneficial to a particular individual*: I follow Solomon in reading '*autwi hoiou*' instead of '*kalon toiouton, autwi hoion*'.

25 *the reason is the same in each case*: it is not clear what the reason is, and how Aristotle can say in the same passage both that new knowledge is the best and that old knowledge is.

36 *or in oneself qua other*: as when the physician heals himself.

37 *being loved is not an activity of the beloved*: I follow Rackham in inserting '*ou*'.

1238a 2 '*a bushel of salt*': the proverb 'Before making a friend, eat a peck of salt with him' passed into many modern languages.

13 *has been rightly said*: by Euripides, *Electra* 941.

34 *Hence the sayings*: again from Euripides, but this time from a lost play.

38 *in itself renders them neither bad nor middling*: the correct reading is uncertain, but it seems clear that the meaning is that the project is not one in virtue of which they are either bad or middling.

BOOK VII, CHAPTER 3

1238b 21 *proportional rather than arithmetical equality*: the difference has been explained in chapters 3 and 4 of Book IV.

25 *the latter is between ruler and subject*: translators disagree about which of the family relationships instantiates the relation of ruler to subject, but I fear it is that of husband and wife. But see below, 1241a33.

28 *for a subject to reproach his ruler*: instead of the words deleted in the OCT, I read '*kai ho archomenos*'.

34 *those who think they are on equal terms . . . passion is proportionate*: let A be the superior and B the inferior. In the utility case A thinks B is as rich as he himself is and complains at the poverty of B's gifts and services. In the pleasure case B thinks he is just as sexy as A, and complains that A's passion does not match his own.

37 *Eunicus*: a writer of old comedy of whom little is known.

39 *think that the proportion is the same*: i.e. think that it is arithmetical.

BOOK VII, CHAPTER 4

1239a 12 *it is right*: I read '*dei*' instead of OCT '*aei*'.

29 *prefers being loved*: I follow Rackham in reading '*philoumenos*' instead of OCT '*philotimos*'.

32 *exercise of love*: I read '*anagkē energounti*' with Richards and Solomon.

37 *like Andromache in Antiphon's tragedy*: Antiphon was a Syracusan tragedian of the fourth century whose tragedy is lost. In Euripides' play of the same name Andromache, widow of Hector of Troy, secretly sends away Molossus, her son by her second marriage, to prevent him from being killed.

BOOK VII, CHAPTER 5

1239b 29 *the hot does not want the cold nor the dry the wet*: as the next paragraph explains, something that is too hot needs to be cooled: but if something has achieved the temperature that is appropriate for it—a hot fire, for instance—it has no need for its contrary.

39 *takes them away from their natural state*: i.e. from an initial excessive or defective state, towards the mean.

BOOK VII, CHAPTER 6

1240a 10 *they use this friendship as a standard*: as does a man who follows the precept to love his neighbour as himself.

16 *it is a matter... of how the parts of the soul are related to each other*: see II.8, 1224b25–7.

23 *in our discussions*: presumably in the Lyceum.

36 *birds share each other's pain*: in the *History of Animals* (IX.612b35) Aristotle tells us that a male pigeon will display extraordinary sympathy to the female pigeon at the time of parturition.

1240b 32 *A horse does not seem good to itself*: I translate Ross's emendation '*ou dokei agathos*'.

BOOK VII, CHAPTER 7

1241a 15 *not friendship itself. . . .* : there is no doubt a lacuna here.

19 *it is possible to think and to desire contrary things*: I accept Richards's emendation '*tanantia noiein kai epithumein*'.

33 *Concord is friendship in citizenship*: see chapters 9 and 10 below.

BOOK VII, CHAPTER 9

1241b 20 *no unity of its own*: in place of '*ouden*', deleted by OCT, I accept Jackson's '*oud' hen*'.

24 *a tool is a sort of inanimate slave*: in *Politics* I.4, 1253b35 ff., Aristotle says that a slave is a living tool, but he goes on to add that if non-living tools could achieve the same purpose, there would be no need for slavery. 'If every instrument could achieve its own work, obeying or anticipating the will of others, like the statues of Daedalus . . . if the shuttle could weave and the plectrum pluck the lyre in a similar manner, overseers would not need servants, nor masters slaves.' So perhaps, in an age of automation, Aristotle would no longer defend slavery.

27 *households*: I accept Fritzsche's reading '*oikiais*'.

28 *constitutions resemble musical modes*: in the *Politics* (e.g. IV.2, 1289a28) Aristotle lists three acceptable forms of polity—monarchy, aristocracy, and constitutional government—and three perversions of these forms—tyranny, oligarchy, and democracy. (By 'democracy' he means

direct democracy, not the representative type favoured nowadays.) He goes on to compare the relation between the good and the bad forms to the relationship between the Dorian and Phrygian mode; we might find a comparison with major and minor keys more accessible.

30 *husband and wife together are an aristocracy*: here there appears a greater equality between the spouses than earlier, at 1238b24.

BOOK VII, CHAPTER 10

1242a 36 *being based on*: I accept Jackson's emendation '*hēi*' for '*hē*'.

35–9 *Never was I . . . No less than Zeus my king*: this appears to be a fragment of a lost play by Sophocles.

1242b 16 *brings together the opposite points of a diagonal*: see IV.5, 1133a6. The four points of the square are the superior, the inferior, the superior's contribution, and the inferior's contribution. The superior thinks that the inferior should contribute more than he does, in proportion to his own superior status; the inferior wants the services rendered to be equal, and thus 'brings together', or equalizes, the points represented by the two contributions.

34 *'fair wages make good friends'*: Hesiod, *Works and Days* 368.

1243a 3 *there are more recriminations in utility friendships than in others*: and most of all, as the previous paragraph has spelt out, in utility friendships masquerading as moral friendships, with the terms of exchange left to the discretion of the partners.

17 *what Theognis says*: this is the fourth time Theognis has been quoted; see above, 1214a6, 1230a12, and 1129b30.

31 *value at the time of repayment*: the possibility of fluctuation in the value of money has already been mentioned at IV.5, 1133b14.

1243b 20 *quarrel as Pytho and Pammenes did*: Pytho was a Byzantine rhetorician who came to Athens in 343 as an ambassador from Philip of Macedon and may indeed have conveyed the invitation to Aristotle to tutor Alexander. From this passage it appears that Pammenes was a pupil with whom he had an affair and then fell out.

22 *the doctor Prodicus*: Prodicus of Selymbria appears in Pliny's apostolic succession of Hippocratic doctors between Hippocrates and Chrysippus, who taught medicine to Aristotle's grandson.

24–7 *There is a similar story . . . had given the harpist pleasure*: some ancient scholars thought the king was Alexander; others thought the story too *infra dig.* for so great a man.

35 *it is clear that A is cheating*: it seems that A has promised to teach wisdom (the more valuable object), but has failed to do so, while taking half his fee in cash (the less valuable object).

BOOK VII, CHAPTER 11

1244a   3 *makes a return*: I retain the MSS reading '*antipoiounti*'.

    10 *Euripides' verses*: from a lost play.

    18 *like this*: I omit OCT's '*toutwi*'.

    30 *you will prefer . . . your pleasant friends*: this is not the first time that Aristotle has expressed his distaste for the company of other generations in his family.

1244b   4 *a good man is self-sufficient*: I accept Fritzsche's '*kai*'.

    23 *because of the comparison*: with the divinity.

    31 *the way it is written in the text*: once again Aristotle makes an obscure reference to a text available to his audience (cf. II.2, 1220b11). At one time I suggested that the text here referred to is *NE* IX.9, 1170a25–9, but few have been convinced.

    36 *to one and the same person*: I have translated '*twi autwi*' rather than the OCT text.

1245a   1 *a series of corresponding items*: Aristotle seems to have in mind a table with two columns, matching determinate and indeterminate items to each other, with the determinate ones being desirable and the indeterminate ones undesirable.

    28 *there is something misleading in the discussion of the question*: the *EE*'s own argument seems to go as follows. Looking at life simply in terms of the possession and communication of knowledge leads to the conclusion that the society of others is superfluous; but it is obvious that we all want to share things with our friends, whether bodily pleasure, or artistic culture, or philosophical inquiry. Hence there must be something wrong with an argument leading to the opposite conclusion.

    35 *being a separate self*: because a friend is an alter ego one can look on his good as one's own.

1245b   2 *If one should live well*: I read '*dei*'.

    15 *the comparison, which was in itself correctly stated*: it was true that God does not need friends, but the virtuous man is not the same as God. If he were, he would think of nothing other than himself, just as God is described as doing in *Metaphysics* Λ.7 and 9.

    29 *the mother of Heracles might have chosen . . . Eurystheus*: Hercules was in fact enslaved to Eurystheus while performing his twelve famous labours.

    32 *a joke like the one made by the Spartan . . . Dioscuri for help*: told to invoke Castor and Pollux, he replied, 'I'm in enough trouble myself; I wouldn't want to involve the Dioscuri too.'

1246a 22 *not be absent*: I read '*apeinai*' for '*einai*'.

BOOK VIII

BOOK VIII, CHAPTER 1

33 *you can use it to err*: the possibility of deliberate misuse of a skill was mentioned at V.5, 1140b23, to contrast art with virtue. Here the point is hammered home that virtue cannot be misused in the way knowledge can. It is used to continue the attack on the Socratic identification of virtue with knowledge, first begun at I.5, 1216b2–10.

1246b 8 *people behaving thus would be acting wisely*: the paragraph up to this point is a *reductio ad absurdum* derived from two premisses that Aristotle rejects: (1) that wisdom is the same as knowledge, (2) that there is only one way of using each thing qua itself. The rest of the paragraph is devoted to showing that the perversion of wisdom is indeed an absurdity, because there is no higher faculty that could pervert it.

10 *what can divert the one that is superior to all*: OCT adds to the MSS the word '*kuria*', but this is unnecessary. '*Poiei ten strophēn*' is tacitly repeated from the previous sentence. Understanding is a virtue that is grander than wisdom, but it is not a controlling virtue in the way that wisdom is; the relationship between the two has been spelt out in the concluding chapters of Book V.

12 *making use of the virtue of the governed*: this assertion of the superiority of wisdom to moral virtue comes as a surprise after Book V described the relationship between the two as a partnership (1144b30). It is treating the relationship between wisdom and virtue as one of governor to governed that allows the formulation of the paradoxical scenarios in the following paragraphs. Neither of them is possible if we recall from Book V that there cannot be wisdom without moral virtue or moral virtue without wisdom. This thesis is now restated at the end of the chapter, 1246b32.

15 *the role of the two will be reversed*: I omit the disjointed letters that occur in the MSS and the OCT's conjectured reconstruction of the text.

BOOK VIII, CHAPTER 2

38 *we say also that the fortunate do well*: the relationship between fortune and happiness was first raised as a problem in the third chapter of Book I (1215a11–16).

1247a 2 *the same results as knowledge*: here being used in a broad sense to include wisdom and art.

4 *is a matter of observation*: having raised the question whether good fortune and bad fortune are inborn or acquired, Aristotle takes a step back to establish whether fortunate people exist at all (1247a3–7). He then puts forward the thesis that being fortunate is something inborn

(1247a7–13), and presents two arguments in favour of this thesis (1247a13–31) before going on to reject it (1247a31–b1).

11 *blue-eyed and black-eyed people differ*: from 1247a37 below it is clear that Aristotle believed black-eyed people to have sharper vision than blue-eyed people. I omit here a nonsensical clause which no commentator has succeeded in amending.

21 *Hippocrates . . . cheated of much money by the customs men at Byzantium*: Hippocrates was a fifth-century geometer, much interested in squaring the circle, who wrote a textbook that anticipated much of Euclid. We do not know how he was cheated.

22 *throws a six*: unlike the OCT, I accept the brilliant emendation of Jackson '*allos de ballei hex*', which corresponds to a medieval Latin version of the text.

29 *it would be strange for a god . . . to favour such a man rather than the best and wisest*: the suggestion in this paragraph that success is due to divine favour reminds a Christian reader of the doctrine of divine grace—a doctrine on whose development this chapter was to have an influence. But this particular sentence presents the heretical Pelagian view that grace is given only to those who have merited it.

34 *would not seem to be*: unlike OCT, I accept Jackson's insertion of '*doxeie*' after '*an*'.

1247b 1 *the fortunate are those whose goods are caused by good luck*: whereas OCT has '*eutucheis tuchēs*', I read, as suggested by the medieval Latin translation, '*eutucheis eutucheis*'.

1 *If this is so, will luck not exist at all*: having reached an impasse on the nature of good fortune (*eutuchia*) Aristotle now raises the more fundamental question: is there anything at all such as luck (*tuchē*)?

9 *That would set us a different problem*: if we take the line that there is no such thing but only hidden causes, we meet the problem that is set out in the following paragraph.

10 *succeeding again through the same cause and yet again*: the text I translate is '*palin alla dia to auto katorthwsai kai palin*'.

14 *there will be no empirical knowledge of it*: the argument seems to be that if luck was really a cloak for hidden causes, whether single or multiple, there would be a science of it, either theoretical or empirical. But there is no such science.

15 *as Socrates said*: in Plato's *Euthydemus* 279d, Socrates states that wisdom is good fortune; but the suggestion is not meant to be taken in the sense Aristotle takes it here, for he goes on to argue that if a man has wisdom, he has no need of good luck (280b).

18 *What follows then?*: Aristotle has not yet finished piling up problems and now starts another hare, starting from the consideration of different kinds of impulse.

21 *everything will march towards the good*: unlike OCT, I preserve the MSS reading '*pan*'.

28 *It will follow that the fortunate are so by nature*: this is the antithesis to the thesis argued for up to 1247a39.

29 *is there more than one sense of 'good fortune'?*: at last Aristotle begins to present his own solution to the problems, by making some preliminary distinctions. Two kinds of good fortune are distinguished on the basis of two kinds of action: action in accordance with impulse and action contrary to impulse. The first kind of good fortune is when someone has healthy impulses, but reasons badly, but nonetheless comes out with the right action. The second kind of good fortune is when someone has bad impulses, but reasons well, and achieves a good that was not what he desired. This is spelt out, not very clearly, in the remainder of the paragraph.

1248a 2 *we see some people succeeding against all sciences and correct reasonings*: these seem to be the people we have already met in the section on natural good fortune (1247a16, b25–7). Aristotle now seems to say that such success is not really good fortune at all. It is the result partly of natural good desire and partly of distorted reason; but it is not something that is caused by luck. Unless, that is, natural good desire is itself caused by luck. But it is not from luck, but from God.

20 *Nor did he think, having thought before thinking, and so on to infinity*: many modern thinkers—usually in ignorance of this passage—have pointed out that if each mental act is caused by a previous mental act of the same kind, then an infinite regress is generated. But Aristotle himself did not hold that view: deliberation arises from a mental state of a different kind, desire, and the question is what is the ultimate trigger of desire. The answer, according to the *EE*, is God.

26 *God moves everything by intelligence*: I read '*kai pan ekei nwi kinei*', adapting a conjecture of Jackson's. The intelligence by which he moves everything in our soul is the same as the divine element in us mentioned in the next sentence.

1248b 3 *there are two kinds of good fortune*: in the course of the discussion we have had four types of candidate for being fortunate. First, there are those to whom God gives a good nature, and who use this in a normally virtuous manner: this is not a genuine case of luck. Secondly, there are those to whom God has given a good nature, which has reached a successful outcome through bad reasoning: this, too, is not fortune through luck, but fortune through nature. The third and the fourth cases are the two that Aristotle regards as genuine cases of luck, and lists here. In the third case God gives us inspiration that leads from good desire to good outcome, without any reasoning, good or bad (this is divine luck). Finally, we have the case in which a person with bad desires, and faulty reasoning, happens to perform a good action—as the Count in the last act of the

Marriage of Figaro, as a result of an evil desire to seduce Susanna, and a misidentification of the Countess, is reconciled with his wife. This is the non-divine, irregular kind of luck mentioned by Aristotle last of all.

BOOK VIII, CHAPTER 3

10 *which we now name nobility*: or perhaps 'which we are accustomed to call nobility'. Nobility (*kalokagathia*) includes all the virtues, but it is more than just the totality of them: as Aristotle goes on to explain, it involves a particular attitude to their value.

26 *A good man is a man for whom natural goods are good*: the natural goods are the same as the goods in the abstract, of which we have heard several times before. It is only if you are a good person that they are good, in the concrete, for you; if you are not good, then being famous or wealthy may be positively bad for you.

38 *a certain civic character, such as the Spartans have*: Spartans are virtuous people, and so they perform virtuous actions for their own sake, because they are the acts that virtue requires. But their evaluation of virtue differs from that of the noble person. To the second-order question 'what is the point of being virtuous?' Spartans answer, 'Because virtue pays'; the noble person answers, 'Because virtue is splendid and noble.'

1249a 10 *To the noble person what is useful is also noble*: for the noble person the noble and the useful are in harmony; but this harmony is highly exceptional. Most people are not good, let alone noble, and for them what is useful is not even good. To the Laconian, whatever is useful is good, but it is not noble since virtue is subordinated to non-noble ends.

17 *Pleasure has already been discussed*: the most relevant conclusion of the discussion in Book VI was that pleasure is identical with action. The truly virtuous man will be exercising all the virtues, and this activity will be the pleasantest possible. Thus we see fulfilled the promise made in the first book, at 1214a1–8, that happiness, besides being the noblest and best of things, is also the pleasantest.

1249b 6 *true but uninformative*: we were given this true but uninformative answer at the beginning of Book V; now, at last, the answer is made more informative, but in a rather surprising manner.

11 *there are two kinds of superior*: the two parts of the intellectual soul, the one whose virtue is understanding, and the one whose virtue is wisdom. The relation here between the two is the same as that elucidated at V.13, 1145a6. Wisdom gives commands, but understanding is the *raison d'être* of those commands.

14 *God is not a superior who issues commands*: the mention of God is surprising here, and some commentators have regarded this as a Christian interpolation. But what Christian would make this statement about the author of the Ten Commandments?

20 *the service and contemplation of God*: there is no warrant for OCT's alteration of the MSS '*ton theon therapeuein*' to '*to en hemin theion therapeuein*'. Admittedly, what Aristotle meant by the service of God is anyone's guess. My own guess (based on the use of the expression in Plato's *Euthyphro*) is that it means acts of moral virtue. Thus, the service of God will be the work of the virtue of one part of the intellectual soul (wisdom) and the contemplation of God will be the work of the virtue of the other part (understanding).

GLOSSARY OF KEY TERMS

abstract, in the	*haplws*	or 'objectively'; see note to III.1, 1228b19
action, conduct	*praxis*	see note to II.6, 1222b20
activity, actuality	*energeia*	
appetite	*epithumia*	sensual appetite; see note to II.7, 1223a27
art	*technē*	includes crafts and skills
belief	*doxa*	
capacity	*dunamis*	also 'faculty', 'capability'
character	*hexis*	
choice	*prohairesis*	see note to II.10, 1225b18
coincidentally	*kata sumbebēkos*	
controlling	*kurios*	also 'superior', 'genuine'
depraved	*mochtheros*	
desire	*orexis*	general term covering will and appetite
equity, equitable	*epieikeia, epiekēs*	the adjective sometimes = decent
error	*agnoia*	also 'ignorance'
final, complete	*teleion*	literally 'end-like'
force, forced	*bia, biaion*	
happiness	*eudaimonia*	
incontinence	*akrasia*	
intelligence	*nous*	
intemperance	*akolasia*	
involuntary	*akousion*	also 'non-voluntary'; see note to II.7, 1223a23
knowledge	*epistēmē*	sometimes 'science'; see notes to I.1, 1214a30, V.3, 1139b19
making	*poiēsis*	contrasted with action; see note to V.4, 1140a10
mean	*meson, mesotēs*	literally 'middle', 'middle state'
movement	*kinēsis*	also 'change'
nature	*phusis*	
necessity	*anagkē*	
nobility	*kalokagathia*	
noble	*kalon*	also 'beautiful'; see note to I.1, 1214a5
pain	*lupē*	includes all kinds of distress, e.g. thirst
passion, emotion	*pathos*	
perception	*aisthēsis*	
perceptions	*phainomena*	see note to I.6, 1216b28
pleasure	*hēdonē*	
pride	*megalopsuchia*	literally 'greatness of soul'
process	*genesis*	literally 'coming into being'
purpose	*hou heneka*	literally 'that for the sake of which'; also '*raison d'être*'

reason	*logos*	versatile word; see note to II.1, 1219b28
source	*archē*	also 'principle'; see note to II.6, 1222b16
task	*ergon*	also 'work'; see note to II.1, 1219a1
temperance	*swphrosune*	
understanding	*sophia*	sometimes 'philosophy'
virtue	*aretē*	also 'excellence'; see note to I.1, 1214a32
voluntary	*hekousion*	
wicked	*ponēros*	
will	*boulēsis*	desire deriving from reason
wisdom	*phronēsis*	

INDEX

abilities 53; *see* powers

absence 139–40

action, human xvi–xvii, 10, 13, 23–4, 69; *see also* conduct

Academy, Plato's vii

activity 15, 107

adultery 21, 55, 59, 63, 70, 73, 165, 167

affirmation 76–7

Agathon 41, 47, 76, 78, 160, 168

Alexander the Great viii, 182

ambiguity 53, 115

analogy 115–17, 179

Anaxagoras 6, 81, 150

Andromache 124, 180

Antiphon 47, 124, 180

anger 22, 39, 44–5, 67, 72, 96–7, 99–100

animal, beast 7, 9, 27, 31, 33, 76, 90, 115, 116, 127

Aphrodite 99

Apis 7, 151

appetite 25, 28–9, 157

Aquinas xxvii, 161

aristocracy 58, 130

Aristotle vii–xii; ethical treatises x–xii; ref. to other works: *Analytics* 9, 24, 34, 77; *De Anima* xiv–xv; *Nicomachean Ethics* x–xii

art, arts 5, 77–8, 80, 108, 138, 169; and wisdom 78–9

assault 21

avoidance 76

babies 7

beauty 43

becoming 78

Being 11, 153

belief 31, 35, 77, 83, 91–4; vs knowledge 91, 93

benefaction 129

Bias 55, 163

blessedness, bliss 5, 106

blind man's buff 29

boars 39

body 129; goods of 109; pleasures of 109; *see* soul

boorishness 104

Brasidas 65, 165

brute i.e. animal 76, 90

brutishness 90, 97–8

calculative faculty 75

candour 50

cannibalism 97–8

categories 11

cause, different kinds distinguished 76

Celts 40

chance 5

character 5, 17–18, 36, 73, 150

Cheiron 41

child, children 6, 38–9, 106, 108, 113, 115, 126–7, 129

choice (purpose) 25–7, 31–6, 42, 66–7, 76, 127, 158–9, 166; and incontinence 102–3

civic friendship 132

cleverness 84, 87, 105, 176

coercion 28–9

comedy 43

commerce 5, 61

common sense 85

company 135–6, 138–9

complete, completeness 15, 147

compulsion 66; *see also* force

concord 128

conduct 23, 27, 76, 79, 156, 168

congratulation 16

contemplation, theoretical knowledge 107–8, 148

continence 25, 27–9, 35–6, 90–106, 172; and temperance 91

contingency 24, 32, 78

contracts 132

contraries 19, 53, 113, 125

convention 62, 65

conviviality 50–1, 162

Coriscus 17, 127

courage 37–42, 47, 52, 54, 70; five kinds of 39

covetousness 54–6

cowardice 37–42, 55–6, 73, 98

cruelty 44–5

danger 37–42
death 39–40
deception 35
decrees 65, 72, 82, 165
deduction 77
defect and excess 18–23, 51–2
deliberate mistake 79, 141, 169, 184
deliberation 32–3, 75, 78, 81, 83–4,
    145, 186
Delos 3
democracy 58
depravity 25, 55, 91, 97
desert 47–9, 57–8
desire 25–6, 31, 43–4, 76, 144–6
dice 143–4
dignity 50
Dioscuri 139
disdain 46–7
disease 6, 107
distributive justice 57–8, 69
divine 5, 10, 81, 109, 151
doctor, physician 32, 34–6, 70, 148;
    see also medicine
dogs 99
drunkenness 20, 94, 105

education 56
emotions 18, 49–51, 94, 103
Empedocles 94, 112
end, aim, goal 13, 32, 34–6, 84, 89
enjoyment, see pleasure
envy 20, 49
epilepsy 98, 102
equality 57–62, 122–4
equity 71–2
error 30, 67–8
eternal 77
Eunicus 122
Euripides 82, 111, 178
Evenus 105, 176
excess and defect 18–23, 51–2, 110–11
exchange 60–4
exoteric works 11, 78, 152
expenditure 49
external goods 14, 109

fair, fairness 56
farmer 62
father 64, 66, 99, 122, 126, 129, 135 166
fear and fearfulness 37–42
felicitation 16
flatterer 20

foolhardiness 19, 37–42, 52
force 27–30
Form of Good, see Good, Idea of
fortune 109, 142–6, 186
fowl 81
friendliness 50
friendship xxvi, 112–40; three kinds
    of 114, 122–3, 132; primary 116–22;
    of utility 116–22, 130; of
    pleasure 116–22; and equality 122–4;
    and likeness 124–5; legal vs
    moral 132, 134
function 154–5; see also task, work

gain 59–60
gentleness 22, 44–5
geometer 82
geometry 23–4, 31–2, 36, 79, 83
geometrical proportion 58
gluttony 20
God 11, 77, 153, 111, 122–3, 134, 138–9,
    145–6, 148, 187–8
gods 71, 89, 90
good, goodness 3, 10–13; Good, Idea
    of 10–12; chief good 10–13, 152;
    someone else's good 55, 64, 163
goods 14, 38; external vs internal 14;
    objective (in the abstract) 38, 54, 71,
    106, 114, 117–18, 120; real vs
    apparent 114; valuable vs
    laudable 147; natural 147
goodwill 128
Graces 61
greatness 47–9
greed 19
grief 126

habit, habituation 3, 18,
happiness xii–xiv, xxii–xxiv, 3–10, 15, 32,
    106, 108–9, 120; three views of 4, 14
health 4, 13, 32, 53, 80, 86, 114, 171
Hector 41, 90
hemlock 30
Heraclitus 26, 94, 113
Hercules 138–9
Herodotus 116
heroic virtue 90
Hippocrates 143, 185
Homer 41, 50, 69, 80, 90, 99, 113
homosexuality 49, 98, 161
honour 97
house, housebuilding 61–3, 78

household 64, 130
human good 79
humility 161

Ideas, Platonic 10–12, 152
ignorance, *see* error
illiberality 45–6
immortality 31
impassivity 19
impetuosity 102
impossibility 31
impulse 28, 144
incontinence 25, 27–9, 69, 90–106, 117, 157, 172; its sphere 91, 95–7; and knowledge 91–5; and wisdom 91, 105–6; of anger 91, 96–7; impetuosity vs weakness 102
India 32
induction 77, 169
infinite regress 32, 145
injustice 53–74
insensibility 19, 42–4
intellectual virtue 75–89
intemperance 19, 42–4, 55–6, 91, 93–6, 101–3
intelligence 77, 85, 169–70
involuntary 24–33, 57, 66–8, 73, 157
irascibility 19, 44

judge 59, 70,
judgement 32, 77, 84–5, 91–2, 171–2
justice xxv–xxvi, 25, 53–74; general vs particular, 53–7; distributive vs rectificatory 57–60, 163; natural vs legal 65–6, 71; justice as mean 63, 165; and friendship 112, 129–30

knowledge 3, 77, 79, 137, 141, 149, 168; possession vs use 30–1, 94; and incontinence 91–5; *see also* science

law 53–6, 64, 72
laws 56
legislation, legislator 71–2, 81
Lesbian rule 72
liberality 45–6, 52
life, lives 6–8; three lives 6, 8, 14, 150
likeness 112–13, 124–5
logic 10, 152
loss 59–60
love 29, 114, 117, 122–4, 134, *see* friendship

luck 3, 5, 109, 142–6
Lyceum viii

madness 4, 40
magnificence 45, 49
making 77; making vs doing 78
malice 49–50, 67
man and wife 64, 122, 125, 130
markets 65
mathematics 23–4; *see also* geometry
mean 18–23, 37, 44, 45, 48, 53, 57, 59–60, 63, 75, 125, 155–6, 161
medicine 32, 81, 86, 115
method in ethics 8–9, 114
Megara 132
Milesians 102, 175
misadventure 67
miser 45, 161
misfortune 120
mistake 67, 79; *see also* error
modesty 50
money 61–3, 133, 182
moral virtue 16–23
morbidity 98
mother 68, 113, 129, 166
multiplication 11
music 43, 121–2, 144

nature 3, 5, 28–30, 65, 85, 88, 142–6
necessary conditions vs constituents 4
necessity 24, 27, 75, 77, 168
need, in exchange 62, 165
negation 76
neighbour 54–5
nemesis 5, 162
Neoptolemus 92, 104
Nicomachus x
Niobe 97, 174
nobility 146–8, 187
noble, the 3, 12, 38, 42, 97, 134, 146–7, 149
numbers 12, 153
nutritive part of soul 16, 87
nymph 3, 149

Odysseus 92
old age 29, 66, 166
operation vs product 14
opinion 77; *see* belief
originator 23

particulars 81–2, 94
pain 27–8, 31, 39, 99–100, 110, 140

partnership 59, 129–30
passion, *see* emotion
past 76
Pelias 30
perception, sensation 76, 137–8
perceptions 8, 36, 90, 114, 116, 151
Pericles 79
persuasion 28
perversion 34–5, 141–2
Phalaris 98
Phidias 80
Philolaus 30
Philoctetes, Sophocles' 92, 104
Philoctetes, Theodectes' 101
Philoxenus 44, 160
philosophers 9, 79–81
philosophy 80, 138
physiologists 94, 110
Plato vii–ix; *see* Ideas, Platonic
pleasure xxii–xxiv, 3–4, 7–8 42–4, 92, 96,
    100, 106–11, 115, 124, 148 151, 176–8,
    187; pleasure and pain 17, 21, 42–4,
    79; necessary vs non-necessary 96, 110;
    natural vs brutish 100, 110; real vs
    apparent 107; intrinsic vs alien 108;
    of the body 109–11; remedial 110–11;
    and friendship 114, 116–24
political justice 64
politics, political skill 7, 13, 81, 112, 117
potentialities 18
powers 14, 154; things in one's
    power 24, 29, 31–3, 66, 156
practical truth 76
practical wisdom, *see* wisdom
praise 15, 17, 36
prayer 54
premeditation 34
premiss 104
pride 46–9, 161
principles 24–5, 156
processes 106–7, 176
Prodicus 134, 182
prodigality 20, 45–6, 52
product, production 14, 17, 76
profit 55, 97
proportion 57–60; geometrical vs
    arithmetical 57–60, 132; continuous vs
    discrete 58
punishment 5, 42, 59
pursuit 76, 103
Pythagoreans 60
Pytho 134, 182

rack, victim on 109
rage, *see* anger
reason, reasoning 16, 28–9, 38, 45, 75,
    88, 99, 144–6, 156
reciprocity 60–4
rectificatory justice 58–60
recrimination 132–3
reductio ad absurdum 23, 156
responsibility 23–4
Rhadamanthus 60
rulers 64

Sardanapallus 7, 151
Schadenfreude 50, 162
science 8, 11, 34, 153; science and
    virtue 8; science of contraries 53
scientific faculty 75
scribes 32
self 138
self-indulgence 22, *see also* intemperance
self-injury 68–70, 72–4
self-love 125–7
self-sufficiency 136–40
series 11
servility 44–5
sex 6, 43, 98, 106, 110
shoe, shoemaker 15, 45, 61–2, 135
sight 34, 115, 141, 143
slave, slavery 64, 125, 129, 131, 181
sleep 7, 15–16, 94, 129
smartness 87
smell 43, 119
Socrates 8, 39, 88, 91, 95, 113, 142, 144,
    151, 160, 174
softness 90, 100–2
Solon 15
sophists 13
Sophocles 92, 104, 166, 173, 182
soul xiv–xv, 15–16, 148, 156;
    parts of 16–17, 28–9, 75, 86–8,
    126, 148, 171
sources 24–5, 156
Sparta, Spartans 90, 140, 147
Speusippus 108, 177
stability 120
state of character 14, 21, 53, 73,
    76, 154
Stratonicus 43, 160
strong-minded 103–4
suicide 72, 140, 167
superior, superiority 122, 131, 141, 148
susceptibilities 21

sweets 95, 174
syllogism 84, 171

task 76, 154–5
taste 43, 95, 115, 174
teacher 134
temper 20, 25–6, 99, 157
temperance 19, 42–4, 79, 91–2, 172
text 12, 137, 153, 183
Theognis 41, 119, 133, 160, 182
thinking, thought 25–7, 30–1, 76, 83, 157
tool 129
touch 43–4
toughness 90, 100–2
Troy 76
truth 76–7; truth vs enlightenment 9, 17, 75, 148, 187

understanding 77, 79–81, 169
universal 81–2, 94–5
use 45, 141, 154–5; proper vs improper 45,

vanity, vain 20
vegetative part of soul 16
vice 79, 90, 96, 99–100, 103
violence 57

virtue in general xvii–xxii, 4, 8, 16–23, 35–6, 46–7, 103, 141, 149, 155, 159; moral vs intellectual xvii–xxii, 16, 21, 75; and knowledge 8; and pleasures and pains 21–3; natural and acquired 51, 87, 172; complete virtue 54, 147; and wisdom 87–8; and friendship 114–22
voluntary and non-voluntary 24–33, 57, 66–8, 73, 157

war 34
weakness 102
wealth 97
wedding 49, 161
wife, see man and wife
will, volition 25–6, 31–3, 157
wisdom 4, 13, 77–88, 141, 143, 149, 154, 169; and understanding 86–7; and virtue 87–8; and incontinence 91–2
women 117
work 14, 154; see also task

Xenophantus 101, 175

Zeus 131, 135

The Oxford World's Classics Website

www.worldsclassics.co.uk

- Browse the full range of Oxford World's Classics online

- Sign up for our monthly e-alert to receive information on new titles

- Read extracts from the Introductions

- Listen to our editors and translators talk about the world's greatest literature with our Oxford World's Classics audio guides

- Join the conversation, follow us on Twitter at OWC_Oxford

- Teachers and lecturers can order inspection copies quickly and simply via our website

www.worldsclassics.co.uk

American Literature

British and Irish Literature

Children's Literature

Classics and Ancient Literature

Colonial Literature

Eastern Literature

European Literature

Gothic Literature

History

Medieval Literature

Oxford English Drama

Poetry

Philosophy

Politics

Religion

The Oxford Shakespeare

A complete list of Oxford World's Classics, including Authors in Context, Oxford English Drama, and the Oxford Shakespeare, is available in the UK from the Marketing Services Department, Oxford University Press, Great Clarendon Street, Oxford OX2 6DP, or visit the website at www.oup.com/uk/worldsclassics.

In the USA, visit www.oup.com/us/owc for a complete title list.

Oxford World's Classics are available from all good bookshops. In case of difficulty, customers in the UK should contact Oxford University Press Bookshop, 116 High Street, Oxford OX1 4BR.

	Classical Literary Criticism
	The First Philosophers: The Presocratics and the Sophists
	Greek Lyric Poetry
	Myths from Mesopotamia
APOLLODORUS	The Library of Greek Mythology
APOLLONIUS OF RHODES	Jason and the Golden Fleece
APULEIUS	The Golden Ass
ARISTOPHANES	Birds and Other Plays
ARISTOTLE	The Nicomachean Ethics
	Physics
	Politics
BOETHIUS	The Consolation of Philosophy
CAESAR	The Civil War
	The Gallic War
CATULLUS	The Poems of Catullus
CICERO	Defence Speeches
	The Nature of the Gods
	On Obligations
	Political Speeches
	The Republic and The Laws
EURIPIDES	Bacchae and Other Plays
	Heracles and Other Plays
	Medea and Other Plays
	Orestes and Other Plays
	The Trojan Women and Other Plays
HERODOTUS	The Histories
HOMER	The Iliad
	The Odyssey

HORACE	The Complete Odes and Epodes
JUVENAL	The Satires
LIVY	The Dawn of the Roman Empire
	Hannibal's War
	The Rise of Rome
MARCUS AURELIUS	The Meditations
OVID	The Love Poems
	Metamorphoses
PETRONIUS	The Satyricon
PLATO	Defence of Socrates, Euthyphro, and Crito
	Gorgias
	Meno and Other Dialogues
	Phaedo
	Republic
	Selected Myths
	Symposium
PLAUTUS	Four Comedies
PLUTARCH	Greek Lives
	Roman Lives
	Selected Essays and Dialogues
PROPERTIUS	The Poems
SOPHOCLES	Antigone, Oedipus the King, and Electra
STATIUS	Thebaid
SUETONIUS	Lives of the Caesars
TACITUS	Agricola and Germany
	The Histories
VIRGIL	The Aeneid
	The Eclogues and Georgics
XENOPHON	The Expedition of Cyrus

THOMAS AQUINAS	Selected Philosophical Writings
FRANCIS BACON	The Essays
WALTER BAGEHOT	The English Constitution
GEORGE BERKELEY	Principles of Human Knowledge and Three Dialogues
EDMUND BURKE	A Philosophical Enquiry into the Origin of Our Ideas of the Sublime and Beautiful Reflections on the Revolution in France
CONFUCIUS	The Analects
DESCARTES	A Discourse on the Method
ÉMILE DURKHEIM	The Elementary Forms of Religious Life
FRIEDRICH ENGELS	The Condition of the Working Class in England
JAMES GEORGE FRAZER	The Golden Bough
SIGMUND FREUD	The Interpretation of Dreams
THOMAS HOBBES	Human Nature and De Corpore Politico Leviathan
DAVID HUME	Selected Essays
NICCOLÒ MACHIAVELLI	The Prince
THOMAS MALTHUS	An Essay on the Principle of Population
KARL MARX	Capital The Communist Manifesto
J. S. MILL	On Liberty and Other Essays Principles of Political Economy and Chapters on Socialism
FRIEDRICH NIETZSCHE	Beyond Good and Evil The Birth of Tragedy On the Genealogy of Morals Thus Spoke Zarathustra Twilight of the Idols

A SELECTION OF   **OXFORD WORLD'S CLASSICS**

Thomas Paine   **Rights of Man, Common Sense, and Other
                            Political Writings**

Jean-Jacques Rousseau   **The Social Contract
                            Discourse on the Origin of Inequality**

Adam Smith   **An Inquiry into the Nature and Causes of
                            the Wealth of Nations**

Mary Wollstonecraft   **A Vindication of the Rights of Woman**

A SELECTION OF   **OXFORD WORLD'S CLASSICS**

Bhagavad Gita

The Bible Authorized King James Version
With Apocrypha

Dhammapada

Dharmasūtras

The Koran

The Pañcatantra

The Sauptikaparvan (from the Mahabharata)

The Tale of Sinuhe and Other Ancient Egyptian Poems

The Qur'an

Upaniṣads

ANSELM OF CANTERBURY   **The Major Works**

THOMAS AQUINAS   **Selected Philosophical Writings**

AUGUSTINE   **The Confessions**
On Christian Teaching

BEDE   **The Ecclesiastical History**

HEMACANDRA   **The Lives of the Jain Elders**

KĀLIDĀSA   **The Recognition of Śakuntalā**

MANJHAN   **Madhumalati**

ŚĀNTIDEVA   **The Bodhicaryàvatàra**